CliffsNotes®
Grade 8
Common Core
Math Review

CliffsNotes®
Grade 8
Common Core
Math Review

By Sandra Luna McCune, Ph.D.

Houghton Mifflin Harcourt
Boston • New York

About the Author

Sandra Luna McCune, Ph.D., is professor emeritus and a former Regents professor in the Department of Elementary Education at Stephen F. Austin State University, where she received the Distinguished Professor Award. She now is a full-time author and consultant and resides near Austin, Texas.

Acknowledgments

I would like to thank Grace Freedson, Greg Tubach, and Christina Stambaugh for their support and encouragement during completion of the book. I also owe a debt of gratitude to Mary Jane Sterling and Tom Page for their meticulous editing and invaluable suggestions.

Dedication

This book is dedicated to my grandchildren—Richard, Rose, Jude, Sophia, Josephine, and Myla Mae. They fill my life with joy!

Editorial

Executive Editor: Greg Tubach
Senior Editor: Christina Stambaugh
Copy Editor: Lynn Northrup
Technical Editors: Mary Jane Sterling and Tom Page
Proofreader: Donna Wright

CliffsNotes® Grade 8 Common Core Math Review

Library of Congress Control Number: 2015944414
ISBN: 978-0-544-37334-1 (pbk)

Printed in the United States of America
DOC 10 9 8 7 6 5 4 3 2 1

For information about permission to reproduce selections from this book, write to Permissions, Houghton Mifflin Harcourt Publishing Company, 215 Park Avenue South, New York, New York 10003.

www.hmhco.com

Table of Contents

Unit 1

Unit 1

Introduction

This book is organized around the Grade 8 Common Core State Standards for Mathematics. These standards define what eighth-grade students are expected to understand and be able to do in their study of mathematics. They include content standards and mathematical practice standards.

In Grade 8, the content standards are grouped under five domains:

- The Number System
- Expressions and Equations
- Functions
- Geometry
- Statistics and Probability

The Number System

Know that There Are Numbers that Are Not Rational, and Approximate Them by Rational Numbers

- **CCSS.Math.Content.8.NS.A.1** Know that numbers that are not rational are called irrational. Understand informally that every number has a decimal expansion; for rational numbers, show that the decimal expansion repeats eventually, and convert a decimal expansion that repeats eventually into a rational number.
- **CCSS.Math.Content.8.NS.A.2** Use rational approximations of irrational numbers to compare the size of irrational numbers, locate them approximately on a number line diagram, and estimate the value of expressions (e.g., π^2). *For example, by truncating the decimal expansion of $\sqrt{2}$, show that $\sqrt{2}$ is between 1 and 2, then between 1.4 and 1.5, and explain how to continue on to get better approximations.*

Expressions and Equations

Work with Radicals and Integer Exponents

- **CCSS.Math.Content.8.EE.A.1** Know and apply the properties of integer exponents to generate equivalent numerical expressions. *For example, $3^2 \times 3^{-5} = 3^{-3} = \dfrac{1}{3^3} = \dfrac{1}{27}$.*
- **CCSS.Math.Content.8.EE.A.2** Use square root and cube root symbols to represent solutions to equations of the form $x^2 = p$ and $x^3 = p$, where p is a positive rational number. Evaluate square roots of small perfect squares and cube roots of small perfect cubes. Know that $\sqrt{2}$ is irrational.

- **CCSS.Math.Content.8.EE.A.3** Use numbers expressed in the form of a single digit times an integer power of 10 to estimate very large or very small quantities and to express how many times as much one is than the other. *For example, estimate the population of the United States as 3 times 10^8 and the population of the world as 7 times 10^9, and determine that the world population is more than 20 times larger than the U.S. population.*

- **CCSS.Math.Content.8.EE.A.4** Perform operations with numbers expressed in scientific notation, including problems where both decimal and scientific notation are used. Use scientific notation and choose units of appropriate size for measurements of very large or very small quantities (e.g., use millimeters per year for seafloor spreading). Interpret scientific notation that has been generated by technology.

Understand the Connections Between Proportional Relationships, Lines, and Linear Equations

- **CCSS.Math.Content.8.EE.B.5** Graph proportional relationships, interpreting the unit rate as the slope of the graph. Compare two different proportional relationships represented in different ways. *For example, compare a distance-time graph to a distance-time equation to determine which of two moving objects has greater speed.*

- **CCSS.Math.Content.8.EE.B.6** Use similar triangles to explain why the slope m is the same between any two distinct points on a nonvertical line in the coordinate plane; derive the equation $y = mx$ for a line through the origin and the equation $y = mx + b$ for a line intercepting the vertical axis at b.

Analyze and Solve Linear Equations and Pairs of Simultaneous Linear Equations

- **CCSS.Math.Content.8.EE.C.7** Solve linear equations in one variable.
  - **CCSS.Math.Content.8.EE.C.7.A** Give examples of linear equations in one variable with one solution, infinitely many solutions, or no solutions. Show which of these possibilities is the case by successively transforming the given equation into simpler forms until an equivalent equation of the form $x = a$, $a = a$, or $a = b$ results (where a and b are different numbers).
  - **CCSS.Math.Content.8.EE.C.7.B** Solve linear equations with rational number coefficients, including equations whose solutions require expanding expressions using the distributive property and collecting like terms.
- **CCSS.Math.Content.8.EE.C.8** Analyze and solve pairs of simultaneous linear equations.
  - **CCSS.Math.Content.8.EE.C.8.A** Understand that solutions to a system of two linear equations in two variables correspond to points of intersection of their graphs, because points of intersection satisfy both equations simultaneously.
  - **CCSS.Math.Content.8.EE.C.8.B** Solve systems of two linear equations in two variables algebraically, and estimate solutions by graphing the equations. Solve simple cases by inspection. *For example, $3x + 2y = 5$ and $3x + 2y = 6$ have no solution because $3x + 2y$ cannot simultaneously be 5 and 6.*

- **CCSS.Math.Content.8.EE.C.8.C** Solve real-world and mathematical problems leading to two linear equations in two variables. *For example, given coordinates for two pairs of points, determine whether the line through the first pair of points intersects the line through the second pair.*

Functions

Define, Evaluate, and Compare Functions

- **CCSS.Math.Content.8.F.A.1** Understand that a function is a rule that assigns to each input exactly one output. The graph of a function is the set of ordered pairs consisting of an input and the corresponding output.
- **CCSS.Math.Content.8.F.A.2** Compare properties of two functions each represented in a different way (algebraically, graphically, numerically in tables, or by verbal descriptions). *For example, given a linear function represented by a table of values and a linear function represented by an algebraic expression, determine which function has the greater rate of change.*
- **CCSS.Math.Content.8.F.A.3** Interpret the equation $y = mx + b$ as defining a linear function whose graph is a straight line; give examples of functions that are not linear. *For example, the function $A = s^2$ giving the area of a square as a function of its side length is not linear because its graph contains the points (1, 1), (2, 4), and (3, 9), which are not on a straight line.*

Use Functions to Model Relationships Between Quantities

- **CCSS.Math.Content.8.F.B.4** Construct a function to model a linear relationship between two quantities. Determine the rate of change and initial value of the function from a description of a relationship or from two (x, y) values, including reading these from a table or from a graph. Interpret the rate of change and initial value of a linear function in terms of the situation it models, and in terms of its graph or a table of values.
- **CCSS.Math.Content.8.F.B.5** Describe qualitatively the functional relationship between two quantities by analyzing a graph (e.g., where the function is increasing or decreasing, linear or nonlinear). Sketch a graph that exhibits the qualitative features of a function that has been described verbally.

Geometry

Understand Congruence and Similarity Using Physical Models, Transparencies, or Geometry Software

- **CCSS.Math.Content.8.G.A.1** Verify experimentally the properties of rotations, reflections, and translations:
  - **CCSS.Math.Content.8.G.A.1.A** Lines are taken to lines, and line segments to line segments of the same length.
  - **CCSS.Math.Content.8.G.A.1.B** Angles are taken to angles of the same measure.
  - **CCSS.Math.Content.8.G.A.1.C** Parallel lines are taken to parallel lines.

- **CCSS.Math.Content.8.G.A.2** Understand that a two-dimensional figure is congruent to another if the second can be obtained from the first by a sequence of rotations, reflections, and translations; given two congruent figures, describe a sequence that exhibits the congruence between them.
- **CCSS.Math.Content.8.G.A.3** Describe the effect of dilations, translations, rotations, and reflections on two-dimensional figures using coordinates.
- **CCSS.Math.Content.8.G.A.4** Understand that a two-dimensional figure is similar to another if the second can be obtained from the first by a sequence of rotations, reflections, translations, and dilations; given two similar two-dimensional figures, describe a sequence that exhibits the similarity between them.
- **CCSS.Math.Content.8.G.A.5** Use informal arguments to establish facts about the angle sum and exterior angle of triangles, about the angles created when parallel lines are cut by a transversal, and the angle-angle criterion for similarity of triangles. *For example, arrange three copies of the same triangle so that the sum of the three angles appears to form a line, and give an argument in terms of transversals why this is so.*

Understand and Apply the Pythagorean Theorem

- **CCSS.Math.Content.8.G.B.6** Explain a proof of the Pythagorean theorem and its converse.
- **CCSS.Math.Content.8.G.B.7** Apply the Pythagorean theorem to determine unknown side lengths in right triangles in real-world and mathematical problems in two and three dimensions.
- **CCSS.Math.Content.8.G.B.8** Apply the Pythagorean theorem to find the distance between two points in a coordinate system.

Solve Real-World and Mathematical Problems Involving Volume of Cylinders, Cones, and Spheres

- **CCSS.Math.Content.8.G.C.9** Know the formulas for the volumes of cones, cylinders, and spheres and use them to solve real-world and mathematical problems.

Statistics and Probability

Investigate Patterns of Association in Bivariate Data

- **CCSS.Math.Content.8.SP.A.1** Construct and interpret scatter plots for bivariate measurement data to investigate patterns of association between two quantities. Describe patterns such as clustering, outliers, positive or negative association, linear association, and nonlinear association.
- **CCSS.Math.Content.8.SP.A.2** Know that straight lines are widely used to model relationships between two quantitative variables. For scatter plots that suggest a linear association, informally fit a straight line, and informally assess the model fit by judging the closeness of the data points to the line.

- **CCSS.Math.Content.8.SP.A.3** Use the equation of a linear model to solve problems in the context of bivariate measurement data, interpreting the slope and intercept. *For example, in a linear model for a biology experiment, interpret a slope of 1.5 cm/hr as meaning that an additional hour of sunlight each day is associated with an additional 1.5 cm in mature plant height.*

- **CCSS.Math.Content.8.SP.A.4** Understand that patterns of association can also be seen in bivariate categorical data by displaying frequencies and relative frequencies in a two-way table. Construct and interpret a two-way table summarizing data on two categorical variables collected from the same subjects. Use relative frequencies calculated for rows or columns to describe possible association between the two variables. *For example, collect data from students in your class on whether or not they have a curfew on school nights and whether or not they have assigned chores at home. Is there evidence that those who have a curfew also tend to have chores?*

Mathematical Practice

- **CCSS.Math.Practice.MP.1** Make sense of problems and persevere in solving them.
- **CCSS.Math.Practice.MP.2** Reason abstractly and quantitatively.
- **CCSS.Math.Practice.MP.3** Construct viable arguments and critique the reasoning of others.
- **CCSS.Math.Practice.MP.4** Model with mathematics.
- **CCSS.Math.Practice.MP.5** Use appropriate tools strategically.
- **CCSS.Math.Practice.MP.6** Attend to precision.
- **CCSS.Math.Practice.MP.7** Look for and make use of structure.
- **CCSS.Math.Practice.MP.8** Look for and express regularity in repeated reasoning.

1. The Number System

In this chapter, you will extend your understanding of the rational numbers, learn about irrational numbers, and recognize the real numbers as the set consisting of all the rational and irrational numbers. You will use rational approximations of irrational numbers to compare the size of irrational numbers, locate them approximately on a real number line, and approximate the value of irrational expressions.

Understanding Rational Numbers

(CCSS.Math.Content.8.NS.A.1)

A **rational number** is any number that can be expressed as $\frac{p}{q}$, where p and q are integers and q is not zero.

The rational numbers include zero and all the numbers that can be written as positive or negative fractions. They are the numbers you are familiar with from your previous work with numbers in arithmetic.

The rational numbers include whole numbers and integers. Here are examples.

The rational numbers include positive and negative fractions. Here are examples.

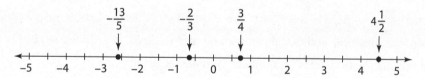

The rational numbers include positive and negative repeating and terminating decimals. (See below for a discussion on repeating and terminating decimals.) Here are examples.

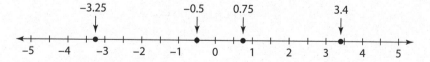

The rational numbers include positive and negative percents. Here are examples.

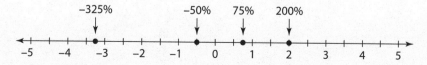

You obtain the equivalent decimal representation of a fraction, such as $\frac{3}{4}$, by performing the indicated division. (*Tip:* Remember, $\frac{3}{4} = 3 \div 4$.) You divide the numerator by the denominator. Insert a decimal point in the numerator and zeros to the right of the decimal point to complete the division.

$$
\begin{array}{r}
0.75 \\
4{\overline{\smash{\big)}\,3.00}} \\
\underline{-28} \\
20 \\
\underline{-20} \\
0
\end{array}
$$

The fraction $\frac{3}{4}$ and the decimal 0.75 are different representations of the same rational number. They are both located at the same location on the number line.

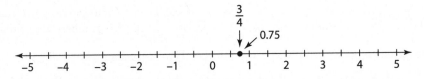

Tip: If the fraction is a negative number, perform the division without the negative sign, and then attach the negative sign to the decimal expansion. For example, $-\frac{3}{4} = -0.75$.

It is important you know the decimal expansion of a rational number either **terminates** in 0s or eventually **repeats**. In the case of $\frac{3}{4}$, you need to insert only two zeros after the decimal point for the division to finally reach a zero remainder. Inserting additional zeros would lead to repeated 0s to the right of 0.75 (like this: 0.75000…). You say that the decimal expansion of $\frac{3}{4}$ **terminates** in 0s.

However, for some rational numbers, the decimal expansion keeps going, but in a block of one or more digits that repeats over and over again. The repeating digits are not all zero. Here is an example.

$$
\frac{5}{11} = 5 \div 11 = 11{\overline{\smash{\big)}\,5.0000...}}
\begin{array}{r}
0.4545... \\
\end{array}
$$

$$
\begin{array}{r}
\underline{-44} \\
60 \\
\underline{-55} \\
50 \\
\underline{-44} \\
60 \\
\underline{-55} \\
\vdots
\end{array}
$$

No matter how long you continue to add zeros and divide, 45 in the quotient continues to repeat without end. You put a bar over one block of the repeating digits to indicate the repetition; thus, $\frac{5}{11} = 0.4545... = 0.\overline{45}$. You say $\frac{5}{11}$ has a **repeating** decimal expansion. It is incorrect to write $\frac{5}{11} = 0.45$. Still, when decimals repeat, they are usually rounded to a specified degree of accuracy. For instance, $\frac{5}{11} \approx 0.45$ when *rounded* to two decimal places.

Pretend you do not know 0.4545... is the decimal expansion of $\frac{5}{11}$. How would you go about converting the repeating decimal expansion 0.4545... into its fractional form $\frac{p}{q}$ $(q \neq 0)$? Here is the way to do it. (***Tip:*** This procedure works for any repeating decimal expansion.)

Let $x = 0.4545...$ Do three steps. First, multiply both sides of the equation $x = 0.4545...$ by 10^r, where r is the number of digits in the repeating block of digits in the decimal expansion. Next, subtract the original equation from the new equation. Then divide both sides of the resulting equation by the coefficient of x.

Step 1. Multiply both sides of the equation $x = 0.4545...$ by $10^2 = 100$ (because two digits repeat).

$$x = 0.4545...$$
$$100 \cdot x = 100(0.4545...)$$
$$100x = 45.4545...$$

Step 2. Subtract the original equation from the new equation.

$$\begin{array}{r} 100x = 45.4545... \\ -x = -0.4545... \\ \hline 99x = 45.0000... \end{array}$$

Step 3. Solve for x by dividing both sides of the resulting equation by the coefficient of x.

$$99x = 45$$
$$\frac{\cancel{99}x}{\cancel{99}} = \frac{45 \div 9}{99 \div 9}$$
$$x = \frac{5}{11}$$

Thus, $0.4545... = \frac{5}{11}$.

Tip: Notice when you multiply 0.4545... by 100, you can write the product as 45.4545.... You can do this because there are infinitely many 45s to the right of the decimal point, so you can write as many as you please.

Here is an additional example of the procedure.

Convert –3.666... to its equivalent fractional form.

Tip: If the number is negative, do the conversion without the negative sign, and then attach the negative sign to the fractional representation.

Let $x = 3.666...$

Step 1. Multiply both sides of the equation $x = 3.666...$ by $10^1 = 10$ (because one digit repeats).

$$x = 3.666...$$
$$10 \cdot x = 10(3.666...)$$
$$10x = 36.666...$$

Step 2. Subtract the original equation from the new equation.

$$10x = 36.666...$$
$$-x = -3.666...$$
$$9x = 33.000...$$

Step 3. Solve for x by dividing both sides of the resulting equation by the coefficient of x.

$$9x = 33$$
$$\frac{9x}{9} = \frac{33 \div 3}{9 \div 3}$$
$$x = \frac{11}{3} = 3\frac{2}{3}$$

Thus, $-3.666... = -\frac{11}{3} = -3\frac{2}{3}$.

☞ Try These

1. Fill in the blank(s).

   (a) A rational number is any number that can be expressed as _____, where p and q are integers and q is not zero.

   (b) The decimal expansion of a rational number either _____ in 0s or eventually _____.

2. Write the decimal expansion for the rational number.

   (a) $\dfrac{3}{8}$

   (b) $\dfrac{2}{7}$

   (c) $-\dfrac{2}{3}$

   (d) $\dfrac{7}{9}$

   (e) $-\dfrac{13}{9}$

3. Convert the decimal expansion to an equivalent fractional form.

   (a)   0.666…
   (b)   0.142857142857…
   (c)   1.1818…

Solutions

1. **(a)** $\dfrac{p}{q}$

   (b) terminates; repeats

2. **(a)** $\dfrac{3}{8} = 0.375$

   (b) $\dfrac{2}{7} = 0.\overline{285714}$

   (c) $-\dfrac{2}{3} = -0.\overline{6}$

   (d) $\dfrac{7}{9} = 0.\overline{7}$

   (e) $-\dfrac{13}{9} = -1.\overline{4}$

3. **(a)** $0.666\ldots = \dfrac{2}{3}$

$$x = 0.666\ldots$$
$$10x = 6.666\ldots$$
$$\underline{-x = -0.666\ldots}$$
$$9x = 6.000\ldots$$
$$\frac{9x}{9} = \frac{6}{9}$$
$$\frac{\cancel{9}x}{\cancel{9}} = \frac{6 \div 3}{9 \div 3}$$
$$x = \frac{2}{3}$$

(b) $0.142857142857\ldots = \dfrac{1}{7}$

$$x = 0.142857142857\ldots$$
$$1{,}000{,}000x = 142{,}857.142857142857\ldots$$
$$\underline{-x = \qquad -\,0.142857142857\ldots}$$
$$999{,}999x = 142{,}857$$
$$\frac{999{,}999x}{999{,}999} = \frac{142{,}857}{999{,}999}$$
$$\frac{\cancel{999{,}999}x}{\cancel{999{,}999}} = \frac{142{,}857 \div 142{,}857}{999{,}999 \div 142{,}857}$$
$$x = \frac{1}{7}$$

(c) $1.1818\ldots = \dfrac{13}{11}$

$$x = 1.1818\ldots$$
$$100x = 118.1818\ldots$$
$$\underline{-x = -1.1818\ldots}$$
$$99x = 117$$
$$\frac{99x}{99} = \frac{117}{99}$$
$$\frac{\cancel{99}x}{\cancel{99}} = \frac{117 \div 9}{99 \div 9}$$
$$x = \frac{13}{11}$$

Recognizing Rational and Irrational Numbers

(CCSS.Math.Content.8.NS.A.1)

Irrational numbers are numbers that cannot be written in the form $\frac{p}{q}$, where p and q are integers and q is not zero. They have nonterminating, nonrepeating decimal expansions. An example of an irrational number is the positive number that multiplies by itself to give 2. This number is the principal square root of 2. Every positive number has two square roots: a positive square root and a negative square root. The positive square root is the **principal square root.** The square root symbol $\left(\sqrt{}\right)$ is used to show the principal square root.

Thus, the principal square root of 2 is written like this: $\sqrt{2}$. The other square root of 2 is $-\sqrt{2}$. It also is an irrational number.

> **Tip: Zero has only one square root; namely, zero (which is a rational number).**

You cannot express $\sqrt{2}$ as $\frac{p}{q}$, where p and q are integers ($q \neq 0$), and you cannot express it precisely in decimal form. No matter how many decimal places you use, you can only approximate $\sqrt{2}$. If you use a calculator to find the square root of the number 2, the display will show a decimal approximation of $\sqrt{2}$. An approximation of $\sqrt{2}$ to nine decimal places is 1.414213562. You can check whether this is $\sqrt{2}$ by multiplying it by itself to see whether you get 2.

$$1.414213562 \cdot 1.414213562 = 1.999999999$$

The number 1.999999999 is very close to 2, but it is not equal to 2. Only $\sqrt{2}$ or $-\sqrt{2}$ will multiply by itself to give 2. Thus, $\sqrt{2} \cdot \sqrt{2} = 2$ and $-\sqrt{2} \cdot -\sqrt{2} = 2$.

Even though an exact value for $\sqrt{2}$ cannot be determined, $\sqrt{2}$ is a number that occurs frequently in the real world. For instance, architects, carpenters, and other builders encounter $\sqrt{2}$ when they measure the length of the diagonal of a square that has sides with lengths of one unit, as shown here.

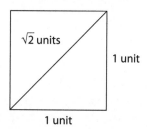

The diagonal of such a square measures $\sqrt{2}$ units.

> **Tip: For most purposes, you can use 1.414 as an approximation for $\sqrt{2}$.**

There are an infinite number of square roots that are irrational. Here are a few examples.

$$\sqrt{3},\ \sqrt{10},\ -\sqrt{24},\ \sqrt{41},\ -\sqrt{89}$$

Another important irrational number is the number represented by the symbol π (pi). The number π also occurs frequently in the real world. For instance, π is the number you get when you divide the circumference of a circle by its diameter. The number π cannot be expressed as a fraction, nor can it be written as a terminating or repeating decimal. Here is an approximation of π to nine decimal places: 3.141592654.

Tip: There is no pattern to the digits of π. In this book, use the rational number 3.14 as an approximation for the irrational number π in problems involving π.

Not all square roots are irrational. For example, the principal square root of 25, denoted $\sqrt{25}$, is not irrational because $\sqrt{25} = 5$, which is a rational number. The number 25 is a **perfect square** because its square root is rational. When you want to find the principal square root of a number, try to find a *nonnegative* number that multiplies by itself to give the number. You will find it helpful to memorize the following principal square roots.

$$\sqrt{1} = 1 \quad \sqrt{25} = 5 \quad \sqrt{81} = 9 \quad \sqrt{169} = 13 \quad \sqrt{289} = 17$$
$$\sqrt{4} = 2 \quad \sqrt{36} = 6 \quad \sqrt{100} = 10 \quad \sqrt{196} = 14 \quad \sqrt{400} = 20$$
$$\sqrt{9} = 3 \quad \sqrt{49} = 7 \quad \sqrt{121} = 11 \quad \sqrt{225} = 15 \quad \sqrt{625} = 25$$
$$\sqrt{16} = 4 \quad \sqrt{64} = 8 \quad \sqrt{144} = 12 \quad \sqrt{256} = 16$$

Make yourself a set of flash cards or make matching cards for a game of "Memory." For the Memory game, turn all the cards facedown. Turn up two cards at a time. If they match (for instance, $\sqrt{144}$ and 12 are a match), remove the two cards; otherwise, turn them facedown again. Repeat until you have matched all the cards.

Here are examples of rational square roots.

$-\sqrt{400}$, which is -20

$\sqrt{\dfrac{36}{49}}$, which is $\dfrac{6}{7}$

$\sqrt{\dfrac{100}{25}}$, which is $\sqrt{4} = 2$

$-\sqrt{\dfrac{9}{4}}$, which is $-\dfrac{3}{2}$

Keep in mind, though, every positive number has <u>two</u> square roots. The two square roots are equal in absolute value, but opposite in sign. For instance, the two square roots of 25 are 5 and –5, with 5 being the *principal* square root. Still, the square root symbol $\left(\sqrt{}\right)$ *always* gives just <u>one</u> square root as the answer, and that square root is either positive or zero. Thus, $\sqrt{25} = 5$, not –5 or ±5 (read "plus or minus 5"). If you want ±5, then do this: $\pm\sqrt{25} = \pm5$.

Tip: Recall that the absolute value of a specific number is just the value of the number with no sign attached.

☞ Try These

1. Fill in the blank(s).

   (a) Irrational numbers are numbers that _____ (can, cannot) be written in the form $\frac{p}{q}$, where p and q are integers and q is not zero.

   (b) Irrational numbers have nonterminating, _____ decimal expansions.

   (c) The square root symbol $\left(\sqrt{} \right)$ is used to show a _____ square root, which is just one number.

   (d) Every positive number has _____ square roots.

   (e) Zero has _____ square root(s).

2. Indicate whether the number is rational or irrational by writing "rational" or "irrational" as your answer.

   (a) $\sqrt{88}$

   (b) $\sqrt{200}$

   (c) $\sqrt{81}$

   (d) $-\sqrt{40}$

   (e) $-3.\overline{45}$

   (f) 62.75

   (g) $\sqrt{\dfrac{25}{36}}$

   (h) $-\sqrt{\dfrac{9}{16}}$

   (i) π

Solutions

1. **(a)** cannot
   (b) nonrepeating
   (c) principal
   (d) two
   (e) one

2. **(a)** irrational
   (b) irrational
   (c) rational
   (d) irrational
   (e) rational
   (f) rational
   (g) rational
   (h) rational
   (i) irrational

Approximating Irrational Numbers and Expressions

(CCSS.Math.Content.8.NS.A.2)

You cannot write an exact decimal representation of an irrational square root. However, you can approximate its value to a desired number of decimal places. Here is an example.

Approximate $\sqrt{40}$ to the nearest hundredth.

Step 1. Approximate $\sqrt{40}$ to the nearest whole number.

Find two consecutive integers such that the square of the first integer is less than 40 and the square of the second integer is greater than 40. You know $6 \times 6 = 36$, which is less than 40, and $7 \times 7 = 49$, which is greater than 40. Thus, $\sqrt{36} < \sqrt{40} < \sqrt{49}$. So, the approximate value of $\sqrt{40}$ is between 6 and 7. It is closer to 6 because 40 is closer to 36 (4 units away) than it is to 49 (9 units away). To the nearest whole number, $\sqrt{40}$ is approximately 6.

Step 2. Approximate $\sqrt{40}$ to the nearest tenth.

Consider that 49 and 36 are 13 units apart and 40 and 36 are 4 units apart. So, 40 is $\frac{4}{13}$ of the distance between 49 and 36. As a rough approximation, $\sqrt{40}$ is about $\frac{4}{13}$ of the distance between 6 and 7. The distance between 6 and 7 is 1 unit. So, $\sqrt{40} \approx 6 + \frac{4}{13}(1) \approx 6 + 0.307 \approx 6.3$. This calculation leads to the guess that $\sqrt{40}$ is between 6.3 and 6.4. Square each of these numbers, $6.3 \times 6.3 = 39.69$ and $6.4 \times 6.4 = 40.96$. The value of $\sqrt{40}$ is closer to 6.3 than it is to 6.4 because 40 is closer to 36.69 (0.31 unit away) than it is to 40.96 (0.96 unit away). To the nearest tenth, $\sqrt{40}$ is approximately 6.3.

Step 3. Approximate $\sqrt{40}$ to the nearest hundredth.

Consider that 40.96 and 39.69 are 1.27 units apart and 40 and 39.69 are 0.31 unit apart. So, 40 is $\frac{0.31}{1.27}$ of the distance between 40.96 and 39.69. As a rough approximation, $\sqrt{40}$ is about $\frac{0.31}{1.27}$ of the distance between 6.3 and 6.4. The distance between 6.3 and 6.4 is 0.1 unit. So, to the nearest hundredth, $\sqrt{40} \approx 6.3 + \frac{0.31}{1.27}(0.1) \approx 6.3 + 0.024 \approx 6.32$. (Checking it, $6.32 \times 6.32 = 39.9424$, which is very close to 40.) On a number line, you would mark $\sqrt{40}$ at approximately 6.32.

To approximate irrational expressions, approximate the irrational component and then evaluate.

Here are examples.

Approximate π^2 to the nearest tenth.

$$\pi^2 \approx (3.14)^2 = 9.8596 \approx 9.9$$

Approximate $5\sqrt{2}$ to the nearest hundredth.

$$5\sqrt{2} \approx 5(1.414) = 7.07$$

☞ Try These

1. Approximate the irrational square root to the nearest tenth.

   (a) $\sqrt{5}$
   (b) $\sqrt{28}$
   (c) $\sqrt{80}$

2. Using the results from question 1, approximate the irrational expression to the nearest tenth.

   (a) $3\sqrt{5}$
   (b) $8\sqrt{28}$
   (c) $\dfrac{\sqrt{80}}{10}$

Solutions

1. **(a)** $\sqrt{5} \approx 2.2$

   Step 1. Approximate $\sqrt{5}$ to the nearest whole number.

   Find two consecutive integers such that the square of the first integer is less than 5 and the square of the second integer is greater than 5. You know $2 \times 2 = 4$, which is less than 5, and $3 \times 3 = 9$, which is greater than 5. Thus, $\sqrt{4} < \sqrt{5} < \sqrt{9}$. So, the approximate value of $\sqrt{5}$ is between 2 and 3. It is closer to 2 because 5 is closer to 4 (1 unit away) than it is to 9 (4 units away). To the nearest whole number, $\sqrt{5}$ is approximately 2.

   Step 2. Approximate $\sqrt{5}$ to the nearest tenth.

   Consider that 9 and 4 are 5 units apart and 5 and 4 are 1 unit apart. So, 5 is $\dfrac{1}{5}$ of the distance between 9 and 4. As a rough approximation, $\sqrt{5}$ is about $\dfrac{1}{5}$ of the distance between 2 and 3. The distance between 2 and 3 is 1 unit. So, $\sqrt{5} \approx 2 + \dfrac{1}{5}(1) \approx 2 + 0.2 \approx 2.2$. This calculation leads to the guess that $\sqrt{5}$ is between 2.2 and 2.3. Square each of these numbers, $2.2 \times 2.2 = 4.84$ and $2.3 \times 2.3 = 5.29$. The value of $\sqrt{5}$ is closer to 2.2 than it is to 2.3 because 5 is closer to 4.84 (0.16 unit away) than it is to 5.29 (0.29 unit away). To the nearest tenth, $\sqrt{5}$ is approximately 2.2.

   (b) $\sqrt{28} \approx 5.3$

   Step 1. Approximate $\sqrt{28}$ to the nearest whole number.

   Find two consecutive integers such that the square of the first integer is less than 28 and the square of the second integer is greater than 28. You know $5 \times 5 = 25$, which is less than 28, and $6 \times 6 = 36$, which is greater than 28. Thus, $\sqrt{25} < \sqrt{28} < \sqrt{36}$. So, the approximate value of $\sqrt{28}$ is between 5 and 6. It is closer to 5 because 28 is closer to 25 (3 units away) than it is to 36 (8 units away). To the nearest whole number, $\sqrt{28}$ is approximately 5.

Step 2. Approximate $\sqrt{28}$ to the nearest tenth.

Consider that 36 and 25 are 11 units apart and 28 and 25 are 3 units apart. So, 28 is $\dfrac{3}{11}$ of the distance between 36 and 25. As a rough approximation, $\sqrt{28}$ is about $\dfrac{3}{11}$ of the distance between 5 and 6. The distance between 5 and 6 is 1 unit. So, $\sqrt{28} \approx 5 + \dfrac{3}{11}(1) \approx 5 + 0.272 \approx 5.3$. This calculation leads to the guess that $\sqrt{28}$ is between 5.3 and 5.4. Square each of these numbers, $5.3 \times 5.3 = 28.09$ and $5.4 \times 5.4 = 29.16$. The value of $\sqrt{28}$ is closer to 5.3 than it is to 6.4 because 28 is closer to 28.09 (0.09 unit away) than it is to 29.16 (1.16 units away). To the nearest tenth, $\sqrt{28}$ is approximately 5.3.

(c) $\sqrt{80} \approx 8.9$

Step 1. Approximate $\sqrt{80}$ to the nearest whole number.

Find two consecutive integers such that the square of the first integer is less than 80 and the square of the second integer is greater than 80. You know $8 \times 8 = 64$, which is less than 80, and $9 \times 9 = 81$, which is greater than 80. Thus, $\sqrt{64} < \sqrt{80} < \sqrt{81}$. So, the approximate value of $\sqrt{80}$ is between 8 and 9. It is closer to 9 because 80 is closer to 81 (1 unit away) than it is to 64 (16 units away). To the nearest whole number, $\sqrt{80}$ is approximately 9.

Step 2. Approximate $\sqrt{80}$ to the nearest tenth.

Consider that 81 and 64 are 17 units apart and 80 and 64 are 16 units apart. So, 80 is $\dfrac{16}{17}$ of the distance between 81 and 64. As a rough approximation, $\sqrt{80}$ is about $\dfrac{16}{17}$ of the distance between 8 and 9. The distance between 8 and 9 is 1 unit. So, $\sqrt{80} \approx 8 + \dfrac{16}{17}(1) \approx 8 + 0.941 \approx 8.9$. This calculation leads to the guess that $\sqrt{80}$ is between 8.9 and 9.0. Square each of these numbers, $8.9 \times 8.9 = 79.21$ and $9.0 \times 9.0 = 81.00$. The value of $\sqrt{80}$ is closer to 8.9 than it is to 9.0 because 80 is closer to 79.21 (0.79 unit away) than it is to 81.00 (1.00 unit away). To the nearest tenth, $\sqrt{80}$ is approximately 8.9.

2. **(a)** $3\sqrt{5} \approx 3(2.2) = 6.6$
   (b) $8\sqrt{28} \approx 8(5.3) = 42.4$
   (c) $\dfrac{\sqrt{80}}{10} \approx \dfrac{8.9}{10} = 0.89 \approx 0.9$

Understanding the Real Numbers

(CCSS.Math.Content.8.NS.A.1, CCSS.Math.Content.8.NS.A.2)

The **real numbers** are made up of all the rational numbers and all the irrational numbers. You can show real numbers on a number line. Every point on the real number line corresponds to a real number, and every real number corresponds to a point on the real number line. Here are examples.

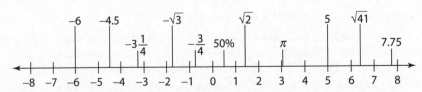

Comparing Real Numbers

When comparing two real numbers, think of their relative locations on the number line. If the numbers have the same location, they are equal. If they don't, they are unequal. Then, the number that is farther to the *right* is the greater number. For example, $-\sqrt{3} > -4.5$ because $-\sqrt{3}$ lies to the right of –4.5 on the number line.

Here are some tips on handling situations that might occur when you are comparing and ordering real numbers:

- If negative numbers are involved, they will be less than all the positive numbers and 0.
- If percents are involved, change the percents to decimals.
- If the problem contains exponential expressions, evaluate them before making comparisons.
- If you have square roots that are rational numbers, find the square roots before making comparisons.
- If you have irrational square roots, approximate the square roots before comparing them to other numbers.

Here is an example.

Order the list of numbers from least to greatest.

$$\sqrt{37},\ 3^2,\ 4.39,\ -4,\ \frac{9}{2}$$

You do not have to proceed in the order the numbers are listed. Start with 3^2, 4.39, –4, and $\frac{9}{2}$. Clearly, –4 is less than all the other numbers. Evaluate 3^2 to obtain 9, and write $\frac{9}{2}$ as 4.50. The order from least to greatest for these four numbers is –4, 4.39, 4.50, 9. Next, approximate $\sqrt{37}$ to be between 6 and 7, because $\sqrt{36} < \sqrt{37} < \sqrt{49}$. So $\sqrt{37}$ lies between 4.50 and 9 in the list. At this point, your ordered list is –4, 4.39, 4.50, $\sqrt{37}$, 9. Substitute in your original numbers to get your final answer: –4, 4.39, $\frac{9}{2}$, $\sqrt{37}$, 3^2.

> **Tip: When you're working with only real numbers, don't try to find square roots of negative numbers because not one real number will multiply by itself to give a negative number. For instance, $\sqrt{-25} \neq -5$. No real number multiplies by itself to give –25.**

☞ Try These

1. Fill in the blank(s).

   (a) A real number is any _____ or _____ number.

   (b) Every _____ on the real number line corresponds to a real number, and every real number corresponds to a _____ on the real number line.

   (c) No real number will multiply by itself to give a _____ number.

2. Which numbers are rational?

   $$-15,\ 0,\ \sqrt{36},\ -3.45,\ 130\%,\ \sqrt{12},\ \frac{6}{10},\ -\frac{1}{20},\ 0.0005,\ \pi,\ 3.14,\ \sqrt{37}$$

3. Which numbers are irrational?

   $$-25,\ 0,\ \sqrt{36},\ -125.4,\ 50\%,\ \sqrt{6},\ -\frac{1}{200},\ 0.0005,\ \pi,\ 3.14,\ 0.\overline{3},\ \sqrt{37}$$

4. Which numbers are real numbers?

$$-16,\ 0,\ \sqrt{37},\ -13.25,\ \sqrt{-64},\ 30\%,\ \sqrt{49},\ \frac{1}{0},\ \frac{3}{5},\ -\frac{12}{24},\ 0.03,\ \pi$$

5. Order the list of numbers from least to greatest.

$$1.25,\ -5,\ \frac{3}{2},\ \left(\frac{1}{2}\right)^2,\ \sqrt{5},\ -\sqrt{36}$$

Solutions

1. **(a)** rational; irrational
   (b) point; point
   (c) negative

2. $-15,\ 0,\ \sqrt{36},\ -3.45,\ 130\%,\ \frac{6}{10},\ -\frac{1}{20},\ 0.0005,$ and 3.14

3. $\sqrt{6},\ \pi,$ and $\sqrt{37}$

4. $-16,\ 0,\ \sqrt{37},\ -13.25,\ 30\%,\ \sqrt{49},\ \frac{3}{5},\ -\frac{12}{24},\ 0.03,\ \pi$

5. $-\sqrt{36}\ -5,\ \left(\frac{1}{2}\right)^2,\ 1.25,\ \frac{3}{2},\ \sqrt{5}$

   Evaluate $-\sqrt{36}$ to obtain –6, which is less than –5. Evaluate $\left(\frac{1}{2}\right)^2$ to obtain $\left(\frac{1}{2}\right)^2=\frac{1}{4}=0.25$, and write $\frac{3}{2}$ as 1.50. Approximate $\sqrt{5}$ as lying between 2 and 3 because $\sqrt{4}<\sqrt{5}<\sqrt{9}$. At this point, the ordered list is –6, –5, 0.25, 1.25, 1.50, $\sqrt{5}$. Substituting in the original numbers gives the final answer: $-\sqrt{36},\ -5,$ $\left(\frac{1}{2}\right)^2,\ 1.25,\ \frac{3}{2},\ \sqrt{5}.$

Computing with Real Numbers

The rules for computing with real numbers are the same as the rules you already know for computing with rational numbers. You do the computations by using the absolute values of the numbers and then assigning the correct sign to the result. The absolute value of a real number is its distance from 0 on the real number line. The absolute value is always positive or zero.

For sums and differences of real numbers, use the following rules.

Rule 1: The sum of 0 and any number is the number.

Rule 2: The sum of a number and its opposite is 0.

Rule 3: To add two nonzero numbers that have the same sign, add their absolute values and give the sum their common sign.

Rule 4: To add two nonzero numbers that have opposite signs, subtract the lesser absolute value from the greater absolute value and give the result the sign of the number with the greater absolute value.

Rule 5: To subtract one number from another, add the opposite of the second number to the first.

For products and quotients of real numbers, use the following rules.

Rule 1: Zero times any number is 0.

Rule 2: To multiply two nonzero numbers that have the same sign, multiply their absolute values and make the product positive.

Rule 3: To multiply two nonzero numbers that have opposite signs, multiply their absolute values and make the product negative.

Rule 4: When 0 is one of the factors, the product is always 0; otherwise, products with an even number of negative factors are positive, whereas those with an odd number of negative factors are negative.

Rule 5: To divide by a nonzero number, follow the same rules for the signs as for multiplication, except divide the absolute values of the numbers instead of multiplying.

Rule 6: The quotient is 0 when the dividend is 0 and the divisor is a nonzero number.

Rule 7: The quotient is undefined when the divisor is 0.

☞ Try These

1. Fill in the blank(s).

   (a) The sum of _____ and any number is the number.
   (b) The sum of a number and its opposite is _____.
   (c) Zero times any number is _____.
   (d) Products with a(n) _____ number of negative factors are positive, whereas those with a(n) _____ number of negative factors are negative.
   (e) The quotient is _____ when the dividend is 0 and the divisor is a nonzero number. For example, $\dfrac{0}{1,000}$ is _____.
   (f) The quotient is _____ when the divisor is 0. For example, $\dfrac{5.6}{0}$ is _____ and $\dfrac{0}{0}$ is _____.

2. Find the sum or difference as indicated.

   (a) $-36 + 20$
   (b) $-105.64 - 235$
   (c) $\dfrac{2}{3} + \dfrac{3}{4}$
   (d) $55 - 100$
   (e) $2\dfrac{3}{4} - \left(-3\dfrac{1}{4}\right)$
   (f) $-58.99 - 0.01$

3. Find the product or quotient as indicated.

   (a) $(-7)(-20)$
   (b) $(105.34)(-238)$
   (c) $\left(\dfrac{2}{3}\right)\left(-\dfrac{3}{4}\right)$
   (d) $\dfrac{50}{-2}$
   (e) $\dfrac{-12.3}{-8.2}$
   (f) $(7.8)(9.1)(0)(-3.4)(125.9)$
   (g) $(2)(-1)(-3)(20)(-10)$
   (h) $(2)(-1)(3)(20)(-10)$

Solutions

1. (a) 0
   (b) 0
   (c) 0
   (d) even; odd
   (e) 0; 0
   (f) undefined; undefined; undefined

2. (a) $-36 + 20 = -16$
   (b) $-105.64 - 235 = -340.64$
   (c) $\dfrac{2}{3} + \dfrac{3}{4} = \dfrac{17}{12} = 1\dfrac{5}{12}$
   (d) $55 - 100 = -45$
   (e) $2\dfrac{3}{4} - \left(-3\dfrac{1}{4}\right) = 2\dfrac{3}{4} + 3\dfrac{1}{4} = 6$
   (f) $-58.99 - 0.01 = -59.00$

3. (a) $(-7)(-20) = 140$
   (b) $(105.34)(-238) = -25,070.92$
   (c) $\left(\dfrac{2}{3}\right)\left(-\dfrac{3}{4}\right) = -\dfrac{6}{12} = -\dfrac{1}{2}$
   (d) $\dfrac{50}{-2} = -25$
   (e) $\dfrac{-12.3}{-8.2} = 1.5$
   (f) $(7.8)(9.1)(0)(-3.4)(125.9) = 0$
   (g) $(2)(-1)(-3)(20)(-10) = -1,200$
   (h) $(2)(-1)(3)(20)(-10) = 1,200$

2. Expressions and Equations

In this chapter, you will work with integer exponents, square roots, and cube roots. You will extend your understanding of the connections between proportional relationships, lines, and linear equations. You will analyze and solve linear equations in one variable and pairs of simultaneous linear equations in two variables. You will also solve mathematical and real-world problems leading to linear equations in one variable and to two linear equations in two variables.

Understanding and Working with Integer Exponents
(CCSS.Math.Content.8.EE.A.1)

In this section, you will extend your understanding of exponents to include all integer exponents. An **exponent** is a small raised number written to the upper right of its **base**. In the **exponential expression** b^n, b is the base and n is the exponent.

$$b^n \leftarrow \text{Exponent}$$
$$\!\leftarrow \text{Base}$$

Here is an example.

In the exponential expression 2^5, 2 is the base and 5 is the exponent.

> **Tip: Exponents are written as superscripts, so they are smaller than the other numbers in an expression. Write an exponent slightly raised and immediately to the right of the number that is its base. Do this carefully so that, for example, 2^5 is not mistaken for 25.**

Understanding Positive Integer Exponents

Consider the product $2 \times 2 \times 2 \times 2 \times 2$. This product is an example of repeated multiplication. **Repeated multiplication** means using the *same* number as a *factor* many times. You use **positive integer exponents** to express repeated multiplication. For the product $2 \times 2 \times 2 \times 2 \times 2$, write 2^5. The expression 2^5 means "use 2 as a factor 5 times."

In general, if b is a real number and n is a positive integer, then $b^n = \underbrace{b \times b \times \cdots b}_{n \text{ factors}}$. The positive integer exponent, n, tells how many times the base, b, is used as a factor. Read b^n as "b to the nth power."

The first power of a number is the number. So, 6^1 is simply 6.

> **Tip: When no exponent is written on a number, the exponent is 1, even though it's not written.**

The second power of a number is its square. So, 6^2 is "six squared." The third power of a number is its cube. So, 6^3 is "six cubed." Beyond the third power, 6^4 is "six to the fourth power," 6^5 is "six to the fifth power," and so on.

To **evaluate** an exponential expression, do to the base what the exponent tells you to do. Evaluating exponential expressions is known as **exponentiation.**

Here are examples when the exponent is a positive integer.

$2^5 = 2 \times 2 \times 2 \times 2 \times 2 = 32$ (***Tip:*** Don't multiply the base by the exponent. 2^5 is *not* 2×5. 2^5 is 32; 2×5 is 10.)

$3^4 = 3 \times 3 \times 3 \times 3 = 81$

$10^6 = 10 \times 10 \times 10 \times 10 \times 10 \times 10 = 1{,}000{,}000$

$6^2 = 6 \times 6 = 36$

$5^3 = 5 \times 5 \times 5 = 125$

$0^4 = 0 \times 0 \times 0 \times 0 = 0$

> **Tip: In an exponentiation expression, which number is the exponent and which is the base makes a difference in the value of the expression. Unlike multiplication, where $5 \times 2 = 2 \times 5 = 10$, exponential expressions do NOT have a commutative property. So $2^5 \neq 5^2$; $2^5 = 2 \times 2 \times 2 \times 2 \times 2 = 32$, $5^2 = 5 \times 5 = 25$.**

When the exponent is a positive integer, the base can be any number. To make the problem easier to read, enclose negative numbers and fractions and decimals in parentheses. Also use parentheses to indicate multiplication. Here are examples.

$(0.1)^5 = (0.1)(0.1)(0.1)(0.1)(0.1) = 0.00001$

$\left(-\dfrac{3}{4}\right)^3 = \left(-\dfrac{3}{4}\right)\left(-\dfrac{3}{4}\right)\left(-\dfrac{3}{4}\right) = -\dfrac{27}{64}$

$(2.5)^2 = (2.5)(2.5) = 6.25$

$\left(3\dfrac{1}{2}\right)^2 = \left(\dfrac{7}{2}\right)^2 = \left(\dfrac{7}{2}\right)\left(\dfrac{7}{2}\right) = \dfrac{49}{4}$

$(-2)^4 = (-2)(-2)(-2)(-2) = 16$

$\left(\sqrt{7}\right)^2 = \left(\sqrt{7}\right)\left(\sqrt{7}\right) = 7$

$\left(-\sqrt{7}\right)^2 = \left(-\sqrt{7}\right)\left(-\sqrt{7}\right) = 7$

$\left(\dfrac{1}{2}\right)^6 = \left(\dfrac{1}{2}\right)\left(\dfrac{1}{2}\right)\left(\dfrac{1}{2}\right)\left(\dfrac{1}{2}\right)\left(\dfrac{1}{2}\right)\left(\dfrac{1}{2}\right) = \dfrac{1}{64}$

Keep in mind that an exponent applies only to the number or grouped quantity to which it is attached. Here are examples.

$3(4)^2 = 3 \cdot 16 = 48$

$5(1+2)^3 = 5(3)^3 = 5 \cdot 27 = 135$

$-6^2 = -36$

$(-6)^2 = 36$

$2^3 \cdot 5^2 = 8 \cdot 25 = 200$

☞ Try These

1. Fill in the blank(s).

   (a) In the exponential expression b^n, _____ is the base and _____ is the exponent.

   (b) A positive integer exponent attached to a number tells how many times the number is used as a _____.

   (c) The second power of a number is its _____.

   (d) The third power of a number is its _____.

2. Express the product as an exponential expression.

   (a) $7 \times 7 \times 7 \times 7 \times 7$

   (b) $\left(-\dfrac{2}{3}\right)\left(-\dfrac{2}{3}\right)\left(-\dfrac{2}{3}\right)\left(-\dfrac{2}{3}\right)$

   (c) $(1.5)(1.5)(1.5)$

   (d) $\left(\sqrt{3}\right)\left(\sqrt{3}\right)$

3. Evaluate the expression.

   (a) $(0.3)^4$

   (b) 5^3

   (c) $\left(-\dfrac{2}{3}\right)^5$

   (d) $\left(-\sqrt{3}\right)^2$

   (e) -5^4

   (f) $2 \cdot 3^2$

Solutions

1. **(a)** b; n
   (b) factor
   (c) square
   (d) cube

2. **(a)** 7^5
   (b) $\left(-\dfrac{2}{3}\right)^4$
   (c) $(1.5)^3$
   (d) $\left(\sqrt{3}\right)^2$

3. **(a)** $(0.3)^4 = (0.3)(0.3)(0.3)(0.3) = 0.0081$
   (b) $5^3 = 5 \times 5 \times 5 = 125$
   (c) $\left(-\dfrac{2}{3}\right)^5 = \left(-\dfrac{2}{3}\right)\left(-\dfrac{2}{3}\right)\left(-\dfrac{2}{3}\right)\left(-\dfrac{2}{3}\right)\left(-\dfrac{2}{3}\right) = -\dfrac{32}{243}$
   (d) $\left(-\sqrt{3}\right)^2 = \left(-\sqrt{3}\right)\left(-\sqrt{3}\right) = 3$
   (e) $-5^4 = -(5 \times 5 \times 5 \times 5) = -(625) = -625$
   (f) $2 \cdot 3^2 = 2 \cdot 9 = 18$

Understanding Zero Exponents

When zero is the exponent on a *nonzero* number, the value of the exponential expression is 1. That is, if b is a number such that $b \neq 0$, then $b^0 = 1$. Here are examples.

$$3^0 = 1$$
$$(-3)^0 = 1$$
$$\left(\frac{3}{4}\right)^0 = 1$$
$$(5.12)^0 = 1$$
$$4(2)^0 = 4 \cdot 1 = 4$$

Tip: $(0)^0$ has no meaning. It is undefined.

☞ Try These

1. Fill in the blank.

    (a) If b is a number such that $b \neq 0$, then $b^0 =$ _____.

    (b) When zero is the exponent, the base cannot be _____.

2. Evaluate the expression.

    (a) $(-7)^0$

    (b) $\left(\frac{2}{3}\right)^0$

    (c) $(7.5)^0$

    (d) $\left(\sqrt{10}\right)^0$

    (e) $(900 + 1{,}000)^0$

    (f) $8(0.3)^0$

Solutions

1. **(a)** 1

    (b) zero

2. **(a)** $(-7)^0 = 1$

    (b) $\left(\frac{2}{3}\right)^0 = 1$

    (c) $(7.5)^0 = 1$

    (d) $\left(\sqrt{10}\right)^0 = 1$

    (e) $(900 + 1{,}000)^0 = 1$

    (f) $8(0.3)^0 = 8(1) = 8$

Understanding Negative Integer Exponents

Negative integer exponents denote reciprocals. If b is a number such that $b \neq 0$, $b^{-n} = \dfrac{1}{b^n}$. Here are examples.

$$2^{-3} = \frac{1}{2^3}$$

$$10^{-4} = \frac{1}{10^4}$$

To evaluate an exponential expression that has a negative integer exponent, first express it as the *reciprocal* of the matching exponential expression that has a *positive* integer exponent. Then perform the repeated multiplication. Here are examples.

$$10^{-4} = \frac{1}{10^4} = \frac{1}{10 \times 10 \times 10 \times 10} = \frac{1}{10,000}$$

$$(-10)^{-4} = \frac{1}{(-10)^4} = \frac{1}{(-10)(-10)(-10)(-10)} = \frac{1}{10,000}$$

$$2^{-3} = \frac{1}{2^3} = \frac{1}{2 \times 2 \times 2} = \frac{1}{8}$$

$$(-2)^{-3} = \frac{1}{(-2)^3} = \frac{1}{(-2)(-2)(-2)} = \frac{1}{-8} = -\frac{1}{8}$$

Tip: Notice $(-2)^{-3}$ is negative because $(-2)^3$ is –8, not because the exponent, –3, is negative. The negative part of the exponent tells you to write a reciprocal; it does not tell you to make your answer negative. For instance,

$$(-3)^{-4} = \frac{1}{(-3)^4} = \frac{1}{(-3)(-3)(-3)(-3)} = \frac{1}{81}.$$

☞ Try These

1. Fill in the blank.

    (a) Negative integer exponents denote _____.

    (b) If b is a number such that $b \neq 0$, $b^{-n} =$ _____.

2. Write the expression as an equivalent expression with a positive exponent.

    (a) 5^{-3}

    (b) $\left(-\dfrac{1}{2}\right)^{-4}$

    (c) 10^{-2}

    (d) $(0.2)^{-5}$

3. Evaluate the expression.

(a) 5^{-3}

(b) $\left(-\dfrac{1}{2}\right)^{-4}$

(c) 10^{-2}

(d) $(0.2)^{-5}$

Solutions

1. (a) reciprocals

(b) $\dfrac{1}{b^n}$

2. (a) $5^{-3} = \dfrac{1}{5^3}$

(b) $\left(-\dfrac{1}{2}\right)^{-4} = \dfrac{1}{\left(-\dfrac{1}{2}\right)^4}$

(c) $10^{-2} = \dfrac{1}{10^2}$

(d) $(0.2)^{-5} = \dfrac{1}{(0.2)^5}$

3. (a) $5^{-3} = \dfrac{1}{5^3} = \dfrac{1}{5\times5\times5} = \dfrac{1}{125}$

(b) $\left(-\dfrac{1}{2}\right)^{-4} = \dfrac{1}{\left(-\dfrac{1}{2}\right)^4} = \dfrac{1}{\left(-\dfrac{1}{2}\right)\left(-\dfrac{1}{2}\right)\left(-\dfrac{1}{2}\right)\left(-\dfrac{1}{2}\right)} = \dfrac{1}{\dfrac{1}{16}} = 16$

(c) $10^{-2} = \dfrac{1}{10^2} = \dfrac{1}{10\times10} = \dfrac{1}{100}$

(d) $(0.2)^{-5} = \dfrac{1}{(0.2)^5} = \dfrac{1}{(0.2)(0.2)(0.2)(0.2)(0.2)} = \dfrac{1}{0.00032}$

Reviewing the Order of Operations

When you evaluate numerical expressions, follow the order of operations.

1. Compute inside **Parentheses** (or other grouping symbols).
2. Do **Exponentiation.**
3. **Multiply** and **Divide** in the order in which they occur from left to right.
4. **Add** and **Subtract** in the order in which they occur from left to right.

Tip: Use the mnemonic "Please Excuse My Dear Aunt Sally"—abbreviated as PEMDAS—to help you remember the order of operations. The first letters stand for "Parentheses, Exponentiation, Multiplication, Division, Addition, and Subtraction."

Here are examples.

Evaluate $80 - 3^2(9 - 7)^3 + (-1)^4(9)^2$.

$$\begin{aligned}
80 - 3^2 (9-7)^3 +(-1)^4 (9)^2 &= 80 - 3^2 (2)^3 +(-1)^4 (9)^2 \\
&= 80 - 9(8) + (1)(81) \\
&= 80 - 72 + 81 \\
&= 89
\end{aligned}$$

Evaluate $(-2)^3 (-3)^2 +\left(\sqrt{5}\right)^2 \left(\sqrt{6}\right)^2 +(123,456,789)^0$.

$$\begin{aligned}
(-2)^3 (-3)^2 +\left(\sqrt{5}\right)^2 \left(\sqrt{6}\right)^2 +(123,456,789)^0 &= (-8)(9) + (5)(6) + 1 \\
&= -72 + 30 + 1 \\
&= -41
\end{aligned}$$

Evaluate $\dfrac{5}{6} + 6^{-1} + \dfrac{8}{9} + 3^{-2} + (1+1)^3$.

$$\begin{aligned}
\frac{5}{6} + 6^{-1} + \frac{8}{9} + 3^{-2} + (1+1)^3 &= \frac{5}{6} + 6^{-1} + \frac{8}{9} + 3^{-2} + (2)^3 \\
&= \frac{5}{6} + \frac{1}{6} + \frac{8}{9} + \frac{1}{3^2} + 8 \\
&= \frac{5}{6} + \frac{1}{6} + \frac{8}{9} + \frac{1}{9} + 8 \\
&= \frac{6}{6} + \frac{9}{9} + 8 \\
&= 1 + 1 + 8 \\
&= 10
\end{aligned}$$

☞ Try These

1. Evaluate $60 - 2^3(9 + 1)^2 + (-1)^2(5)^3$.
2. Evaluate $(2)^3 (-4)^2 +\left(\sqrt{7}\right)^2 \left(-\sqrt{3}\right)^2 +(90,000 + 23,999)^0$.
3. Evaluate $\dfrac{2}{3} + 3^{-1} + \dfrac{24}{25} + 5^{-2} + (3+1)^3 - 2^4$.

Solutions

1. $\begin{aligned}[t]
60 - 2^3 (9+1)^2 +(-1)^2 (5)^3 &= 60 - 2^3 (10)^2 +(-1)^2 (5)^3 \\
&= 60 - 8(100) + (1)(125) \\
&= 60 - 800 + 125 \\
&= -615
\end{aligned}$

2. $\begin{aligned}[t]
(2)^3 (-4)^2 +\left(\sqrt{7}\right)^2 \left(-\sqrt{3}\right)^2 +(90,000 + 23,999)^0 &= (8)(16) + (7)(3) + 1 \\
&= 128 + 21 + 1 \\
&= 150
\end{aligned}$

3. $\dfrac{2}{3}+3^{-1}+\dfrac{24}{25}+5^{-2}+(3+1)^3-2^4 = \dfrac{2}{3}+3^{-1}+\dfrac{24}{25}+5^{-2}+(4)^3-2^4$

$$= \dfrac{2}{3}+\dfrac{1}{3}+\dfrac{24}{25}+\dfrac{1}{25}+64-16$$

$$= \dfrac{3}{3}+\dfrac{25}{25}+48$$

$$= 1+1+48$$

$$= 50$$

Understanding and Applying the Properties of Integer Exponents

If a and b are any nonzero real numbers and m and n are integers, you can transform exponential expressions by applying the properties detailed here.

Property 1: When you multiply exponential expressions that have the *same* base, add the exponents and keep the same base.

$$b^m b^n = b^{m+n}$$

For instance, when m and n are positive integer exponents, b^m is m factors of b and b^n is n factors of b. When you multiply b^m by b^n, you get a total of $(m+n)$ factors of b.

Tip: This property works only if the bases are the same. Notice the base b appears twice in $b^m b^n$.

Here is an example.

$4^2 4^3 = 4^{2+3} = 4^5$ [because $4^2 4^3 = (4 \times 4) \times (4 \times 4 \times 4) = 4^5$]

Property 2: When you divide exponential expressions that have the *same* base, subtract the divisor exponent from the dividend exponent and keep the same base.

$$\dfrac{b^m}{b^n} = b^{m-n}$$

For instance, when m and n are positive integer exponents with $m > n$, b^m is m factors of b and b^n is n factors of b. When you divide b^m by b^n, n factors of b in the denominator will cancel n factors of b in the numerator, leaving $(m-n)$ factors of b in the numerator.

Tip: This property works only if the bases are the same. Notice the base b appears twice in $\dfrac{b^m}{b^n}$.

Here is an example.

$\dfrac{4^5}{4^2} = 4^{5-2} = 4^3 \left[\text{because } \dfrac{4^5}{4^2} = \dfrac{4\times4\times4\times4\times4}{4\times4} = \dfrac{\cancel{4}\times\cancel{4}\times4\times4\times4}{\cancel{4}\times\cancel{4}} = 4^3 \right]$

Property 3: When you raise an exponential expression to a power, keep the base and multiply its exponent by the power.

$$(b^m)^n = b^{mn}$$

For instance, when m and n are positive integer exponents, b^m is m factors of b and $(b^m)^n$ is n factors of b^m. So, using Property 1,

$$(b^m)^n = \underbrace{b^m \times b^m \times \cdots b^m}_{n \text{ factors of } b^m} = b^{\overbrace{m+m+\cdots+m}^{n \text{ times}}} = b^{mn} \text{ for a total of } mn \text{ factors of } b.$$

Here is an example.

$$(5^2)^3 = 5^{2 \cdot 3} = 5^6 \text{ [because } (5^2)^3 = (5^2)(5^2)(5^2) = 5^{2+2+2} = 5^6]$$

Property 4: A product of two or more factors raised to a power is the product of each factor raised to the power.

$$(ab)^n = a^n b^n$$

For instance, when n is a positive integer exponent,

$$(ab)^n = \underbrace{ab \times ab \times \cdots ab}_{n \text{ factors}} = \left(\underbrace{a \times a \times \cdots a}_{n \text{ factors}}\right)\left(\underbrace{b \times b \times \cdots b}_{n \text{ factors}}\right) = a^n b^n$$

This property means that you get the same answer whether you multiply two factors first and then raise the product to a power, or you raise each factor to a power and then multiply the results. Here is an example.

$$(2 \cdot 5)^3 = (10)^3 = 1,000 \text{ and } (2 \cdot 5)^3 = 2^3 \cdot 5^3 = 8 \cdot 125 = 1,000$$

Property 5: If $a \neq 0$, $a^{-n} = \dfrac{1}{a^n}$, by definition.

Applying a negative exponent to a nonzero number results in a reciprocal. Here is an example.

$$4^{-3} = \frac{1}{4^3} = \frac{1}{64}$$

Property 6: If $a \neq 0$, $a^0 = 1$, by definition.

When zero is the exponent on any nonzero number or quantity, the value of the expression is always 1. Here is an example.

$$(-658.89)^0 = 1$$

Sometimes, you might find it convenient to transform exponential expressions by applying the above properties *before* proceeding through the order of operations.

Here is an example.

Evaluate $(3 \cdot 10)^2 - \dfrac{5^7}{5^4}$.

Tip: Transforming exponential expressions *first* simplifies the calculations in this problem.

$(3 \cdot 10)^2 - \dfrac{5^7}{5^4} = 3^2 \cdot 10^2 - \dfrac{5^7}{5^4}$ Transform $(3 \cdot 10)^2$ instead of doing its parentheses first.

$\qquad\qquad\qquad = 3^2 \cdot 10^2 - 5^3$ Transform $\dfrac{5^7}{5^4}$ instead of doing its exponentiation first.

$\qquad\qquad\qquad = 9 \cdot 100 - 125$

$\qquad\qquad\qquad = 900 - 125$

$\qquad\qquad\qquad = 775$

A word of caution: Be careful when transforming exponential expressions when you have grouping symbols. It is very important when you have *addition* or *subtraction* inside the grouping symbol that you perform operations in grouping symbols first.

The exception is when the exponent on a grouping symbol is zero. If you are certain that the sum or difference inside the grouping symbol is nonzero, you can evaluate the expression to be 1 without performing the operations inside the grouping symbol first.

Here are examples.

$(1+5)^3 = (6)^3 = 216$ Add first, then do exponentiation.

Note: $(1+5)^3 \neq 1^3 + 5^3 = 1 + 125 = 126$ Exponentiation does not "distribute" over addition.

$(7-4)^3 = 3^3 = 27$ Subtract first, then do exponentiation.

Note: $(7-4)^3 \neq 7^3 - 4^3 = 343 - 64 = 279$ Exponentiation does not "distribute" over subtraction.

$(1{,}254 + 51{,}000)^0 = 1$ A nonzero number raised to the zero power is 1.

Here is a summary of the properties of exponents.

Properties of Exponents

If a and b are any nonzero real numbers and m and n are integers, the following properties hold.

1. $b^m b^n = b^{m+n}$
2. $\dfrac{b^m}{b^n} = b^{m-n}$
3. $(b^m)^n = b^{mn}$
4. $(ab)^n = a^n b^n$
5. If $a \neq 0$, $a^{-n} = \dfrac{1}{a^n}$
6. If $a \neq 0$, $a^0 = 1$

☞ Try These

1. Fill in the blank(s).

    (a) When you multiply exponential expressions that have the *same* base, _____ the exponents and keep the same base.

    (b) When you divide exponential expressions that have the *same* base, subtract the _____ exponent from the _____ exponent and keep the same base.

    (c) When you raise an exponential expression to a power, keep the base and _____ its exponent by the power.

    (d) A product of two or more factors raised to a power is the _____ of each factor raised to the power.

2. Use the properties of exponents to obtain an equivalent exponential expression.

    (a) $10^3 \times 10^5$

    (b) $10^{-3} \times 10^5$

    (c) $\dfrac{10^5}{10^3}$

    (d) $(10^3)^5$

3. Use the properties of exponents to perform the indicated operation.

    (a) $(2a)^3$

    (b) $b^0 \cdot b^5$

    (c) $(x^{-6})^{-2}$

    (d) $x \cdot x^2$

    (e) $\dfrac{y^4}{y^0}$

    (f) $\dfrac{a^6}{a^2}$

4. Evaluate. Use the property of exponents when appropriate.

    (a) $\dfrac{(5 \cdot 10)^3}{5^2} - \dfrac{4^9}{4^7} + \left(\dfrac{3}{4} - \dfrac{5}{6} + \dfrac{1}{2} \right)^0$

    (b) $(2 + 10)^2 - (2 \cdot 10)^2$

Solutions

1. **(a)** add
    (b) divisor; dividend
    (c) multiply
    (d) product

2. **(a)** $10^3 \times 10^5 = 10^8$
    (b) $10^{-3} \times 10^5 = 10^2$
    (c) $\dfrac{10^5}{10^3} = 10^2$
    (d) $(10^3)^5 = 10^{15}$

3. **(a)** $(2a)^3 = 2^3a^3 = 8a^3$

   (b) $b^0 \cdot b^5 = 1 \cdot b^5 = b^5$

   (c) $(x^{-6})^{-2} = x^{12}$

   (d) $x \cdot x^2 = x^3$

   (e) $\dfrac{y^4}{y^0} = \dfrac{y^4}{1} = y^4$

   (f) $\dfrac{a^6}{a^2} = a^4$

4. **(a)** $\dfrac{(5\cdot10)^3}{5^2} - \dfrac{4^9}{4^7} + \left(\dfrac{3}{4} - \dfrac{5}{6} + \dfrac{1}{2}\right)^0 = \dfrac{5^3\cdot10^3}{5^2} - 4^2 + 1$

   $= 5^1\cdot10^3 - 4^2 + 1$

   $= 5\cdot1{,}000 - 16 + 1$

   $= 5{,}000 - 16 + 1$

   $= 4{,}985$

   (b) $(2+10)^2 - (2\cdot10)^2 = (12)^2 - 2^2\cdot10^2$

   $= 144 - 4\cdot100$

   $= 144 - 400$

   $= -256$

Understanding and Working with Scientific Notation

(CCSS.Math.Content.8.EE.A.3, CCSS.Math.Content.8.EE.A.4)

Scientific notation is a way to write very large or very small numbers in a shortened form. Scientific notation helps keep track of the decimal places and makes performing computations with these numbers easier.

A number written in scientific notation is written as a product of two factors. The first factor is a number that is greater than or equal to 1 but less than 10. The second factor is an integer power of 10. The idea is to make a product that will equal the given number. Any decimal number can be written in scientific notation.

Writing Large Numbers in Scientific Notation

Follow these steps to write a large number in scientific notation.

Step 1. Create the first factor. Move the decimal point left, to the immediate right of the first *nonzero* digit of the number.

Step 2. Create the second factor. The second factor will be an integer power of 10. The exponent for the power of 10 is the number of places you moved the decimal point in Step 1. For numbers greater than or equal to 10, it will be a positive integer.

Tip: As the exponent increases by 1, the value of the number increases by a factor of 10.

Here is an example.

Write 34,000 in scientific notation.

Step 1. Create the first factor. Move the decimal point left, to the immediate right of the first *nonzero* digit of the number.

$$3.\,4000$$
$$\underset{\substack{4\text{ places} \\ \text{left}}}{\underleftarrow{}}$$

Step 2. Create the second factor. The exponent for the power of 10 is the number of places you moved the decimal point in Step 1. It is a positive integer.

$$34,000 = 3.\,4000 \times 10^? = 3.4 \times 10^4$$
$$\underset{\substack{4\text{ places} \\ \text{left}}}{\underleftarrow{}}$$

Tip: When you move the decimal point to the left, the exponent on 10 is positive.

As long as you make sure your first factor is greater than or equal to 1 and less than 10, you can always check whether you wrote the number in scientific notation correctly. Expand your answer to decimal notation by multiplying to see whether you get your original number back.

Tip: A shortcut for multiplying by 10^n is to move the decimal point n places to the right, inserting zeros as needed.

$$3.4 \times 10^4 = 3\,4000. = 34,000 \checkmark$$
$$\underset{\substack{4\text{ places} \\ \text{right}}}{\underrightarrow{}}$$

☞ Try These

1. Fill in the blank.

   (a) The first factor of a number written in scientific notation is greater than or equal to 1, but less than _____.

   (b) Exponential expressions such as 10^1, 10^2, 10^3, and so on are _____ of 10.

2. Write the number in scientific notation.

   (a) 456,000,000

   (b) 93,000,000

   (c) 26

   (d) 130

   (e) 1,760

3. Write the number in decimal notation.

   (a) 2.68×10^9

   (b) 5.3×10^4

   (c) 1.5×10^2

   (d) 3.25×10^8

   (e) 2×10^5

4. The diameter of the sun is about 1,400,000 kilometers. Express this measurement in scientific notation.

Solutions

1. (a) 10
   (b) powers

2. (a) $456,000,000 = 4.56 \times 10^8$
   (b) $93,000,000 = 9.3 \times 10^7$
   (c) $26 = 2.6 \times 10^1$
   (d) $130 = 1.3 \times 10^2$
   (e) $1,760 = 1.76 \times 10^3$

3. (a) $2.68 \times 10^9 = 2,680,000,000$
   (b) $5.3 \times 10^4 = 53,000$
   (c) $1.5 \times 10^2 = 150$
   (d) $3.25 \times 10^8 = 325,000,000$
   (e) $2 \times 10^5 = 200,000$

4. 1.4×10^6

Writing Small Numbers in Scientific Notation

Follow these steps to write a small number in scientific notation.

Step 1. Create the first factor. Move the decimal point right, to the immediate right of the first *nonzero* digit of the number.

Step 2. Create the second factor. The second factor will be an integer power of 10. The exponent for the power of 10 is the negative of the number of places you moved the decimal point in Step 1. For numbers between 0 and 1, it will be a negative integer.

Tip: As the exponent decreases by 1, the value of the number decreases by a factor of 10.

Here is an example.

Write 0.00047 in scientific notation.

Step 1. Create the first factor. Move the decimal point right, to the immediate right of the first *nonzero* digit of the number.

$$0\ 0004\ .7$$
4 places right

Step 2. Create the second factor. The exponent for the power of 10 is the negative of the number of places you moved the decimal point in Step 1. It is a negative integer.

$$0.00047 = 0\ 0004\ .7 \times 10^? = 4.7 \times 10^{-4}$$
4 places right

Tip: When you move the decimal point to the right, the exponent on 10 is negative.

After you make sure your first factor is greater than or equal to 1 and less than 10, check whether you wrote the number in scientific notation correctly. Expand your answer to decimal notation by multiplying to see whether you get your original number back.

Tip: A shortcut for multiplying by 10^{-n} is to move the decimal point n places to the left, inserting zeros as needed.

$$4.7 \times 10^{-4} = 0.\ 0004\ 7 = 0.00047 \checkmark$$

$$\underbrace{\qquad\qquad}_{\substack{4 \text{ places} \\ \text{left}}}$$

☞ Try These

1. Write the number in scientific notation.

    (a) 0.00004
    (b) 0.000000975
    (c) 0.3
    (d) 0.0064
    (e) 0.000000047

2. Write the number in decimal notation.

    (a) 2.6×10^{-9}
    (b) 1.572×10^{-3}
    (c) 2×10^{-4}
    (d) 8.6×10^{-2}
    (e) 9×10^{-10}

3. A dollar bill is about 0.0043 inches thick. Express this measurement in scientific notation.

Solutions

1. **(a)** $0.00004 = 4 \times 10^{-5}$
    (b) $0.000000975 = 9.75 \times 10^{-7}$
    (c) $0.3 = 3 \times 10^{-1}$
    (d) $0.0064 = 6.4 \times 10^{-3}$
    (e) $0.000000047 = 4.7 \times 10^{-8}$

2. Write the number in decimal notation.
    (a) $2.6 \times 10^{-9} = 0.0000000026$
    (b) $1.572 \times 10^{-3} = 0.001572$
    (c) $2 \times 10^{-4} = 0.0002$
    (d) $8.6 \times 10^{-2} = 0.086$
    (e) $9 \times 10^{-10} = 0.0000000009$

3. 4.3×10^{-3}

Selecting Appropriate Units for Measurements of Very Large or Very Small Quantities

The units for measurements of very large or very small quantities should be appropriate for the situation. Make sure your choice of units communicates the size of the measurement in a meaningful way to your intended audience. Here are examples.

Delphina tells her friend Jason that she spends about 144,000 seconds working on homework each month during the school year. About how many hours does Delphina spend on homework each month?

There are 60 minutes in an hour and 60 seconds in a minute. (See the appendix for measurement conversions.) So, there are $60 \times 60 = 3,600$ seconds in an hour.

$$144,000 \text{ sec} \div \frac{3,600 \text{ sec}}{1 \text{ hr}} = 144,000 \text{ sec} \times \frac{1 \text{ hr}}{3,600 \text{ sec}} = \frac{144,000}{3,600} \text{ hr} = 40 \text{ hr}$$

If Delphina spends about 40 hours on homework each month, which choice of measurement unit would better communicate the size of the measurement in a meaningful way to Jason: seconds or hours?

Hours would better communicate the size of the measurement in a meaningful way to Jason.

Andrew tells his 10-year-old brother that the diameter of a dime is about 0.0000179 kilometer.

(a) How many centimeters is 0.0000179 kilometer?

(b) Which choice of measurement unit would better communicate the size of the measurement in a meaningful way to Andrew's brother: kilometers or centimeters?

(a) There are 1,000 meters in a kilometer and 100 centimeters in a meter. (See the appendix for measurement conversions.) So, there are $1,000 \times 100 = 100,000$ centimeters in a kilometer.

$$0.0000179 \text{ km} \times \frac{100,000 \text{ cm}}{1 \text{ km}} = 1.79 \text{ cm}$$

0.0000179 kilometer is 1.79 centimeters.

(b) Centimeters would better communicate the size of the measurement in a meaningful way to Andrew's brother.

☞ Try These

1. Talia tells her classmate Dangelo that the distance from her house to school is 316,800 inches.

    (a) How many miles is Talia's house from school?

    (b) Which choice of measurement unit would better communicate the size of the measurement in a meaningful way to Dangelo: inches or miles?

2. Marcos tells his friend Mona that the naked human eye can see objects as small as 0.0000001 kilometer.

    (a) How many millimeters is 0.0000001 kilometer?

    (b) Which choice of measurement unit would better communicate the size of the measurement in a meaningful way to Mona: kilometers or millimeters?

Solutions

1. (a) There are 5,280 feet in a mile and 12 inches in a foot. (See the appendix for measurement conversions.) So, there are 5,280 × 12 = 63,360 inches in a mile.

$$316{,}800 \text{ in} \div \frac{63{,}360 \text{ in}}{1 \text{ mi}} = 316{,}800 \text{ in} \times \frac{1 \text{ mi}}{63{,}360 \text{ in}} = \frac{316{,}800}{63{,}360} \text{ mi} = 5 \text{ mi}$$

Talia's house is 5 miles from school.

   (b) Miles would better communicate the size of the measurement in a meaningful way to Dangelo.

2. (a) There are 1,000 meters in a kilometer and 1,000 millimeters in a meter. (See the appendix for measurement conversions.) So, there are 1,000 × 1,000 = 1,000,000 millimeters in a kilometer.

$$0.0000001 \text{ km} \times \frac{1{,}000{,}000 \text{ mm}}{1 \text{ km}} = 0.1 \text{ mm}$$

0.0000001 kilometer is 0.1 millimeter.

   (b) Millimeters would better communicate the size of the measurement in a meaningful way to Mona.

Interpreting Scientific Notation Generated by Technology

Many scientific and graphing calculators and other technology devices display scientific calculators using E notation. Here are examples.

2.1E5 means $2.1 \times 10^5 = 210{,}000$

6.4E⁻5 means $6.4 \times 10^{-5} = 0.000064$

> **Tip:** Calculators have a special key for entering negative signs. Do not use the subtraction key. Check your calculator manual for instructions.

☞ Try These

1. Write 1.3E6 in decimal notation.

2. Write 4.35E⁻4 in decimal notation.

Solutions

1. $1.3\text{E}6 = 1.3 \times 10^6 = 1{,}300{,}000$

2. $4.35\text{E}⁻4 = 4.35 \times 10^{-4} = 0.000435$

Multiplying and Dividing Numbers Written in Scientific Notation

You can compute with numbers written in scientific notation. When your answer is a very large or a very small number, you should express it in proper scientific notation. Otherwise, express your answer in decimal notation.

Multiplying

To multiply two numbers written in scientific notation, follow these steps.

Step 1. Multiply the first factors of each number.

Step 2. Using the properties of exponents, multiply the second factors of each number.

Step 3. If the result of Step 1 is greater than 10, rewrite it in scientific notation. Simplify the resulting expression so that your final answer is in proper scientific notation.

Here is an example.

Compute $(3 \times 10^7)(2 \times 10^4)$.

$$(3 \times 10^7)(2 \times 10^4) = \underbrace{(3 \times 2)}_{\text{First factors}} \times \underbrace{(10^7 \times 10^4)}_{\text{Second factors}} = \underset{\text{Step 1}}{6} \times \underset{\text{Step 2}}{10^{11}} = 6 \times 10^{11}$$

Tip: Step 3 is not needed in the above example because the answer is in proper scientific notation.

Here is an example in which Step 3 is needed.

Compute $(5 \times 10^9)(4 \times 10^3)$.

$$(5 \times 10^9)(4 \times 10^3) = \underbrace{(5 \times 4)}_{\text{First factors}} \times \underbrace{(10^9 \times 10^3)}_{\text{Second factors}} = \underset{\text{Step 1}}{20} \times \underset{\text{Step 2}}{10^{12}} = \underbrace{2.0 \times 10^1 \times 10^{12} = 2 \times 10^{13}}_{\text{Step 3}}$$

Here are additional examples.

Compute $(2 \times 10^5)(3 \times 10^{-9})$.

$$(2 \times 10^5)(3 \times 10^{-9}) = (2 \times 3) \times (10^5 \times 10^{-9}) = 6 \times 10^{-4}$$

Compute $(3.5 \times 10^{-7})(2 \times 10^{-2})$.

$$(3.5 \times 10^{-7})(2 \times 10^{-2}) = (3.5 \times 2) \times (10^{-7} \times 10^{-2}) = 7 \times 10^{-9}$$

Compute $(50 \times 10^{-4})(6 \times 10^{-2})$.

$$(50 \times 10^{-4})(6 \times 10^{-2}) = (50 \times 6) \times (10^{-4} \times 10^{-2}) = 300 \times 10^{-6} = 3.00 \times 10^2 \times 10^{-6} = 3 \times 10^{-4}$$

Dividing

To divide two numbers written in scientific notation, follow these steps.

Step 1. Divide the first factors of each number.

Step 2. Using the properties of exponents, divide the second factors of each number.

Step 3. If the result of Step 1 is less than 1, rewrite it in scientific notation. Simplify the resulting expression so that your final answer is in proper scientific notation.

Here are examples.

Compute $\dfrac{8\times10^5}{2\times10^3}$.

$$\frac{8\times10^5}{2\times10^3} = \underbrace{\left(\frac{8}{2}\right)}_{\text{First factors}} \times \underbrace{\left(\frac{10^5}{10^3}\right)}_{\text{Second factors}} = \underset{\text{Step 1}}{4} \times \underset{\text{Step 2}}{10^2} = 4\times10^2$$

Compute $\dfrac{6\times10^4}{2\times10^9}$.

$$\frac{6\times10^4}{2\times10^9} = \underbrace{\left(\frac{6}{2}\right)}_{\text{First factors}} \times \underbrace{\left(\frac{10^4}{10^9}\right)}_{\text{Second factors}} = \underset{\text{Step 1}}{3} \times \underset{\text{Step 2}}{10^{-5}} = 3\times10^{-5}$$

Compute $\dfrac{4\times10^{12}}{8\times10^3}$.

$$\frac{4\times10^{12}}{8\times10^3} = \underbrace{\left(\frac{4}{8}\right)}_{\text{First factors}} \times \underbrace{\left(\frac{10^{12}}{10^3}\right)}_{\text{Second factors}} = \underset{\text{Step 1}}{0.5} \times \underset{\text{Step 2}}{10^9} = \underset{\text{Step 3}}{5\times10^{-1}\times10^9 = 5\times10^8}$$

☞ Try These

1. Compute as indicated. Express your answer in proper scientific notation.

   (a) $(4 \times 10^7)(1.5 \times 10^6)$

   (b) $(4 \times 10^{-5})(2 \times 10^4)$

   (c) $(5 \times 10^6)(2.4 \times 10^4)$

   (d) $\dfrac{9\times10^8}{3\times10^5}$

   (e) $\dfrac{6.4\times10^3}{1.6\times10^5}$

2. The mass of the planet Jupiter is approximately 2×10^{27} kilograms. The mass of Earth is approximately 6×10^{24} kilograms. The mass of Jupiter is approximately how many times larger than the mass of Earth? Express your answer in proper scientific notation and, if appropriate, in decimal notation as well.

3. The mass of a hydrogen atom is about 2×10^{-24} grams. The mass of an electron is about 9×10^{-28} grams. How many times heavier is a hydrogen atom than an electron? Express your answer in proper scientific notation and, if appropriate, in decimal notation as well.

Solutions

1. (a) $(4 \times 10^7)(1.5 \times 10^6) = 6 \times 10^{13}$
   (b) $(4 \times 10^{-5})(2 \times 10^4) = 8 \times 10^{-1}$
   (c) $(5 \times 10^6)(2.4 \times 10^4) = 12 \times 10^{10} = 1.2 \times 10^1 \times 10^{10} = 1.2 \times 10^{11}$
   (d) $\dfrac{9\times10^8}{3\times10^5} = 3\times10^3$
   (e) $\dfrac{6.4\times10^3}{1.6\times10^5} = 4\times10^{-2}$

2. $\dfrac{2\times10^{27}}{6\times10^{24}} \approx 0.3\times10^3 = 3\times10^{-1}\times10^3 = 3\times10^2$

The mass of Jupiter is about $3 \times 10^2 = 300$ times the mass of Earth.

3. $\dfrac{2\times10^{-24}}{9\times10^{-28}} \approx 0.2\times10^4 = 2\times10^{-1}\times10^4 = 2\times10^3$

A hydrogen atom is about $2 \times 10^3 = 2{,}000$ times heavier than an electron.

Solving One-Variable Linear Equations

(CCSS.Math.Content.8.EE.C.7.A, CCSS.Math.Content.8.EE.C.7.B)

An **equation** is a statement that two mathematical expressions are equal. An equation has two sides. Whatever is on the left side of the equal sign is the **left side (LS)** of the equation, and whatever is on the right side of the equal sign is the **right side (RS)** of the equation.

In a **one-variable linear equation,** there is only one variable, the variable has an unwritten exponent of 1, and no product of variables or variable divisors are allowed.

A **solution** to a one-variable linear equation is a number that when substituted for the variable makes the equation true. An equation is true when the left side has the same value as the right side. For example, -5 is a solution to the equation $2x + 8 = -2$. It is a number that when substituted for x makes the equation $2x + 8 = -2$ a true statement.

The set consisting of all solutions to an equation is the equation's **solution set.** If the solution set is all real numbers, the equation is an **identity.** For example, $x + 5 = x + 2 + 3$ is an identity because any number substituted for x will make the equation true. Thus, an identity has an infinite number of solutions. If the solution set is empty, the equation has **no solution.** For example, $x + 5 = x + 2$ has no solution because there is no number that will make this equation true. Equations that have the same solution set are **equivalent equations.**

To **solve a linear equation** in one variable means to find its solution set. Unless the equation is an identity or has no solution, the solution set will consist of one number. To determine whether a number is a solution to a one-variable equation, replace the variable with the number and perform the operations indicated on each side of the equation. If a true equation results, the number is a solution. This process is called **checking** a solution. For example, -5 is a solution to the equation $2x + 8 = -2$ because $2(-5) + 8 = -10 + 8 = -2$ is a true statement.

The equal sign in an equation is like a balance point. To keep the equation in balance, whatever you do to one side of the equation you must do to the other side of the equation. The strategy in solving an equation is to proceed through a series of "undoing" steps until you produce an equivalent equation that has this form:

$$\text{variable} = \text{solution}$$

A one-variable linear equation is solved when you succeed in getting the variable by itself on one side of the equation only, the variable's coefficient is understood to be 1, and the other side of the equation is a single number all by itself.

> **Tip:** Getting the variable term by itself on one side of the equation is referred to as *isolating the variable.*

The main actions that will result in equivalent equations as you proceed through the undoing process are

- Adding the same number to both sides of the equation.
- Subtracting the same number from both sides of the equation.
- Multiplying both sides of the equation by the same nonzero number.
- Dividing both sides of the equation by the same nonzero number.

Tip: Never multiply or divide both sides of an equation by 0.

What has been done to the variable determines which operation you should do. You do it to both sides of the equation to keep it balanced. You "undo" an operation by using the inverse of the operation. Addition and subtraction undo each other, and multiplication and division (or multiplying by the reciprocal) undo each other.

With that said, how do you proceed?

To solve an equation, follow these six steps.

Step 1. If the equation has parentheses, use the distributive property to remove them.

Step 2. Combine like terms, if any, on each side of the equation.

Step 3. If the variable appears on both sides of the equation, eliminate the variable from one side of the equation. Add a variable expression to both sides of the equation or subtract a variable expression from both sides so that the variable appears on only one side of the equation. Then combine like terms.

Step 4. Isolate the variable term. If a number is added to the variable term, subtract that number from both sides of the equation. If a number is subtracted from the variable term, add that number to both sides of the equation. Then combine like terms.

Step 5. Divide both sides of the equation by the coefficient of the variable. If the coefficient is a fraction, divide by multiplying both sides of the equation by the fraction's reciprocal. (*Tip:* This step should always result in 1 being understood as the coefficient of the variable because you have divided out like factors.)

Step 6. Check the solution by substituting it into the original equation.

Tip: Skip steps that are not needed for the equation you are solving.

One Solution

Here are examples of solving one-variable linear equations in which there is exactly one solution.

Solve $5(x + 8) - 35 = 2x - 46$.

Step 1. Use the distributive property to remove parentheses.

$$5(x+8) - 35 = 2x - 46$$
$$5x + 40 - 35 = 2x - 46$$

Step 2. Combine like terms.

$$5x + 5 = 2x - 46$$

Step 3. Eliminate the variable from the RS of the equation by subtracting $2x$ from both sides of the equation. Then combine like terms.

$$5x + 5 - 2x = 2x - 46 - 2x$$
$$5x - 2x + 5 = 2x - 2x - 46$$
$$3x + 5 = -46$$

Step 4. Isolate the variable term by subtracting 5 from both sides of the equation. Then combine like terms.

$$3x + 5 - 5 = -46 - 5$$
$$3x = -51$$

Step 5. Divide both sides of the equation by the coefficient of the variable.

$$\frac{3x}{3} = \frac{-51}{3}$$
$$\frac{\cancel{3}x}{\cancel{3}} = -17$$
$$x = -17$$

Step 6. Check the solution.

$$5(x + 8) - 35 = 2x - 46$$
$$5(-17 + 8) - 35 \overset{?}{=} 2(-17) - 46$$
$$5(-9) - 35 \overset{?}{=} -34 - 46$$
$$-45 - 35 \overset{?}{=} -34 - 46$$
$$-80 \overset{\checkmark}{=} -80$$

Here's another example.

Solve $\dfrac{2}{3}x - 45 = -\left(\dfrac{1}{2}x + 24\right)$.

Step 1. Use the distributive property to remove parentheses.

$$\frac{2}{3}x - 45 = -\frac{1}{2}x - 24$$

Tip: When a negative sign immediately precedes a parentheses, remove the parentheses, but change the sign of every term inside the parentheses.

Step 2: Skip this step.

Step 3. Eliminate the variable from the RS of the equation by adding $\frac{1}{2}x$ to both sides of the equation. Then combine like terms.

$$\frac{2}{3}x - 45 + \frac{1}{2}x = -\frac{1}{2}x - 24 + \frac{1}{2}x$$

$$\frac{2}{3}x + \frac{1}{2}x - 45 = -\frac{1}{2}x + \frac{1}{2}x - 24$$

$$\frac{4}{6}x + \frac{3}{6}x - 45 = -\frac{1}{2}x + \frac{1}{2}x - 24$$

$$\frac{7}{6}x - 45 = -24$$

Step 4. Isolate the variable term by adding 45 to both sides of the equation. Then combine like terms.

$$\frac{7}{6}x - 45 + 45 = -24 + 45$$

$$\frac{7}{6}x = 21$$

Step 5. Multiply both sides of the equation by $\frac{6}{7}$, the reciprocal of $\frac{7}{6}$, the coefficient of the variable.

$$\frac{6}{7} \cdot \frac{7}{6}x = \frac{6}{7} \cdot \frac{21}{1}$$

$$\frac{\cancel{6}}{\cancel{7}} \cdot \frac{\cancel{7}}{\cancel{6}}x = \frac{6}{{}_1\cancel{7}} \cdot \frac{\cancel{21}^3}{1}$$

$$x = 18$$

Step 6. Check the solution.

$$\frac{2}{3}x - 45 = -\left(\frac{1}{2}x + 24\right)$$

$$\frac{2}{3}(18) - 45 \overset{?}{=} -\left(\frac{1}{2}(18) + 24\right)$$

$$\frac{2}{{}_1\cancel{3}}\left(\cancel{18}^6\right) - 45 \overset{?}{=} -\left(\frac{1}{{}_1\cancel{2}}\left(\cancel{18}^9\right) + 24\right)$$

$$12 - 45 \overset{?}{=} -(9 + 24)$$

$$-33 \overset{?}{=} -(33)$$

$$-33 \overset{\checkmark}{=} -33$$

Infinite Number of Solutions

When you attempt to solve an identity, you obtain an equation that has the form $a = a$, where a is a real number. You have an infinite number of solutions because any number substituted for x will make the equation true. Here is an example.

Solve $x + 5 = x + 2 + 3$.

$$x + 5 = x + 2 + 3$$
$$x + 5 = x + 5$$
$$x + 5 - x = x + 5 - x$$
$$x - x + 5 = x - x + 5$$
$$5 = 5$$

No Solution

When you attempt to solve an equation that has no solution, you obtain an equation that has the form $a = b$, where a and b are unequal real numbers. There is no number that will make the equation true. Here is an example.

Solve $x + 5 = x + 2$.

$$x + 5 = x + 2$$
$$x + 5 - x = x + 2 - x$$
$$x - x + 5 = x - x + 2$$
$$5 \neq 2$$

Using Shortcuts

As you become a skillful equation solver, you likely will modify the equation-solving process based on the particular equation you are trying to solve. For instance, you might divide both sides of an equation by a number before removing parentheses.

Here is an example.

Solve $100(2x + 40) = 600$.

Looking at the equation, you see that both sides are divisible by 100. Dividing both sides of the equation by 100 first will simplify the calculations.

$$100(2x + 40) = 600$$
$$\frac{\cancel{100}\,(2x + 40)}{\cancel{100}} = \frac{\cancel{600}^{\,6}}{\cancel{100}^{\,1}}$$
$$(2x + 40) = 6$$
$$2x + 40 = 6$$
$$2x + 40 - 40 = 6 - 40$$
$$2x = -34$$
$$\frac{2x}{2} = \frac{-34}{2}$$
$$\frac{\cancel{2}x}{\cancel{2}} = -17$$
$$x = -17$$

Check:

$$100(2x+40)=600$$

$$100(2(-17)+40)\overset{?}{=}600$$

$$100(-34+40)\overset{?}{=}600$$

$$100(6)\overset{?}{=}600$$

$$600\overset{\checkmark}{=}600$$

Real-World Problems

Many real-world problems can be modeled and solved using one-variable linear equations. To solve such problems, read the problem carefully. Look for a sentence that contains words or phrases such as "what is," "what was," "find," "how many," and "determine" to help you identify what you are to find. Let the variable represent this unknown quantity. (*Tip:* Be precise in specifying a variable. State its units, if any.) Then write and solve an equation that represents the facts given in the problem.

Here is an example.

> Jaidee is twice as old as Davon. In 5 years, Jaidee's age will be 55 years minus Davon's age. What is Jaidee's age now?

You don't know Jaidee's age or Davon's age now. *Tip:* For one-variable linear equations, when you have two unknowns and one of them is described in terms of the other one, designate the variable as the other one. For instance, Jaidee's age now is described as "twice as old as Davon," so designate the variable as Davon's age now.

Let d = Davon's age in years now, and $2d$ = Jaidee's age in years now.

Make a chart to organize the information in the question.

When?	Davon's Age	Jaidee's Age
Now	d	$2d$
5 years from now	$d + 5$ years	$2d + 5$ years

From the question, you know that Jaidee's age 5 years from now is 55 years minus Davon's age 5 years from now. Use the information in the chart to set up an equation to match the facts in the question.

$$2d + 5 \text{ years} = 55 \text{ years} - (d + 5 \text{ years})$$

Solve the equation, omitting the units for convenience.

$$2d + 5 = 55 - (d + 5)$$
$$2d + 5 = 55 - d - 5$$
$$2d + 5 = 50 - d$$
$$2d + 5 + d = 50 - d + d$$
$$2d + d + 5 = 50$$
$$3d + 5 = 50$$
$$3d + 5 - 5 = 50 - 5$$
$$3d = 45$$
$$\frac{3d}{3} = \frac{45}{3}$$
$$\frac{\cancel{3}d}{\cancel{3}} = 15$$
$$d = 15$$
$$2d = 30$$

Jaidee is 30 years old.

Tip: Make sure you answer the question asked. In this question, after you obtain Davon's age now, calculate Jaidee's age now.

☞ Try These

1. Fill in the blank.

    (a) An equation is a statement that two mathematical expressions are _____.
    (b) A solution to an equation is a number that when substituted for the variable makes the equation _____.
    (c) If the solution set is all real numbers, the equation is an _____.
    (d) If the solution set is _____, the equation has no solution.
    (e) Equations that have the same solution set are _____ equations.
    (f) To solve a one-variable linear equation, you _____ what has been done to the variable.
    (g) To keep an equation in balance, whatever you do to one side of the equation you must do to the _____ side of the equation.

2. Solve for the variable.

    (a) $3x - 4.6 = x + 1.8$
    (b) $5(y + 13) = 50 - 3y$
    (c) $\frac{1}{2}x - 7 = 14 - \frac{5}{2}x$
    (d) $-4x + 9 = -5 + 3x$
    (e) $-2(z - 1) = 20 + 3z$

3. A truck leaves a location traveling due east at a constant speed of 55 miles per hour. One hour later, a car leaves the same location traveling in the same direction at a constant speed of 65 miles per hour. If both vehicles continue in the same direction at their same respective speeds, how many hours will it take the car to catch up to the truck?

Solutions

1. **(a)** equal
   (b) true
   (c) identity
   (d) empty
   (e) equivalent
   (f) undo
   (g) other

2. **(a)**

$$3x - 4.6 = x + 1.8$$
$$3x - 4.6 - x = x + 1.8 - x$$
$$3x - x - 4.6 = x - x + 1.8$$
$$2x - 4.6 = 1.8$$
$$2x - 4.6 + 4.6 = 1.8 + 4.6$$
$$2x = 6.4$$
$$\frac{2x}{2} = \frac{6.4}{2}$$
$$\frac{\cancel{2}x}{\cancel{2}} = 3.2$$
$$x = 3.2$$

Check:

$$3x - 4.6 = x + 1.8$$
$$3(3.2) - 4.6 \overset{?}{=} 3.2 + 1.8$$
$$9.6 - 4.6 \overset{?}{=} 5.0$$
$$5.0 \overset{\checkmark}{=} 5.0 \checkmark$$

(b)

$$5(y + 13) = 50 - 3y$$
$$5 \cdot y + 5 \cdot 13 = 50 - 3y$$
$$5y + 65 = 50 - 3y$$
$$5y + 65 + 3y = 50 - 3y + 3y$$
$$5y + 3y + 65 = 50 - 3y + 3y$$
$$8y + 65 = 50$$
$$8y + 65 - 65 = 50 - 65$$
$$8y = -15$$
$$\frac{8y}{8} = \frac{-15}{8}$$
$$\frac{\cancel{8}y}{\cancel{8}} = -1.875$$
$$y = -1.875$$

Check:

$$5(y+13) = 50 - 3y$$

$$5(-1.875 + 13) \overset{?}{=} 50 - 3(-1.875)$$

$$5(11.125) \overset{?}{=} 50 + 5.625$$

$$55.625 \overset{\checkmark}{=} 55.625$$

(c) $\quad \dfrac{1}{2}x - 7 = 14 - \dfrac{5}{2}x$

$$\dfrac{1}{2}x - 7 + \dfrac{5}{2}x = 14 - \dfrac{5}{2}x + \dfrac{5}{2}x$$

$$\dfrac{1}{2}x + \dfrac{5}{2}x - 7 = 14$$

$$\dfrac{6}{2}x - 7 = 14$$

$$3x - 7 = 14$$

$$3x - 7 + 7 = 14 + 7$$

$$3x = 21$$

$$\dfrac{3x}{3} = \dfrac{21}{3}$$

$$\dfrac{\cancel{3}x}{\cancel{3}} = 7$$

$$x = 7$$

Check:

$$\dfrac{1}{2}x - 7 = 14 - \dfrac{5}{2}x$$

$$\dfrac{1}{2}(7) - 7 \overset{?}{=} 14 - \dfrac{5}{2}(7)$$

$$3.5 - 7 \overset{?}{=} 14 - 17.5$$

$$-3.5 \overset{\checkmark}{=} -3.5$$

(d) $\quad -4x + 9 = -5 + 3x$

$$-4x + 9 - 3x = -5 + 3x - 3x$$

$$-4x - 3x + 9 = -5$$

$$-7x + 9 - 9 = -5 - 9$$

$$-7x = -14$$

$$\dfrac{-7x}{-7} = \dfrac{-14}{-7}$$

$$\dfrac{\cancel{-7}x}{\cancel{-7}} = 2$$

$$x = 2$$

Check:

$$-4x+9=-5+3x$$

$$-4(2)+9\stackrel{?}{=}-5+3(2)$$

$$-8+9\stackrel{?}{=}-5+6$$

$$1\stackrel{\checkmark}{=}1$$

(e) $$-2(z-1)=20+3z$$

$$-2(z+-1)=20+3z$$

$$-2\cdot z+-2\cdot-1=20+3z$$

$$-2z+2=20+3z$$

$$-2z+2-3z=20+3z-3z$$

$$-2z-3z+2=20$$

$$-5z+2-2=20-2$$

$$-5z=18$$

$$\frac{-5z}{-5}=\frac{18}{-5}$$

$$\frac{\cancel{-5}z}{\cancel{-5}}=-3.6$$

$$z=-3.6$$

Check:

$$-2(z-1)=20+3z$$

$$-2(-3.6-1)\stackrel{?}{=}20+3(-3.6)$$

$$-2(-4.6)\stackrel{?}{=}20+(-10.8)$$

$$9.2\stackrel{\checkmark}{=}9.2$$

3. Let t = the time in hours the car will travel before it catches up to the truck. Then $t + 1$ hour = the time in hours that the truck travels before the car catches up to it.

Make a chart to organize the information in the question.

Vehicle	Rate (in mph)	Time (in hours)	Distance (in miles)
car	65	t	$65t$
truck	55	$t + 1$	$55(t + 1)$

Tip: Distance = Rate × Time.

Using the chart, write an equation to represent the facts given in the question.

When the car catches up to the truck, both vehicles have traveled the same distance. Thus, $65t = 55(t + 1)$.

Solve the equation.

$$65t = 55(t+1)$$
$$65t = 55t + 55$$
$$65t - 55t = 55t + 55 - 55t$$
$$10t = 55t - 55t + 55$$
$$10t = 55$$
$$\frac{10t}{10} = \frac{55}{10}$$
$$\frac{\cancel{10}t}{\cancel{10}} = 5.5$$
$$t = 5.5$$

The car will catch up to the truck in 5.5 hours.

Solving Equations of the Forms $x^2 = k$ and $x^3 = c$

(CCSS.Math.Content.8.EE.A.2B)

To solve an equation that has the form $x^2 = k$ or $x^3 = c$, you find the solution set for the equation. Recall from the previous section that the set consisting of all solutions to an equation is the equation's solution set.

Solving Equations of the Form $x^2 = k$

If k is a positive real number, the solution of the equation $x^2 = k$ is $x = \sqrt{k}$ or $x = -\sqrt{k}$. The solution set contains two numbers, $\sqrt{k}$ and $-\sqrt{k}$. The number $\sqrt{k}$ is the positive number whose square is k. The number $-\sqrt{k}$ is the negative number whose square is k.

The two numbers, $\sqrt{k}$ and $-\sqrt{k}$, are the two square roots of k. If k is a perfect square, its square roots are rational. If k is not a perfect square, its square roots are irrational.

> **Tip:** See the section "Recognizing Rational and Irrational Numbers" in Chapter 1 for a list of square roots of perfect squares (page 8).

Here are examples.

Solve $x^2 = 25$.

$$x^2 = 25$$
$$x = \sqrt{25} \text{ or } -\sqrt{25}$$
$$x = 5 \text{ or } -5$$

Check:

$$x^2 = 25$$

$$(5)^2 \overset{?}{=} 25 \text{ and } (-5)^2 \overset{?}{=} 25$$

$$25 \overset{\checkmark}{=} 25 \text{ and } 25 \overset{\checkmark}{=} 25$$

Solve $x^2 = 7$.

$$x^2 = 7$$

$$x = \sqrt{7} \text{ or } -\sqrt{7}$$

Check:

$$x^2 = 7$$

$$\left(\sqrt{7}\right)^2 \overset{?}{=} 7 \text{ and } \left(-\sqrt{7}\right)^2 \overset{?}{=} 7$$

$$7 \overset{\checkmark}{=} 7 \text{ and } 7 \overset{\checkmark}{=} 7$$

Tip: $\sqrt{7}$ is simply $\sqrt{7}$, an irrational number, because 7 is not a perfect square.

☞ Try These

1. Fill in the blank(s).

   (a) If k is a positive real number, the solution of the equation $x^2 = k$ is $x =$ _____ or $x =$ _____.

   (b) If k is a positive real number, the solution set of $x^2 = k$ contains _____ (one real number, two real numbers, three real numbers).

   (c) If k is a perfect square, its square roots are _____ (irrational, rational). If k is not a perfect square, its square roots are _____ (irrational, rational).

2. Solve the equation.

   (a) $x^2 = 64$

   (b) $x^2 = 30$

   (c) $x^2 = 100$

   (d) $x^2 = 11$

Solutions

1. **(a)** $\sqrt{k}; -\sqrt{k}$
   (b) two real numbers
   (c) rational; irrational

2. **(a)** $x^2 = 64$

$\qquad x = \sqrt{64}$ or $-\sqrt{64}$

$\qquad x = 8$ or -8

Check:

$\qquad\qquad x^2 = 64$

$\qquad (8)^2 \overset{?}{=} 64$ and $(-8)^2 \overset{?}{=} 64$

$\qquad\quad 64 \overset{\checkmark}{=} 64$ and $64 \overset{\checkmark}{=} 64$

(b) $x^2 = 30$

$\qquad x = \sqrt{30}$ or $-\sqrt{30}$

Check:

$\qquad\qquad x^2 = 30$

$\qquad \left(\sqrt{30}\right)^2 \overset{?}{=} 30$ and $\left(-\sqrt{30}\right)^2 \overset{?}{=} 30$

$\qquad\quad 30 \overset{\checkmark}{=} 30$ and $30 \overset{\checkmark}{=} 30$

(c) $x^2 = 100$

$\qquad x = \sqrt{100}$ or $-\sqrt{100}$

$\qquad x = 10$ or -10

Check:

$\qquad\qquad x^2 = 100$

$\qquad (10)^2 \overset{?}{=} 100$ and $(-10)^2 \overset{?}{=} 100$

$\qquad\quad 100 \overset{\checkmark}{=} 100$ and $100 \overset{\checkmark}{=} 100$

(d) $x^2 = 11$

$\qquad x = \sqrt{11}$ or $-\sqrt{11}$

Check:

$\qquad\qquad x^2 = 11$

$\qquad \left(\sqrt{11}\right)^2 \overset{?}{=} 11$ and $\left(-\sqrt{11}\right)^2 \overset{?}{=} 11$

$\qquad\quad 11 \overset{\checkmark}{=} 11$ and $11 \overset{\checkmark}{=} 11$

Solving Equations of the Form $x^3 = c$

If c is a positive real number, the solution of the equation $x^3 = c$ is $x = \sqrt[3]{c}$, where $\sqrt[3]{c}$ denotes the "cube root of c." The solution set contains one real number, $\sqrt[3]{c}$. The number $\sqrt[3]{c}$ is the number whose cube is c. If c is a **perfect cube,** its cube root is rational. If c is not a perfect cube, its cube root is irrational.

Here are examples.

Solve $x^3 = 8$.

$$x^3 = 8$$
$$x = \sqrt[3]{8}$$
$$x = 2$$

Check:

$$x^3 = 8$$
$$(2)^3 \stackrel{?}{=} 8$$
$$(2)(2)(2) \stackrel{?}{=} 8$$
$$8 \stackrel{\checkmark}{=} 8$$

Solve $x^3 = 100$.

$$x^3 = 100$$
$$x = \sqrt[3]{100}$$

Check:

$$x^3 = 100$$
$$\left(\sqrt[3]{100}\right)^3 \stackrel{?}{=} 100$$
$$\left(\sqrt[3]{100}\right)\left(\sqrt[3]{100}\right)\left(\sqrt[3]{100}\right) \stackrel{?}{=} 100$$
$$100 \stackrel{\checkmark}{=} 100$$

Tip: $\sqrt[3]{100}$ **is simply** $\sqrt[3]{100}$ **, an irrational number, because 100 is not a perfect cube.**

You will find it helpful to memorize the following cube roots of perfect cubes.

$$\sqrt[3]{1} = 1 \quad \sqrt[3]{8} = 2 \quad \sqrt[3]{27} = 3 \quad \sqrt[3]{64} = 4 \quad \sqrt[3]{125} = 5 \quad \sqrt[3]{216} = 6 \quad \sqrt[3]{343} = 7 \quad \sqrt[3]{1,000} = 10$$

☞ Try These

1. Fill in the blank(s)

   (a) If c is a positive real number, the solution of the equation $x^3 = c$ is $x =$ _____.

   (b) The solution set of $x^3 = c$ contains _____ (one real number, two real numbers, three real numbers).

   (c) If c is a perfect cube, its cube root is _____ (irrational, rational). If c is not a perfect cube, its cube root is _____ (irrational, rational).

2. Solve the equation.

   (a) $x^3 = 64$

   (b) $x^3 = 75$

   (c) $x^3 = 1,000$

   (d) $x^3 = 25$

Solutions

1. **(a)** $\sqrt[3]{c}$
   (b) one real number
   (c) rational; irrational

2. **(a)** $x^3 = 64$

   $x = \sqrt[3]{64}$

   $x = 4$

   Check:

   $$x^3 = 64$$

   $$(4)^3 \overset{?}{=} 64$$

   $$(4)(4)(4) \overset{?}{=} 64$$

   $$64 \overset{\checkmark}{=} 64$$

   (b) $x^3 = 75$

   $x = \sqrt[3]{75}$

   Check:

   $$x^3 = 75$$

   $$\left(\sqrt[3]{75}\right)^3 \overset{?}{=} 75$$

   $$\left(\sqrt[3]{75}\right)\left(\sqrt[3]{75}\right)\left(\sqrt[3]{75}\right) \overset{?}{=} 75$$

   $$75 \overset{\checkmark}{=} 75$$

   (c) $x^3 = 1,000$

   $x = \sqrt[3]{1,000}$

   $x = 10$

   Check:

   $$x^3 = 1,000$$

   $$(10)^3 \overset{?}{=} 1,000$$

   $$(10)(10)(10) \overset{?}{=} 1,000$$

   $$1,000 \overset{\checkmark}{=} 1,000$$

(d) $x^3 = 25$

$x = \sqrt[3]{25}$

Check:

$$x^3 = 25$$

$$\left(\sqrt[3]{25}\right)^3 \overset{?}{=} 25$$

$$\left(\sqrt[3]{25}\right)\left(\sqrt[3]{25}\right)\left(\sqrt[3]{25}\right) \overset{?}{=} 25$$

$$25 \overset{\checkmark}{=} 25$$

Graphing Two-Variable Linear Equations of the Form $y = mx + b$

(CCSS.Math.Content.8.EE.B.5, CCSS.Math.Content.8.EE.B.6, CCSS.Math.Content.8.F.A.3)

The equation $y = mx + b$ is a linear equation in two variables. The graph of $y = mx + b$ is a line. The **slope** of the line is the coefficient m. The number b is the y-coordinate of the point where the graph intersects the y-axis. It is the **y-intercept**.

Here is an example.

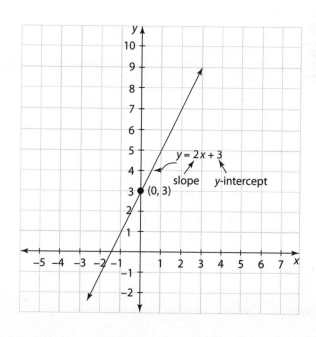

Understanding the Slope and *y*-Intercept

The slope *m* of a line tells you important information about the line. The slope is its **rate of change.** For any two points on the line,

$$\text{slope} = \frac{\text{vertical change between the two points}}{\text{horizontal change between the two points}} = \frac{\text{rise}}{\text{run}}$$

Tip: The vertical change between two points on a line is the *rise* between the points. The horizontal change between two points on a line is the *run* between the points.

The slope of a line is the same no matter which two points on the line you choose.

Here is an example.

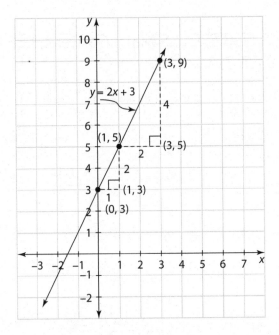

On the graph of the line $y = 2x + 3$, the slope between the points (0, 3) and (1, 5) is

$$\frac{\text{vertical change between the two points}}{\text{horizontal change between the two points}} = \frac{\text{rise}}{\text{run}} = \frac{5-3}{1-0} = \frac{2}{1} = 2$$

Similarly, the slope between the points (1, 5) and (3, 9) is

$$\frac{\text{vertical change between the two points}}{\text{horizontal change between the two points}} = \frac{\text{rise}}{\text{run}} = \frac{9-5}{3-1} = \frac{4}{2} = 2$$

The slope is the same whether you use (0, 3) and (1, 5) or (1, 5) and (3, 9). The rate of change for the line is $\frac{2}{1}$. For every 1-unit change horizontally, there is a 2-unit change vertically.

In general, if (x_1, y_1) and (x_2, y_2) are points on a nonvertical line, the slope of the line is

$$\frac{\text{vertical change between the two points}}{\text{horizontal change between the two points}} = \frac{\text{rise}}{\text{run}} = \frac{y_2 - y_1}{x_2 - x_1}$$

Tip: The order in which you subtract is important. Put y_2 first in the numerator and x_2 first in the denominator.

The slope describes the steepness or slant of the line. If m is positive, the line slants up from left to right. If m is negative, the line slants down from left to right. If $m = 0$, the line is horizontal with no slant. The greater the absolute value of m, the steeper the line and the faster the rate of change.

For example, as shown below, the graph of $y = 6x + 3$ is much steeper than the graph of $y = 2x + 3$.

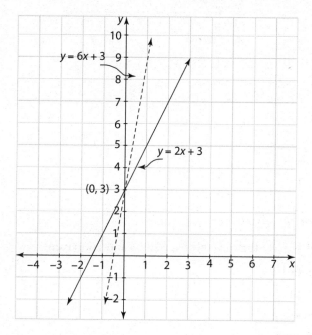

The slope of $y = 6x + 3$ is three times as steep as that of $y = 2x + 3$. The graph of $y = 6x + 3$ is changing three times as fast as the graph of $y = 2x + 3$ because its slope is three times as large ($6 = 2 \times 3$).

The y-intercept also provides useful information. It tells you what happens when the x-value is zero. If zero is the starting value for the variable x, the y-intercept lets you know whether the initial y-value is zero or perhaps some other value.

Tip: When the y-intercept is 0, the line passes through the origin.

For instance, suppose the starting value of the variable x is zero for the graphs of $y = 2x + 3$, $y = 2x - 1$, and $y = 2x$ as shown below. Look at the y-intercept of each line. Although the three lines have the same slope, each has a different y-value corresponding to $x = 0$.

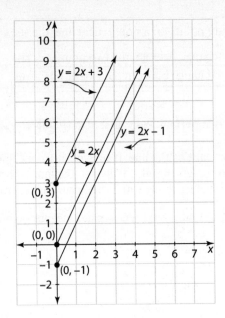

☞ Try These

1. Fill in the blank.

   (a) The graph of the equation $y = 3x + 5$ is a _____.

   (b) The slope of a line is its _____ of change.

   (c) The slope of $y = \dfrac{1}{2}x + 4$ is _____.

   (d) The y-intercept of $y = \dfrac{1}{2}x + 4$ is _____.

2. Write the equation of the line that has the given slope and y-intercept.

   (a) slope 2; y-intercept 10

   (b) slope $\dfrac{2}{3}$; y-intercept −5

   (c) slope −4; y-intercept 7

   (d) slope $\dfrac{3}{4}$; y-intercept 0

3. Find the slope and y-intercept of the line shown.

(a)

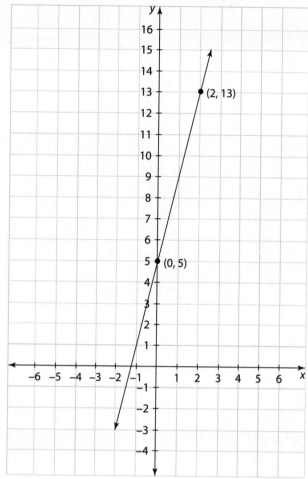

(b)

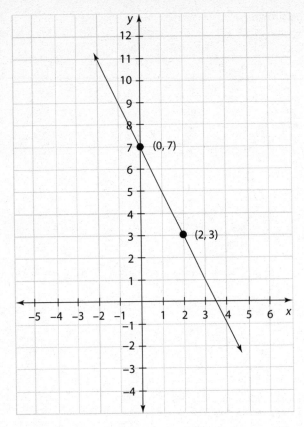

(c)

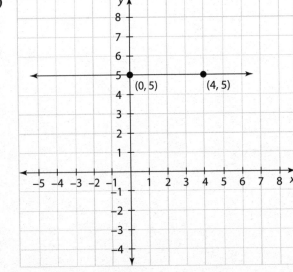

Solutions

1. **(a)** line
   (b) rate
   (c) $\dfrac{1}{2}$
   (d) 4

2. **(a)** $y = 2x + 10$
   (b) $y = \dfrac{2}{3}x - 5$
   (c) $y = -4x + 7$
   (d) $y = \dfrac{3}{4}x$

3. **(a)** The points $(0, 5)$ and $(2, 13)$ are two points on the line.

$$\text{slope} = \frac{\text{vertical change between the two points}}{\text{horizontal change between the two points}} = \frac{y_2 - y_1}{x_2 - x_1} = \frac{13 - 5}{2 - 0} = \frac{8}{2} = 4; \ y\text{-intercept} = 5$$

   (b) The points $(0, 7)$ and $(2, 3)$ are two points on the line.

$$\text{slope} = \frac{\text{vertical change between the two points}}{\text{horizontal change between the two points}} = \frac{y_2 - y_1}{x_2 - x_1} = \frac{3 - 7}{2 - 0} = \frac{-4}{2} = -2; \ y\text{-intercept} = 7$$

   (c) The points $(0, 5)$ and $(4, 5)$ are two points on the line.

$$\text{slope} = \frac{\text{vertical change between the two points}}{\text{horizontal change between the two points}} = \frac{y_2 - y_1}{x_2 - x_1} = \frac{5 - 5}{4 - 0} = \frac{0}{4} = 0; \ y\text{-intercept} = 5$$

Graphing $y = mx + b$

There are two common methods for graphing $y = mx + b$. Here are examples of each.

Graph $y = \dfrac{3}{2}x - 7$.

Method 1:

Step 1. Set up an x-y table and determine two ordered pairs that make the equation true. ***Tip:*** Pick convenient values for x, and then compute the corresponding y values.

x	$y = \dfrac{3}{2}x - 7$
0	$\dfrac{3}{2}(0) - 7 = 0 - 7 = -7$
2	$\dfrac{3}{2}(2) - 7 = 3 - 7 = -4$

Step 2. Graph the ordered pairs from Step 1. Connect them with a line extending in both directions.

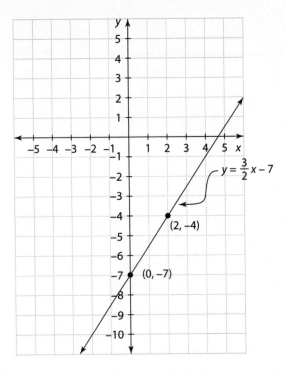

Method 2:

Step 1. Identify the slope m of the line (the coefficient of x) and b, the y-intercept (the constant).

$$\text{slope } m = \frac{3}{2} \text{ ; } y\text{-intercept } b = -7$$

Step 2. Graph the point $(0, b)$. Use the slope to find a second point. Connect the two points with a line extending in both directions.

$(0, b) = (0, -7)$. Given $m = \dfrac{\text{vertical change}}{\text{horizontal change}} = \dfrac{3}{2}$, when x changes 2 units, y changes 3 units. Start at $(0, -7)$.

Move 2 units right, and from there move 3 units up to locate a second point. Connect the two points with a line extending in both directions.

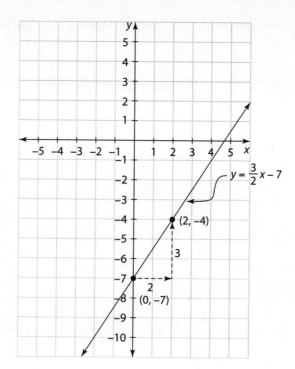

☞ Try These

1. Graph using Method 1.

    (a) $y = 3x + 5$

    (b) $y = -\dfrac{3}{4}x + \dfrac{1}{2}$

2. Graph using Method 2.

    (a) $y = 4x - 9$

    (b) $y = \dfrac{1}{2}x + 4$

Solutions

1. **(a)** *Step 1.* Set up an *x-y* table and determine two ordered pairs that make the equation true.

x	y = 3x + 5
0	5
2	11

Step 2. Graph the ordered pairs from Step 1. Connect them with a line extending in both directions.

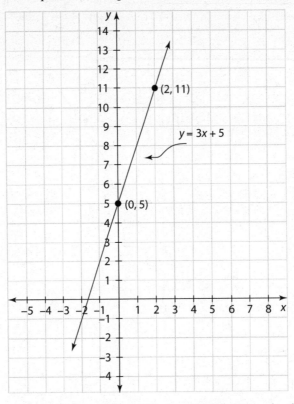

(b) *Step 1.* Set up an x-y table and determine two ordered pairs that make the equation true.

x	$y = -\dfrac{3}{4}x + \dfrac{1}{2}$
0	$\dfrac{1}{2}$
2	-1

Step 2. Graph the ordered pairs from Step 1. Connect them with a line extending in both directions.

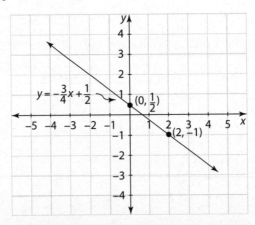

2. **(a)** *Step 1.* Identify the slope m of the line (the coefficient of x) and b, the y-intercept (the constant).

$$\text{slope } m = 4; \; y\text{-intercept } b = -9$$

Step 2. Graph the point $(0, -9)$. Use the slope to find a second point. Connect the two points with a line extending in both directions.

Given $m = \dfrac{\text{vertical change}}{\text{horizontal change}} = \dfrac{4}{1}$, when x changes 1 unit, y changes 4 units. Start at $(0, -9)$. Move 1 unit right, and from there move 4 units up to locate a second point. Connect the two points with a line extending in both directions.

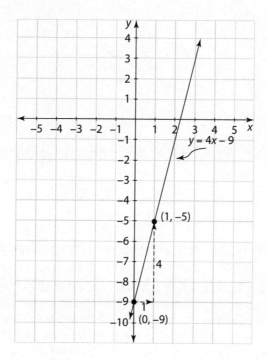

(b) *Step 1.* Identify the slope m of the line (the coefficient of x) and b, the y-intercept (the constant).

$$\text{slope } m = \frac{1}{2}; \; y\text{-intercept } b = 4$$

Step 2. Graph the point (0, 4). Use the slope to find a second point. Connect the two points with a line extending in both directions.

Given $m = \dfrac{\text{vertical change}}{\text{horizontal change}} = \dfrac{1}{2}$, when x changes 2 units, y changes 1 unit. Start at (0, 4). Move 2 units right, and from there move 1 unit up to locate a second point. Connect the two points with a line extending in both directions.

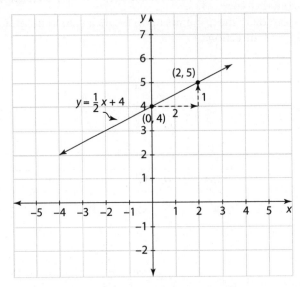

Graphing and Comparing Proportional Relationships

(CCSS.Math.Content.8.EE.B.6, CCSS.Math.Content.8.F.A.2)

When the y-intercept is zero, the equation $y = mx + b$ has the form $y = mx$. The graph of the equation $y = mx$ is a proportional relationship. The slope m is the *unit rate* of the proportional relationship. Graph proportional relationships using Method 1 or Method 2 of the previous section.

Here is an example.

> Rafael walks at a constant rate of 4 miles per hour. The equation $d = 4t$ represents the proportional relationship between the distance, d (in miles), traveled in time, t (in hours). Graph $d = 4t$.

Graph $d = 4t$ using Method 2 of the previous section. *Tip:* In the graph of $d = 4t$, t is the horizontal axis and d is the vertical axis.

Step 1. Identify the slope m of the line and b, the d-intercept.

$$\text{slope } m = \frac{4}{1}; \ d\text{-intercept } b = 0$$

Step 2. Graph the point (0, 0) and use the slope to find a second point. Connect the two points with a line.

Given $m = \dfrac{\text{vertical change}}{\text{horizontal change}} = \dfrac{4}{1}$, for every 1 hour change in time t, the distance d changes 4 miles. Start at (0, 0). Move 1 unit right, and from there move 4 units up to locate a second point. Connect the two points with a ray extending away from the origin (because both time and distance are nonnegative).

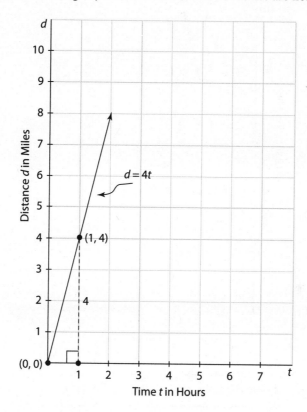

Compare the rates of change of two proportional relationships by identifying and comparing the unit rates (slopes) of their equations. The proportional relationship that has the greater unit rate has the faster rate of change. Here is an example.

Compare the two situations to determine who walks faster: Rafael or Bartolo. Justify your answer.

Situation 1: The graph shows the proportional relationship between the distance, d (in miles), traveled in time, t (in hours), by Rafael.

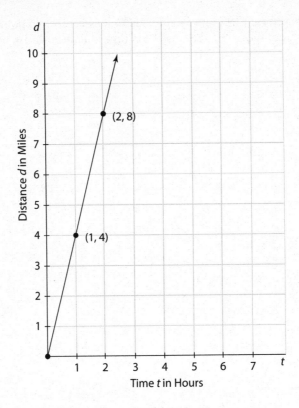

Situation 2: Bartolo walks at a constant rate. The table shows the proportional relationship between the distance, d (in miles), traveled in time, t (in hours), by Bartolo.

Time, t (in hours)	Distance, d (in miles)
$\frac{2}{5}$	1.4
$\frac{1}{2}$	1.75
$1\frac{1}{2}$	5.25
$3\frac{1}{5}$	11.2

Situation 1: Calculate Rafael's unit rate of miles per hour walking speed. Using the two points shown, calculate the unit rate (slope) of the graph.

$$\text{unit rate } = \text{ slope } = \frac{y_2 - y_1}{x_2 - x_1} = \frac{8-4}{2-1} = \frac{4}{1} = 4$$

Rafael's unit rate of miles per hour walking speed is 4.

Situation 2: Calculate Bartolo's unit rate of miles per hour walking speed.

$$\frac{1.4}{\frac{2}{5}} = \frac{1.4}{.4} = 3.5; \quad \frac{1.75}{\frac{1}{2}} = \frac{1.75}{.5} = 3.5; \quad \frac{5.25}{1\frac{1}{2}} = \frac{5.25}{1.5} = 3.5; \quad \frac{11.2}{3\frac{1}{5}} = \frac{11.2}{3.2} = 3.5$$

Bartolo's unit rate of miles per hour walking speed is 3.5.

Because Rafael's unit rate of 4 is greater than Bartolo's unit rate of 3.5, Rafael walks faster than Bartolo.

☞ Try These

1. Fill in the blank.

    (a) The graph of the equation $y = mx$ is a _____ relationship.
    (b) The slope m of $y = mx$ is its _____ _____ (two words).

2. Graph the proportional relationship.

    (a) $y = 2.5x$
    (b) $y = \frac{1}{3}x$
    (c) $c = 6n$
    (d) $d = 60t$

3. Compare the proportional relationships in the two situations to determine which vehicle is traveling faster: the car or the truck.

Situation 1: A car is traveling at a constant rate of 65 miles per hour. The equation $d = 65t$ represents the proportional relationship between the distance, d (in miles), traveled in time, t (in hours), by the car.

Situation 2: The graph shows the proportional relationship between the distance d (in miles), a truck travels in time t (in hours).

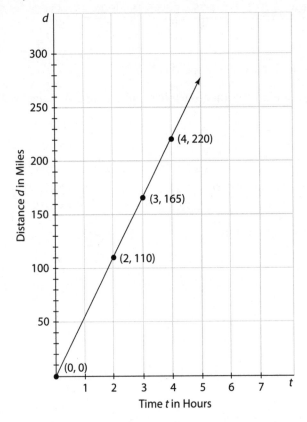

Solutions

1. **(a)** proportional
   (b) unit rate

2. **(a)**

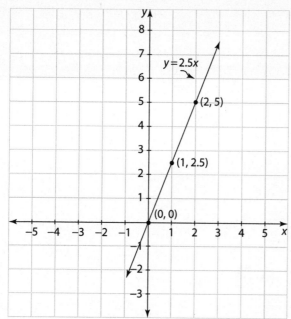

(b)

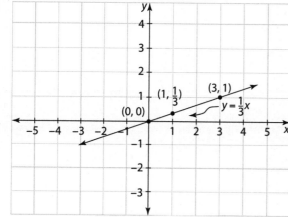

(c)

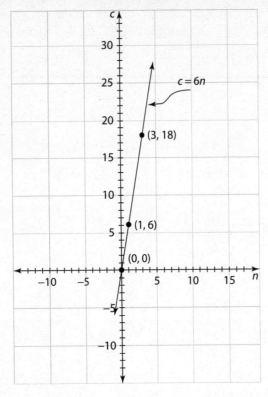

(d)

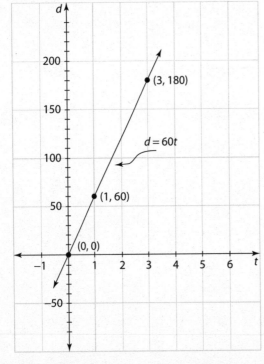

3. **Situation 1:** The car's unit rate of miles per hour is 65.
   Situation 2: Calculate the truck's unit rate of miles per hour. Using the points (3, 165) and (4, 220) shown on the graph, calculate the unit rate (slope) of the graph.

$$\text{unit rate} = \text{slope} = \frac{y_2 - y_1}{x_2 - x_1} = \frac{220 - 165}{4 - 3} = \frac{55}{1} = 55$$

Because the car's unit rate of 65 is greater than the truck's unit rate of 55, the car is traveling at a faster speed.

Solving Pairs of Simultaneous Two-Variable Linear Equations

(CCSS.Math.Content.8.EE.C.8.A, CCSS.Math.Content.8.EE.C.8.B, CCSS.Math.Content.8.EE.C.8.C)

The **standard form** of a two-variable linear equation is $Ax + By = C$, where A and B are not both zero. For example, $3x + 4y = 2$ and $4x - y = 9$ are linear equations in standard form.

A set of two linear equations, each with the same two variables, is a **system** when the two equations are considered **simultaneously,** meaning at the same time.

Here is an example of a system of two linear equations with variables x and y.

$$3x + 4y = 2$$
$$4x - y = 9$$

To solve a system of two equations in two variables, find an ordered pair of values; for example, an x-value paired with a corresponding y-value, written as (x, y), that makes *both* equations true at the same time. An ordered pair that makes an equation in two variables true **satisfies the equation.** When an ordered pair makes *both* equations in a system of two equations true, the ordered pair **satisfies the system.**

The system has a **solution** when the two equations in the system are both satisfied by at least one ordered pair. A system that has a solution is **consistent.** A system that has no solution is **inconsistent.** The **solution set** is the collection of all solutions. There are three possibilities: the system has *exactly one solution, infinitely many solutions,* or *no solution.*

Determining Whether an Ordered Pair Satisfies a System of Two Linear Equations

To determine whether an ordered pair satisfies a system of two equations, check whether the ordered pair satisfies both equations in the system. Do this by plugging the x and y values of the ordered pair into the two equations. Be careful to enclose in parentheses the values that you put in. Here is an example.

Given the system $\begin{array}{l} 3x+4y=2 \\ 4x-\ y=9 \end{array}$

(a) Determine whether the ordered pair $(1, -2)$ satisfies the system.
(b) Determine whether the ordered pair $(2, -1)$ satisfies the system.

(a) First, check whether $(1, -2)$ satisfies $3x + 4y = 2$.

On the LS of the equation, substitute 1 for x and -2 for y. Then evaluate and compare the result to the RS of the equation.

$$3x + 4y = 3(1) + 4(-2) = 3 + -8 = -5$$

The RS of the equation is 2. Because $-5 \neq 2$, $(1, -2)$ does not satisfy $3x + 4y = 2$. Therefore, $(1, -2)$ does *not* satisfy the given system because it fails to satisfy one of the equations in the system.

(b) First, check whether $(2, -1)$ satisfies $3x + 4y = 2$.

On the LS of the equation, substitute 2 for x and -1 for y. Then evaluate and compare the result to the RS of the equation.

$$3x + 4y = 3(2) + 4(-1) = 6 + -4 = 2$$

The RS of the equation is also 2, so $(2, -1)$ satisfies $3x + 4y = 2$.

Next, check whether $(2, -1)$ satisfies $4x - y = 9$.

On the LS of the equation, substitute 2 for x and -1 for y. Then evaluate and compare the result to the RS of the equation.

$$4x - y = 4(2) - (-1) = 8 + 1 = 9$$

The RS of the equation is also 9, so $(2, -1)$ satisfies $4x - y = 9$. Therefore, $(2, -1)$ satisfies the given system because it satisfies both equations in the system.

☞Try These

1. Fill in the blank(s).

   (a) A set of two linear equations, each with the same two variables, is a system when the two equations are considered _____.
   (b) When an ordered pair makes both equations in a system of two equations true, the ordered pair _____ the system.
   (c) A system that has a solution is _____ (consistent, inconsistent).
   (d) A system that has no solution is _____ (consistent, inconsistent).
   (e) There are three possibilities for the solution set of a system: the system has exactly _____ solution, _____ many solutions, or _____ solution.

2. Given the system $\begin{array}{l} 5x-2y=-1 \\ 2x-\ y=0 \end{array}$

   (a) Determine whether the ordered pair $(1, 3)$ satisfies the system.
   (b) Determine whether the ordered pair $(-1, -2)$ satisfies the system.

Solutions

1. **(a)** simultaneously
   (b) satisfies
   (c) consistent
   (d) inconsistent
   (e) one; infinitely; no

2. **(a)** First, check whether $(1, 3)$ satisfies $5x - 2y = -1$.

   On the LS of the equation, substitute 1 for x and 3 for y. Then evaluate and compare the result to the RS of the equation.

   $$5x - 2y = 5(1) - 2(3) = 5 - 6 = -1$$

   The RS of the equation is also -1, so $(1, 3)$ satisfies $5x - 2y = -1$.

   Next, check whether $(1, 3)$ satisfies $2x - y = 0$.

   On the LS of the equation, substitute 1 for x and 3 for y. Then evaluate and compare the result to the RS of the equation.

   $$2x - y = 2(1) - (3) = 2 - 3 = -1$$

   The RS of the equation is 0. Because $-1 \neq 0$, $(1, 3)$ does not satisfy $2x - y = 0$. Therefore, $(1, 3)$ does *not* satisfy the given system because it fails to satisfy one of the equations in the system.

   (b) First, check whether $(-1, -2)$ satisfies $5x - 2y = -1$.

   On the LS of the equation, substitute -1 for x and -2 for y. Then evaluate and compare the result to the RS of the equation.

   $$5x - 2y = 5(-1) - 2(-2) = -5 + 4 = -1$$

   The RS of the equation is also -1, so $(-1, -2)$ satisfies $5x - 2y = -1$.

   Next, check whether $(-1, -2)$ satisfies $2x - y = 0$.

   On the LS of the equation, substitute -1 for x and -2 for y. Then evaluate and compare the result to the RS of the equation.

   $$2x - y = 2(-1) - (-2) = -2 + 2 = 0$$

   The RS of the equation is also 0, so $(-1, -2)$ satisfies $2x - y = 0$. Therefore, $(-1, -2)$ satisfies the given system because it satisfies both equations in the system.

Interpreting Systems of Two Linear Equations Geometrically

In the coordinate plane, the graphs of the two equations in a system of two linear equations are two lines. The graph of $Ax + By = C$ is a line with slope $m = -\dfrac{A}{B}$ and y-intercept $= \dfrac{C}{B}$ (provided $B \neq 0$). For the two equations, there are three possibilities that can occur. The three possibilities are exactly one solution, infinitely many solutions, or no solution. If the system is consistent and has exactly one solution, the two lines intersect in exactly one point in the plane. The point of intersection is the solution to the system.

Here is an example.

Graph the system $\begin{array}{l} 3x+4y=2 \\ 4x-\ y=9 \end{array}$.

The equation $3x + 4y = 2$ has slope $m = -\dfrac{A}{B} = -\dfrac{3}{4}$ and y-intercept $= \dfrac{C}{B} = \dfrac{2}{4} = \dfrac{1}{2}$. The equation $4x - y = 9$ has

slope $m = -\dfrac{A}{B} = -\dfrac{4}{-1} = \dfrac{4}{1}$ and y-intercept $= \dfrac{C}{B} = \dfrac{9}{-1} = -9$. Use Method 1 or Method 2 from the section

"Graphing $y = mx + b$" earlier in this chapter to graph the two equations in the same coordinate plane.

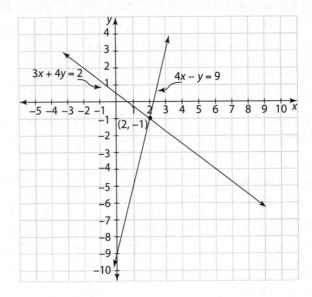

The two lines intersect in exactly one point $(2, -1)$. This point is the solution to the system $\begin{array}{l} 3x+4y=2 \\ 4x-\ y=9 \end{array}$.

If the system is consistent and has infinitely many solutions, the two lines are **coincident** (that is, they have all points in common).

Here is an example.

Graph the system $\begin{array}{l} 3x+4y=2 \\ 6x+8y=4 \end{array}$.

The equation $3x + 4y = 2$ has slope $m = -\dfrac{A}{B} = -\dfrac{3}{4}$ and y-intercept $= \dfrac{C}{B} = \dfrac{2}{4} = \dfrac{1}{2}$. The equation $6x + 8y = 4$ has

slope $m = -\dfrac{6}{8} = -\dfrac{3}{4}$ and y-intercept $= \dfrac{C}{B} = \dfrac{4}{8} = \dfrac{1}{2}$. The two lines representing the equations have the same slope

and the same y-intercept, so their graphs will lie on top of each other. Use Method 2 from the section
"Graphing $y = mx + b$" earlier in this chapter to graph the two equations in the same coordinate plane.

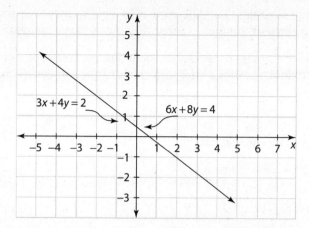

Notice that when both sides of the equation $6x + 8y = 4$ are divided by 2, the result is $3x + 4y = 2$. Thus, $3x + 4y = 2$ and $6x + 8y = 4$ are equivalent equations with the same solutions. All points on the line that has slope $-\frac{3}{4}$ and y-intercept $\frac{1}{2}$ will satisfy both equations at the same time. So, the system has infinitely many solutions.

If the system is inconsistent and has no solution, the two lines are parallel in the plane.

Here is an example.

Graph the system $\begin{array}{l} 3x + 4y = 2 \\ 6x + 8y = 16 \end{array}$.

The equation $3x + 4y = 2$ has slope $m = -\frac{A}{B} = -\frac{3}{4}$ and y-intercept $= \frac{C}{B} = \frac{2}{4} = \frac{1}{2}$. The equation $6x + 8y = 16$ has slope $m = -\frac{6}{8} = -\frac{3}{4}$ and y-intercept $= \frac{C}{B} = \frac{16}{8} = 2$. The two lines representing the equations have the same slope, but different y-intercepts. Use Method 2 from the section "Graphing $y = mx + b$" earlier in this chapter to graph the two equations in the same coordinate plane.

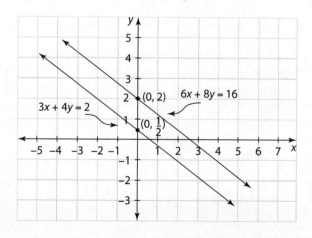

73

The two lines have exactly the same slant but different y-intercepts, so they are parallel and will never intersect. The system has no common solution. Therefore, the system is inconsistent and has no solution.

A quick way to decide whether a system of two linear equations has exactly one solution, infinitely many solutions, or no solution is to look at ratios of the coefficients of the two equations. Consider the system
$$A_1x+B_1y=C_1$$
$$A_2x+B_2y=C_2.$$

If $\dfrac{A_1}{A_2} \neq \dfrac{B_1}{B_2}$, the system has exactly one solution.

For example, in the system $\begin{matrix}3x+4y=2\\4x-\ y=9\end{matrix}, \dfrac{3}{4} \neq \dfrac{4}{-1}$. So, the system has exactly one solution. As previously shown in this section, the solution is (2, –1).

If $\dfrac{A_1}{A_2} = \dfrac{B_1}{B_2} = \dfrac{C_1}{C_2}$, the system has infinitely many solutions.

For example, in the system $\begin{matrix}3x+4y=2\\6x+8y=4\end{matrix}, \dfrac{3}{6}=\dfrac{4}{8}=\dfrac{2}{4}=\dfrac{1}{2}$. So, the system has infinitely many solutions. As

previously shown in this section, $3x + 4y = 2$ and $6x + 8y = 4$ are equivalent equations with the same

solutions. All points on the line that has slope $-\dfrac{3}{4}$ and y-intercept $\dfrac{1}{2}$ will satisfy both equations at the same time.

If $\dfrac{A_1}{A_2} = \dfrac{B_1}{B_2} \neq \dfrac{C_1}{C_2}$, the system has no solution.

For example, in the system $\begin{matrix}3x+4y=2\\6x+8y=16\end{matrix}, \dfrac{3}{6}=\dfrac{4}{8}=\dfrac{1}{2} \neq \dfrac{2}{16}=\dfrac{1}{8}$. So, the system has no solution. As previously

shown in this section, the two lines have exactly the same slant, but different y-intercepts. So they are parallel and will never intersect. The system is inconsistent and has no common solution.

☞ Try These

1. Fill in the blank(s).

   (a) The graph of $Ax + By = C$ is a line with slope $m =$ _____ and y-intercept $=$ _____ (provided $B \neq 0$).

   (b) If a system of two equations is consistent with exactly one solution, the graphs of the two equations are two lines that _____ in exactly one point in the plane.

   (c) If a system of two equations is consistent and has infinitely many solutions, the graphs of the two equations are two lines that have _____ points in common.

   (d) If a system of two equations is inconsistent and has no solution, the graphs of the two equations are two lines that are _____ in the plane.

2. Determine whether the given system has exactly one solution, infinitely many solutions, or no solution. Justify your answer.

(a)
$$3x + y = 4$$
$$4x - y = 3$$

(b)
$$2x - 3y = 5$$
$$4x - 6y = 8$$

(c)
$$4x + 3y = 10$$
$$8x + 6y = 20$$

Solutions

1. (a) $-\dfrac{A}{B}$; $\dfrac{C}{B}$

   (b) intersect

   (c) all

   (d) parallel

2. (a) The system $\begin{array}{l} 3x + y = 4 \\ 4x - y = 3 \end{array}$ has exactly one solution because $\dfrac{3}{4} \neq \dfrac{1}{-1}$.

   (b) The system $\begin{array}{l} 2x - 3y = 5 \\ 4x - 6y = 8 \end{array}$ has no solution because $\dfrac{2}{4} = \dfrac{-3}{-6} = \dfrac{1}{2} \neq \dfrac{5}{8}$.

   (c) The system $\begin{array}{l} 4x + 3y = 10 \\ 8x + 6y = 20 \end{array}$ has infinitely many solutions because $\dfrac{4}{8} = \dfrac{3}{6} = \dfrac{10}{20} = \dfrac{1}{2}$.

Solving a System of Two Linear Equations by Substitution

To solve a system of two linear equations by the method of substitution, do these steps.

Step 1. Select the simpler equation and solve for one of the variables in terms of the other. ***Tip:*** You can solve for either variable. Use your judgment to decide.

Step 2. Substitute this expression into the other equation, simplify, and solve for the variable.

Step 3. Substitute the answer to Step 2 into one of the original equations and solve for the other variable.

Step 4. State the solution and check it in the original equations.

Here is an example.

Solve the system $\begin{array}{l} 3x - y = 1 \\ x + y = -5 \end{array}$ by the method of substitution.

The system has exactly one solution because $\dfrac{3}{1} \neq \dfrac{-1}{1}$.

Step 1. Select the simpler equation and solve for one of the variables in terms of the other. ***Tip:*** Treat the other variable as a constant while you solve.

Solve $x + y = -5$ for x in terms of y.

$$x+y=-5$$
$$x+y-y=-5-y$$
$$x=-5-y$$

Step 2. Substitute this expression into the other equation, simplify, and solve for the variable.

$$3x-y=1$$
$$3(-5-y)-y=1$$
$$-15-3y-y=1$$
$$-15-4y=1$$
$$-15-4y+15=1+15$$
$$-4y-15+15=16$$
$$-4y=16$$
$$\frac{-4y}{-4}=\frac{16}{-4}$$
$$\frac{\cancel{-4}y}{\cancel{-4}}=-4$$
$$y=-4$$

Step 3. Substitute the answer to Step 2 into one of the original equations and solve for the other variable. *Tip:* You can substitute into either equation. Use your judgment to decide.

$$x+y=-5$$
$$x+(-4)=-5$$
$$x+-4+4=-5+4$$
$$x=-1$$

Step 4. State the solution and check it in the original equations.

The ordered pair $(-1, -4)$ is the solution of the system $\begin{matrix} 3x-y=1 \\ x+y=-5 \end{matrix}$.

Check:

$$\begin{matrix} 3x-y=1 \\ x+y=-5 \end{matrix} \rightarrow \begin{matrix} 3(-1)-(-4)\overset{?}{=}1 \\ (-1)+(-4)\overset{?}{=}-5 \end{matrix} \rightarrow \begin{matrix} -3+4\overset{?}{=}1 \\ (-1)+(-4)\overset{?}{=}-5 \end{matrix} \rightarrow \begin{matrix} 1\overset{\checkmark}{=}1 \\ -5\overset{\checkmark}{=}-5 \end{matrix}$$

☞ Try These

1. Solve the system $\begin{matrix} 3x+y=4 \\ 4x-y=3 \end{matrix}$ by the method of substitution.

2. Solve the system $\begin{matrix} 2x-3y=5 \\ 4x-6y=8 \end{matrix}$ by the method of substitution.

3. Solve the system $\begin{matrix} x+y=48 \\ 0.25x+0.10y=7.50 \end{matrix}$ by the method of substitution.

Solutions

1. The system $\begin{array}{l} 3x+y=4 \\ 4x-y=3 \end{array}$ has exactly one solution because $\dfrac{3}{4} \neq \dfrac{1}{-1}$.

Step 1. Solve $3x + y = 4$ for y in terms of x.

Isolate the y term by subtracting $3x$ from both sides of the equation. Then combine like terms.

$$3x+y=4$$
$$3x+y-3x=4-3x$$
$$y+3x-3x=4-3x$$
$$y=4-3x$$

Step 2. Substitute $y = 4 - 3x$ into the equation $4x - y = 3$, simplify, and solve for x.

$$4x-y=3$$
$$4x-(4-3x)=3$$
$$4x-4+3x=3$$
$$4x+3x-4=3$$
$$7x-4=3$$
$$7x-4+4=3+4$$
$$7x=7$$
$$\frac{7x}{7}=\frac{7}{7}$$
$$\frac{\cancel{7}x}{\cancel{7}}=1$$
$$x=1$$

Step 3. Substitute $x = 1$ into the equation $3x + y = 4$ and solve for y.

$$3x+y=4$$
$$3(1)+y=4$$
$$3+y=4$$
$$3+y-3=4-3$$
$$y+3-3=4-3$$
$$y=4-3$$
$$y=1$$

Step 4. The ordered pair $(1, 1)$ is the solution of the system $\begin{array}{l} 3x+y=4 \\ 4x-y=3 \end{array}$.

Check:

$$\begin{array}{l} 3x+y=4 \\ 4x-y=3 \end{array} \rightarrow \begin{array}{l} 3(1)+(1)\overset{?}{=}4 \\ 4(1)-(1)\overset{?}{=}3 \end{array} \rightarrow \begin{array}{l} 3+1\overset{?}{=}4 \\ 4-1\overset{?}{=}3 \end{array} \rightarrow \begin{array}{l} 4\overset{\checkmark}{=}4 \\ 3\overset{\checkmark}{=}3 \end{array}$$

2. The system $\dfrac{2x-3y=5}{4x-6y=8}$ has no solution because $\dfrac{2}{4}=\dfrac{-3}{-6}=\dfrac{1}{2}\neq\dfrac{5}{8}$.

3. The system $\dfrac{x+y=48}{0.25x+0.10y=7.50}$ has exactly one solution because $\dfrac{1}{0.25}\neq\dfrac{1}{0.10}$.

Step 1. Solve $x + y = 48$ for x in terms of y.

Isolate the x term by subtracting y from both sides of the equation. Then combine like terms.

$$x+y=48$$
$$x+y-y=48-y$$
$$x=48-y$$

Step 2. Substitute $x = 48 - y$ into the equation $0.25x + 0.10y = 7.50$, simplify, and solve for y.

$$0.25x+0.10y=7.50$$
$$0.25(48-y)+0.10y=7.50$$
$$12-0.25y+0.10y=7.50$$
$$12-0.15y=7.50$$
$$12-0.15y-12=7.50-12$$
$$-0.15y+12-12=7.50-12$$
$$\dfrac{-0.15y}{-0.15}=\dfrac{-4.5}{-0.15}$$
$$\dfrac{\cancel{-0.15}y}{\cancel{-0.15}}=30$$
$$y=30$$

Step 3. Substitute $y = 30$ into the equation $x + y = 48$ and solve for x.

$$x+y=48$$
$$x+(30)=48$$
$$x+30=48$$
$$x+30-30=48-30$$
$$x=18$$

Step 4. The ordered pair (18, 30) is the solution of the system $\dfrac{x+y=48}{0.25x+0.10y=7.50}$.

Check:

$$\begin{matrix} x+y=48 \\ 0.25x+0.10y=7.50 \end{matrix} \rightarrow \begin{matrix} (18)+(30)\overset{?}{=}48 \\ 0.25(18)-0.10(30)\overset{?}{=}7.50 \end{matrix} \rightarrow \begin{matrix} 18+30\overset{?}{=}48 \\ 4.50+3.00\overset{?}{=}7.50 \end{matrix} \rightarrow \begin{matrix} 48\overset{\checkmark}{=}48 \\ 7.50\overset{\checkmark}{=}7.50 \end{matrix}$$

Solving a System of Two Linear Equations by Elimination

To solve a system of linear equations by the method of elimination, do these steps.

Step 1. Write both equations in standard form: $Ax + By = C$.

Step 2. Eliminate one of the variables. If necessary, multiply one or both of the equations by a nonzero constant or constants to make the coefficients of one of the variables sum to 0. ***Tip:*** You can eliminate either variable. Use your judgment to decide.

Step 3. Add the equations and solve for the variable that was not eliminated.

Step 4. Substitute the answer to Step 3 into one of the original equations and solve for the other variable.

Step 5. State the solution and check it in the original equations.

Here is an example.

Solve the system $\begin{array}{l} 2x - 3y = 12 \\ 5x + 2y = 11 \end{array}$ by the method of elimination.

The system has exactly one solution because $\dfrac{2}{5} \neq \dfrac{-3}{2}$.

Step 1. Write both equations in standard form: $Ax + By = C$.

$$2x - 3y = 12$$
$$5x + 2y = 11$$

Step 2. To eliminate y, multiply the first equation by 2 and the second equation by 3.

$$\begin{array}{l} 2x - 3y = 12 \\ 5x + 2y = 11 \end{array} \rightarrow \begin{array}{l} 2(2x - 3y) = 2(12) \\ 3(5x + 2y) = 3(11) \end{array} \rightarrow \begin{array}{l} 4x - 6y = 24 \\ 15x + 6y = 33 \end{array}$$

Step 3. Add the transformed equations and solve for x.

$$4x - 6y = 24$$
$$\underline{15x + 6y = 33}$$
$$19x + 0 = 57$$
$$19x = 57$$
$$\frac{19x}{19} = \frac{57}{19}$$
$$\frac{\cancel{19}x}{\cancel{19}} = \frac{57}{19}$$
$$x = 3$$

Step 4. Substitute $x = 3$ into the equation $2x - 3y = 12$ and solve for y.

$$2x - 3y = 12$$
$$2(3) - 3y = 12$$
$$6 - 3y = 12$$
$$6 - 3y - 6 = 12 - 6$$
$$-3y + 6 - 6 = 12 - 6$$
$$-3y = 6$$
$$\frac{-3y}{-3} = \frac{6}{-3}$$
$$\frac{\cancel{-3}y}{\cancel{-3}} = -2$$
$$y = -2$$

Step 5. State the solution and check it in the original equations.

The ordered pair $(3, -2)$ is the solution of the system $\begin{matrix} 2x - 3y = 12 \\ 5x + 2y = 11 \end{matrix}$.

Check:

$$\begin{matrix} 2x - 3y = 12 \\ 5x + 2y = 11 \end{matrix} \rightarrow \begin{matrix} 2(3) - 3(-2) \overset{?}{=} 12 \\ 5(3) + 2(-2) \overset{?}{=} 11 \end{matrix} \rightarrow \begin{matrix} 6 + 6 \overset{?}{=} 12 \\ 15 + -4 \overset{?}{=} 11 \end{matrix} \rightarrow \begin{matrix} 12 \overset{\checkmark}{=} 12 \\ 11 \overset{\checkmark}{=} 11 \end{matrix}$$

☞ Try These

1. Solve the system $\begin{matrix} x = -1 - y \\ 4x - 3y = 3 \end{matrix}$ by the method of elimination.

2. Solve the system $\begin{matrix} 3x - y = 2 \\ 9x - 3y = 8 \end{matrix}$ by the method of elimination.

3. Solve the system $\begin{matrix} x + y = 500 \\ 0.02x + 0.03y = 13 \end{matrix}$ by the method of elimination.

Solutions

1. *Step 1.* Write both equations in standard form: $Ax + By = C$.

$$x + y = -1$$
$$4x - 3y = 3$$

The system $\begin{matrix} x + y = -1 \\ 4x - 3y = 3 \end{matrix}$ has exactly one solution because $\frac{1}{4} \neq \frac{1}{-3}$.

Step 2. To eliminate y, multiply the first equation by 3.

$$\begin{matrix} x + y = -1 \\ 4x - 3y = 3 \end{matrix} \rightarrow \begin{matrix} 3(x + y) = 3(-1) \\ 4x - 3y = 3 \end{matrix} \rightarrow \begin{matrix} 3x + 3y = -3 \\ 4x - 3y = 3 \end{matrix}$$

Step 3. Add the transformed equations and solve for x.

$$3x + 3y = -3$$
$$4x - 3y = 3$$
$$\overline{}$$
$$7x + 0 = 0$$
$$7x = 0$$
$$\frac{7x}{7} = \frac{0}{7}$$
$$\frac{\cancel{7}x}{\cancel{7}} = 0$$
$$x = 0$$

Step 4. Substitute $x = 0$ into the equation $x = -1 - y$ and solve for y.

$$x = -1 - y$$
$$0 = -1 - y$$
$$0 + y = -1 - y + y$$
$$y = -1$$

Step 5. State the solution and check it in the original equations.

The ordered pair $(0, -1)$ is the solution of the system $\begin{array}{l} x = -1 - y \\ 4x - 3y = 3 \end{array}$.

Check:

$$\begin{array}{l} x = -1 - y \\ 4x - 3y = 3 \end{array} \rightarrow \begin{array}{l} (0) \overset{?}{=} -1 - (-1) \\ 4(0) - 3(-1) \overset{?}{=} 3 \end{array} \rightarrow \begin{array}{l} 0 \overset{?}{=} -1 + 1 \\ 0 + 3 \overset{?}{=} 3 \end{array} \rightarrow \begin{array}{l} 0 \overset{\checkmark}{=} 0 \\ 3 \overset{\checkmark}{=} 3 \end{array}$$

2. The system $\begin{array}{l} 3x - y = 2 \\ 9x - 3y = 8 \end{array}$ has no solution because $\frac{3}{9} = \frac{-1}{-3} = \frac{1}{3} \neq \frac{2}{8} = \frac{1}{4}$.

3. *Step 1.* Write both equations in standard form: $Ax + By = C$.

$$x + y = 500$$
$$0.02x + 0.03y = 13$$

The system $\begin{array}{l} x + y = 500 \\ 0.02x + 0.03y = 13 \end{array}$ has exactly one solution because $\frac{1}{0.02} \neq \frac{1}{0.03}$.

Step 2. To eliminate x, multiply the first equation by -0.02.

$$\begin{array}{l} x + y = 500 \\ 0.02x + 0.03y = 13 \end{array} \rightarrow \begin{array}{l} -0.02(x + y) = -0.02(500) \\ 0.02x + 0.03y = 13 \end{array} \rightarrow \begin{array}{l} -0.02x - 0.02y = -10 \\ 0.02x + 0.03y = 13 \end{array}$$

Step 3. Add the transformed equations and solve for y.

$$-0.02x - 0.02y = -10$$
$$\underline{0.02x + 0.03y = 13}$$
$$0 + 0.01y = 3$$
$$0.01y = 3$$
$$\frac{0.01y}{0.01} = \frac{3}{0.01}$$
$$\frac{\cancel{0.01}y}{\cancel{0.01}} = 300$$
$$y = 300$$

Step 4. Substitute $y = 300$ into the equation $x + y = 500$ and solve for x.

$$x + y = 500$$
$$x + (300) = 500$$
$$x + 300 = 500$$
$$x + 300 - 300 = 500 - 300$$
$$x = 200$$

Step 5. State the solution and check it in the original equations.

The ordered pair (200, 300) is the solution of the system $\begin{array}{l} x + y = 500 \\ 0.02x + 0.03y = 13 \end{array}$.

Check:

$$\begin{array}{l} x + y = 500 \\ 0.02x + 0.03y = 13 \end{array} \rightarrow \begin{array}{l} (200) + (300) \overset{?}{=} 500 \\ 0.02(200) + 0.03(300) \overset{?}{=} 13 \end{array} \rightarrow \begin{array}{l} 200 + 300 \overset{?}{=} 500 \\ 4 + 9 \overset{?}{=} 13 \end{array} \rightarrow \begin{array}{l} 500 \overset{\checkmark}{=} 500 \\ 13 \overset{\checkmark}{=} 13 \end{array}$$

Solving Real-World Problems Leading to Two Linear Equations in Two Variables

You can use systems of two linear equations to model real-world problems in which there are two unknowns. Here is an example.

> Rashid has $7.50 in dimes and quarters. The total number of coins is 48. How many dimes and how many quarters does Rashid have?

There are two unknowns. The number of dimes is unknown, and the number of quarters is unknown. Represent the two unknowns with variables.

Let d = the number of dimes and q = the number of quarters.

Make a chart to organize the information.

	Dimes	Quarters	Total
Value per coin	$0.10	$0.25	
Number of coins	d	q	48
Value of coins	$0.10d	$0.25q	$7.50

Using the chart, write two equations that represent the facts of the question.

$$d + q = 48$$
$$\$0.10d + \$0.25q = \$7.50$$

Tip: When you have two variables, you must write two equations in order to determine a solution.

Solve the system, omitting the units for convenience.

Using the method of substitution, solve $d + q = 48$ for q in terms of d.

$$d + q = 48$$
$$d + q - d = 48 - d$$
$$q = 48 - d$$

Substitute $q = 48 - d$ into the equation $0.10d + 0.25q = 7.50$ and solve for d.

$$0.10d + 0.25q = 7.50$$
$$0.10d + 0.25(48 - d) = 7.50$$
$$0.10d + 12 - 0.25d = 7.50$$
$$0.10d - 0.25d + 12 = 7.50$$
$$-0.15d + 12 = 7.50$$
$$-0.15d + 12 - 12 = 7.50 - 12$$
$$-0.15d = -4.50$$
$$\frac{-0.15d}{-0.15} = \frac{-4.50}{-0.15}$$
$$\frac{\cancel{-0.15}d}{\cancel{-0.15}} = 30$$
$$d = 30$$

Substitute $d = 30$ into the equation $d + q = 48$ and solve for q.

$$d + q = 48$$
$$(30) + q = 48$$
$$30 + q - 30 = 48 - 30$$
$$q = 18$$

Rashid has 30 dimes and 18 quarters.

Check:

$$d + q = 48 \qquad \xrightarrow{} \qquad 30 + 18 \overset{?}{=} 48 \qquad \xrightarrow{} \qquad 48 \overset{\checkmark}{=} 48 \qquad \xrightarrow{} \qquad 48 \overset{\checkmark}{=} 48$$

$$\$0.10d + \$0.25q = \$7.50 \qquad \$0.10(30) + \$0.25(18) \overset{?}{=} \$7.50 \qquad \$3.00 + \$4.50 \overset{?}{=} \$7.50 \qquad \$7.50 \overset{\checkmark}{=} \$7.50$$

☞ Try These

1. The sum of two numbers is 100. Their difference is 50. Find the numbers.

2. The length of a garden is 3 meters more than its width. The garden's perimeter is 54 meters. Find the garden's dimensions.

3. The admission at a zoo is $9 for adults and $6 for children. On a certain day, 1,950 people enter the zoo and $13,950 is collected for their admission. How many adult tickets and how many children tickets were sold on that day?

Solutions

1. There are two unknowns. The larger number is unknown, and the smaller number is unknown. Represent the two unknowns with variables.

   Let x = the larger number and y = the smaller number.

   Write two equations that represent the facts of the question.

   $$x + y = 100$$
   $$x - y = 50$$

   Solve the system.

   Using the method of elimination, add the two equations to eliminate y.

   $$x + y = 100$$
   $$\underline{x - y = 50}$$
   $$2x + 0 = 150$$
   $$2x = 150$$
   $$\frac{2x}{2} = \frac{150}{2}$$
   $$\frac{\cancel{2}x}{\cancel{2}} = 75$$
   $$x = 75$$

Substitute $x = 75$ into the equation $x + y = 100$ and solve for y.

$$x + y = 100$$
$$(75) + y = 100$$
$$75 + y = 100$$
$$75 + y - 75 = 100 - 75$$
$$y = 25$$

The larger number is 75 and the smaller number is 25.

Check:

$$\begin{array}{c} x + y = 100 \\ x - y = 50 \end{array} \rightarrow \begin{array}{c} 75 + 25 \overset{?}{=} 100 \\ 75 - 25 \overset{?}{=} 50 \end{array} \rightarrow \begin{array}{c} 100 \overset{\checkmark}{=} 100 \\ 50 \overset{\checkmark}{=} 50 \end{array}$$

2. There are two unknowns. The length of the garden is unknown, and its width is unknown. Represent the two unknowns with variables.

   Let l = the garden's length in meters and w = the garden's width in meters.

   Make a sketch.

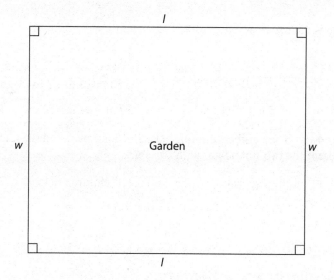

   Write two equations that represent the facts of the question.

$$l = w + 3 \text{ meters}$$
$$2l + 2w = 54 \text{ meters}$$

   Solve the system, omitting the units for convenience.

Using the method of substitution, substitute $l = w + 3$ into the equation $2l + 2w = 54$ and solve for w.

$$2l + 2w = 54$$
$$2(w+3) + 2w = 54$$
$$2w + 6 + 2w = 54$$
$$4w + 6 = 54$$
$$4w + 6 - 6 = 54 - 6$$
$$4w = 48$$
$$\frac{4w}{4} = \frac{48}{4}$$
$$\frac{\cancel{4}w}{\cancel{4}} = 12$$
$$w = 12$$

Substitute $w = 12$ into the equation $l = w + 3$ and solve for l.

$$l = w + 3$$
$$l = 12 + 3$$
$$l = 15$$

The garden's length is 15 meters and its width is 12 meters.

Check:

$$
\begin{array}{llll}
l = w + 3 \text{ m} & (15 \text{ m}) \overset{?}{=} (12 \text{ m}) + 3 \text{ m} & 15 \text{ m} \overset{?}{=} 12 \text{ m} + 3 \text{ m} & 15 \text{ m} \overset{\checkmark}{=} 15 \text{ m} \\
\rightarrow & \rightarrow & \rightarrow & \\
2l + 2w = 54 \text{ m} & 2(15 \text{ m}) + 2(12 \text{ m}) \overset{?}{=} 54 \text{ m} & 30 \text{ m} + 24 \text{ m} \overset{?}{=} 54 \text{ m} & 54 \text{ m} \overset{\checkmark}{=} 54 \text{ m}
\end{array}
$$

3. There are two unknowns. The number of adult tickets is unknown, and the number of children tickets is unknown. Represent the two unknowns with variables.

Let a = the number of adult tickets and c = the number of children tickets.

Write two equations that represent the facts of the question.

$$a + c = 1,950$$
$$\$9a + \$6c = \$13,950$$

Solve the system, omitting the units for convenience.

Using the method of substitution, solve $a + c = 1,950$ for a in terms of c.

$$a + c = 1,950$$
$$a + c - c = 1,950 - c$$
$$a = 1,950 - c$$

Substitute $a = 1,950 - c$ into the equation $9a + 6c = 13,950$ and solve for c.

$$9a + 6c = 13,950$$
$$9(1,950 - c) + 6c = 13,950$$
$$17,550 - 9c + 6c = 13,950$$
$$17,550 - 3c = 13,950$$
$$17,550 - 3c - 17,550 = 13,950 - 17,550$$
$$-3c = -3,600$$
$$\frac{-3c}{-3} = \frac{-3,600}{-3}$$
$$\frac{\cancel{-3}c}{\cancel{-3}} = 1,200$$
$$c = 1,200$$

Substitute $c = 1,200$ into the equation $a + c = 1,950$ and solve for a.

$$a + c = 1,950$$
$$a + 1,200 = 1,950$$
$$a + 1,200 - 1,200 = 1,950 - 1,200$$
$$a = 750$$

The zoo sold 750 adult tickets and 1,200 children tickets.

Check:

$a + c = 1,950$ $\rightarrow$ $(750) + (1,200) \overset{?}{=} 1,950$ $\rightarrow$ $750 + 1,200 \overset{?}{=} 1,950$ $\rightarrow$ $1,950 \overset{\checkmark}{=} 1,950$

$\$9a + \$6c = \$13,950$ $\$9(750) + \$6(1,200) \overset{?}{=} \$13,950$ $\$6,750 + \$7,200 \overset{?}{=} \$13,950$ $\$13,950 \overset{\checkmark}{=} \$13,950$

3. Functions

In this chapter, you are introduced to the concept of a function. You will evaluate and compare functions, construct a function to model a linear relationship between two quantities, and describe qualitatively the functional relationship between two quantities by analyzing a graph.

Understanding Function Concepts

(CCSS.Math.Content.8.F.A.1)

A **function** is rule that assigns to each **input** exactly one **output.** For instance, when x represents the input and y represents the output, a function pairs each x value with exactly one y value. Here are examples.

> For every input, x, the function $y = 2x + 1$ produces exactly one output, y. For instance, when $x = -5$, $y = 2(-5) + 1 = -10 + 1 = -9$; when $x = 3$, $y = 2(3) + 1 = 6 + 1 = 7$; and so on.
>
> For every input, x, the function $y = x^2$ produces exactly one output, y. For instance, when $x = -2$, $y = (-2)^2 = 4$; when $x = 2$, $y = (2)^2 = 4$; and so on. *Tip:* Notice in this example that the output for the input -2 is the same as the output for the input 2. This situation is permissible in a function. It's okay that the outputs are the same, as long as their inputs are different.

The **graph** of a function is the set of ordered pairs consisting of an input and its corresponding output. An ordered pair of numbers is written in a definite order so that one number is first and the other is second. In the graph of a function, the inputs are the first numbers and their corresponding outputs are the second numbers of the ordered pairs.

Graphs and numerical tables are useful partial representations of functions. These representations are "partial" representations because unless you know otherwise, the functions they represent have an infinite number of ordered pairs in their graphs. Therefore, you cannot graph or list all the possible input and output pairs.

Here are examples.

> The function $y = 2x + 1$

The graph of the function $y = 2x + 1$ is shown below.

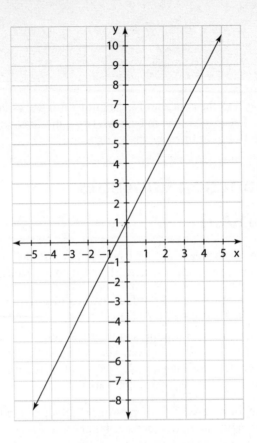

The graph shows that every input on the *x*-axis has exactly one output on the *y*-axis.

A table of input and output ordered pairs for the function $y = 2x + 1$ is shown below.

Input x	Output y
−5	−9
−2	−3
0	1
2	5
5	11

For the ordered pairs shown in the table, each value in the input column is paired with exactly one value in the output column.

The function $y = x^2$

The graph of the function $y = x^2$ is shown below.

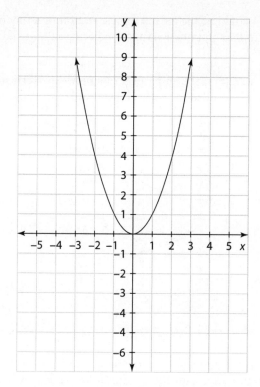

The graph shows that every input on the x-axis has exactly one output on the y-axis.

A table of inputs and outputs for the function $y = x^2$ is shown below.

Input x	Output y
−3	9
−2	4
0	0
2	4
3	9

For the ordered pairs shown in the table, each value in the input column is paired with exactly one value in the output column.

In the graph of a function, no two ordered pairs have the same x value but different y values.

Compare the following two tables of ordered pairs.

Table 1	
x	y
−5	−9
−2	−3
0	1
2	5
5	11

Table 2	
x	y
4	2
9	3
9	−3
16	4
25	5

Only the ordered pairs in Table 1 could be the partial representation of a function. The ordered pairs in Table 2 could *not* be the partial representation of a function because (9, 3) and (9, –3) have the same input, 9, but different outputs, 3 and –3.

You can visually check whether a graph is the graph of a function. Any vertical line can intersect a function's graph at only one point. This check is called the **vertical line test.** Here is an example.

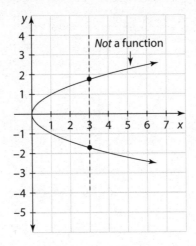

The dashed vertical line intersects the graph at two points, so the graph is *not* the graph of a function. As you can see, there are two different y values for the x value 3. *Remember:* A function cannot have two different y values assigned to the same x value.

☞Try These

1. Fill in the blank.

   (a) A function is a rule that assigns to each input exactly _____ output.

   (b) In a function, it _____ (is, is not) permissible for an input to be paired with two or more different outputs.

   (c) In a function, it _____ (is, is not) permissible for an output to be paired with two or more different inputs.

   (d) The _____ of a function is the set of ordered pairs consisting of the function's inputs and their corresponding outputs.

2. Could the ordered pairs in each of the following tables be a partial representation of a function? State yes or no. Explain your answer.

(a)

Input x	Output y
–3	1
–2	2
–2	4
2	6
3	1

(b)

Input x	Output y
1	1
2	1
3	1
4	1
5	1

(c)

Input x	Output y
–3	–6
–2	–4
0	0
2	4
3	6

(d)

Input x	Output y
$-\dfrac{1}{3}$	–3
$-\dfrac{1}{2}$	–2
0	0
$\dfrac{1}{2}$	2
$\dfrac{1}{3}$	3

3. Could the graph be a partial representation of a function? State yes or no. Explain your answer.

(a)

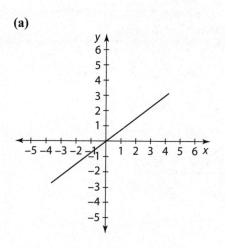

(b)

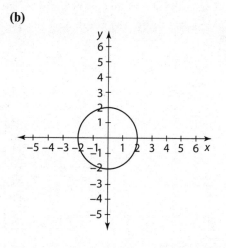

(c)

(d)

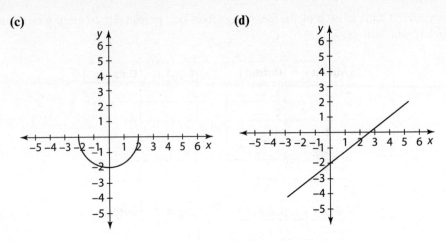

Solutions

1. **(a)** one
   (b) is not
   (c) is
   (d) graph

2. **(a)** No. The ordered pairs could not be the partial representation of a function because (–2, 2) and (–2, 4) have the same input, –2, but different outputs, 2 and 4.
   (b) Yes. Each value in the input column is paired with exactly one value in the output column.
   (c) Yes. Each value in the input column is paired with exactly one value in the output column.
   (d) Yes. Each value in the input column is paired with exactly one value in the output column.

3. **(a)** Yes. The graph shows that every input on the x-axis has exactly one output on the y-axis.
   (b) No. As shown below, the graph does not pass the vertical line test.

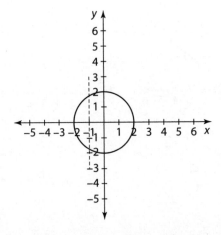

   (c) Yes. The graph shows that every input on the x-axis has exactly one output on the y-axis.
   (d) Yes. The graph shows that every input on the x-axis has exactly one output on the y-axis.

Understanding and Comparing Linear Functions

(CCSS.Math.Content.8.F.A.2, CCSS.Math.Content.8.F.A.3)

The function $y = mx + b$ is a **linear function.** The function is called linear because its graph is a straight *nonvertical* line. The slope of the line is the coefficient m. The number b is the y-coordinate of the point where the graph intersects the y-axis. It is the y-intercept (or simply the **intercept**). (See "Graphing Two-Variable Linear Equations of the Form $y = mx + b$" in Chapter 2 for an additional discussion of slope and y-intercept.)

Here is an example.

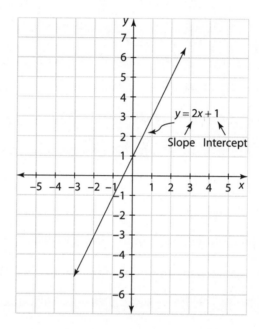

The slope m of a linear function's graph is the function's **rate of change.** Because the slope of a line is constant, a linear function's rate of change is constant over the entire graph. The rate of change describes how the output changes in relation to the input. For every 1-unit change in the input, there are m units of change in the output. If the input changes by k units, the output changes by km units.

For example, for the function $y = 2x + 1$, for every 1-unit change in x, there is a 2-unit change in y.

In general, if (x_1, y_1) and (x_2, y_2) are any two ordered pairs in a linear function's graph, the function's rate of change is $\dfrac{\text{change in } y}{\text{change in } x} = \dfrac{y_2 - y_1}{x_2 - x_1}$.

Rates of change can be positive, negative, or zero. A **positive rate of change** corresponds to an increase in the output when the input increases. When you trace the input, *x*, as it increases from left to right, you will observe that the output, *y*, increases from lower to higher values. The result is that the graph slants upward from left to right. Here is a graphical illustration.

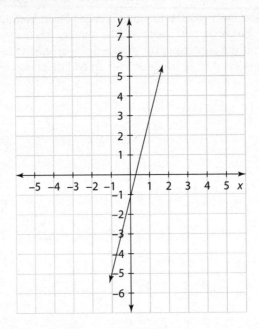

A **negative rate of change** corresponds to a decrease in the output when the input increases. When you trace the input, *x*, as it increases from left to right, you will observe that the output, *y*, decreases from higher to lower values. The result is that the graph slants downward from left to right. Here is a graphical illustration.

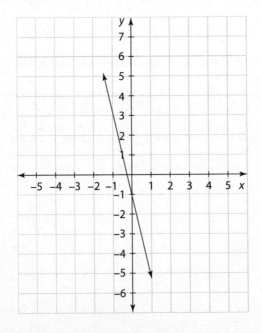

A **zero rate of change** occurs when the output does not change as the input increases. When you trace the input, x, as it increases from left to right, you will observe that the value of the output, y, does not change. That is, the output's value remains constant. The result is that the graph is a horizontal line. Here is a graphical illustration.

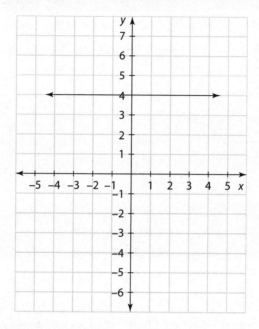

Therefore, linear functions are either increasing, decreasing, or remaining constant, from left to right, at a steady rate. Their graphs do not change direction.

Compare the following representations of three linear functions to determine which function has the greatest rate of change.

Function 1: $y = 2x + 5$

Function 2:

Input x	Output y
−1	−5
0	−2
1	1

Function 3:

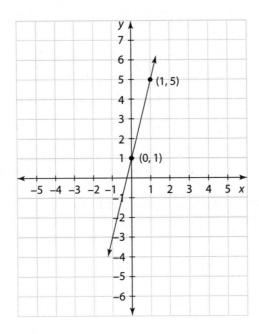

Function 1: The rate of change is 2 because the coefficient of x is 2.

Function 2: The rate of change is 3 because $\dfrac{\text{change in } y}{\text{change in } x} = \dfrac{y_2 - y_1}{x_2 - x_1} = \dfrac{-2-(-5)}{0-(-1)} = \dfrac{-2+5}{0+1} = \dfrac{3}{1} = 3.$

Tip: You can pick any two (x, y) pairs in the table to determine the rate of change.

Function 3: The rate of change is 4 because $\dfrac{\text{change in } y}{\text{change in } x} = \dfrac{y_2 - y_1}{x_2 - x_1} = \dfrac{5-1}{1-0} = \dfrac{4}{1} = 4.$

Tip: You can pick any two (x, y) pairs on the graph to determine the rate of change.

Function 3 has the greatest rate of change.

When a function's output starts at zero, the y-intercept of its graph is the function's **initial value.** The initial value is the output value that corresponds to an input of zero. For example, in the following table of input-output pairs, the initial value is 3.

Input x	Output y
0	3
2	4
6	6

The graphs of three functions are shown below. The three functions have the same rate of change, but different initial values. Which one has the least initial value?

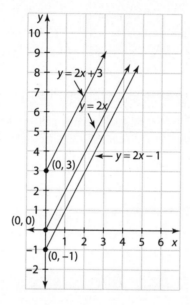

The initial value for $y = 2x + 3$ is 3. The initial value for $y = 2x$ is 0. The initial value for $y = 2x - 1$ is -1. The function $y = 2x - 1$ has the least initial value.

The function $y = x^2$ is a nonlinear function. As shown below, its graph is not a straight line. The shape of the graph is a **parabola.** The rate of change of $y = x^2$ is not constant.

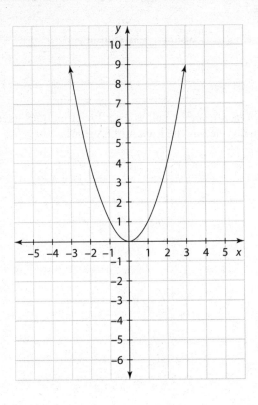

☞ Try These

1. Fill in the blank(s).

   (a) The function $y = mx + b$ is a _____ function.

   (b) The _____ of a function's graph is the function's rate of change.

   (c) A linear function's rate of change is _____ over the entire graph.

   (d) A function's rate of change m describes how the _____ changes in relation to the input. For every _____ unit change in the input, there are m units of change in the output. And if the input changes by k units, the output changes by _____ units.

   (e) A positive rate of change corresponds to a(n) _____ (decrease, increase) in the output when the input increases. A negative rate of change corresponds to a(n) _____ (decrease, increase) in the output when the input increases.

   (f) A zero rate of change occurs when the output _____ (does, does not) change as the input increases.

   (g) When a function's output starts at zero, the _____ of its graph is the function's initial value.

   (h) A function's initial value is the output value that corresponds to an input of _____ .

2. Compare the following representations of three linear functions to determine which function has the greatest rate of change.

   Function 1: $y = \dfrac{5}{2}x + 1$

   Function 2:

Input x	Output y
−5	−1
0	3
5	7

   Function 3:

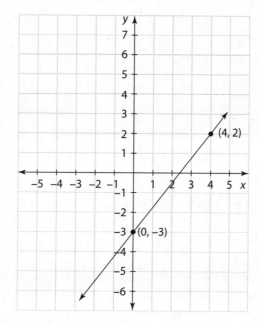

3. Compare the partial representations of the two linear functions and determine which has a negative rate of change.

   Function 1:

Input x	Output y
0	25
2	18
3	14.50
5	7.50

   Function 2:

Input x	Output y
0	−100
2	−80
3	−70
5	−50

4. Compare the partial representations of the two linear functions and determine which has the least *y*-intercept.

Function 1:

Input *x*	Output *y*
−5	−6
−1	−2.8
0	−2
5	2

Function 2:

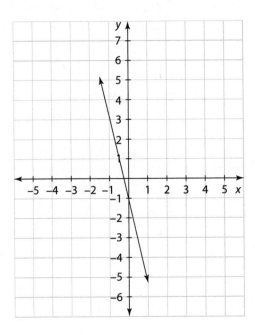

Solutions

1. (a) linear
   (b) slope
   (c) constant
   (d) output; 1; *mk*
   (e) increase; decrease
   (f) does not
   (g) *y*-intercept
   (h) zero

2. Function 1 has the greatest rate of change.

   Function 1: The rate of change is $\frac{5}{2}$ because the coefficient of x is $\frac{5}{2}$.

   Function 2: The rate of change is $\frac{4}{5}$ because $\dfrac{\text{change in } y}{\text{change in } x} = \dfrac{y_2 - y_1}{x_2 - x_1} = \dfrac{3-(-1)}{0-(-5)} = \dfrac{3+1}{0+5} = \dfrac{4}{5}$.

   Function 3: The rate of change is $\frac{5}{4}$ because $\dfrac{\text{change in } y}{\text{change in } x} = \dfrac{y_2 - y_1}{x_2 - x_1} = \dfrac{2-(-3)}{4-0} = \dfrac{2+3}{4} = \dfrac{5}{4}$.

3. Function 1 has a negative rate of change because the output values decrease as the input values increase.

   Function 2 has a positive rate of change because the output values increase as the input values increase.

4. Function 1 has the least y-intercept.

   The y-intercept for Function 1 is –2.

   The y-intercept for Function 2 is –1.

Proportional Relationships

(CCSS.Math.Content.8.F.A.1, CCSS.Math.Content.8.F.A.3, CCSS.Math.Content.8.F.B.4)

When the y-intercept, b, is zero, the linear function $y = mx + b$ has the form $y = mx$. This function models a proportional relationship. The coefficient m is the **constant of proportionality** (or unit rate) of the proportional relationship. In other words, a function is a proportional function when the output is equal to the input multiplied by a constant. If the graph of a linear function passes through the origin, the linear function is a proportional relationship. Here is an example.

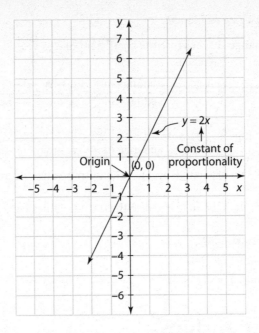

Write a linear function that represents the proportional relationship shown in the table below.

Time, t, in Hours	Distance, d, in Miles
0	0
2	8
3	12

The intercept is 0. The rate of change is $\dfrac{8-0}{2-0} = \dfrac{8}{2} = \dfrac{4}{1} = 4$. The function is $d = 4t$.

☞ Try These

1. Fill in the blank(s).

   (a) The linear function $y = mx$ models a _____ relationship. Its graph passes through the _____.

   (b) The coefficient m of the function $y = mx$ is the _____ of proportionality.

2. For the proportional relationship shown in the table below,

   (a) Determine the intercept and rate of change.

   (b) Write a linear function that represents the proportional relationship.

Amount of Fuel, g, in Gallons	Cost, c, in Dollars
0	0
2	6.90
5	17.25

Solutions

1. **(a)** proportional; origin
   (b) constant

2. **(a)** The intercept is 0. The rate of change is $\dfrac{6.90-0}{2-0}=\dfrac{6.90}{2}=\dfrac{3.45}{1}=3.45.$
   (b) The function is $c = 3.45g$.

Modeling Linear Relationships Between Two Quantities

(CCSS.Math.Content.8.F.B.4)

To construct a function that models a linear relationship, determine the rate of change and initial value (that is, when the input is zero) of the function. Then write the function as y = (rate of change)x + (initial value). Here is an example.

Write a function that models the linear relationship in the table below.

x	y
0	1
1	−3
2	−7

The input-output ordered pairs are (0, 1), (1, −3) and (2, −7). Use any two pairs to find the rate of change.

Using (0, 1) and (1, −3), the rate of change is $\dfrac{-3-1}{1-0}=\dfrac{-4}{1}=-4.$ The initial value is 1. The function is $y = -4x + 1$.

In real-world problems, you use linear functions to model situations that involve change at a constant rate. You determine the rate of change and initial value of the linear function from a description of the situation it is intended to model. Here is an example.

A tank contains 350 gallons of water. Suppose water is added to the tank at a constant rate of 100 gallons per hour. Write an expression that models the amount in gallons, g, of water in the tank as a function of t, the elapsed time in hours.

The rate of change is 100 (the rate of gallons per hour). The initial value is 350 (the amount in gallons in the tank when t is 0). The function is $g = 100t + 350$.

☞ Try These

1. Write a function that models the linear relationship in the table below.

Input x	Output y
0	25
2	18
3	14.5
5	7.5

2. A train is initially 50 miles from a city and moving away from the city at 60 miles per hour. Write an expression that models the train's distance, d, from the city as a function of t, the elapsed time in hours.

Solutions

1. The function is $y = -3.50x + 25$.

   The input-output ordered pairs are (0, 25), (2, 18), (3, 14.5), and (5, 7.5). Using (0, 25) and (2, 18), the rate of change is $\dfrac{18-25}{2-0} = \dfrac{-7}{2} = -\dfrac{3.5}{1} = -3.5$. The initial value is 25.

2. The function is $d = 60t + 50$.

   The rate of change is 60 (the rate of miles per hour). The initial value is 50 (the distance when t is 0).

Qualitatively Describing Functional Relationships Between Two Quantities

(CCSS.Math.Content.8.F.B.5)

To describe qualitatively the functional relationship between two quantities, proceed from left to right. Verbally describe the behavior of the output (for example, it is increasing or decreasing) as the input is increasing.

Here is an example of describing the height of a ball thrown straight up in the air.

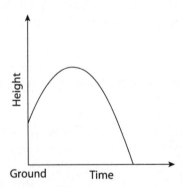

Description: The initial height is greater than zero. The height increases until the ball stops, at which time maximum height is reached. Then gravity starts to pull the ball down, and the height decreases as the ball returns to the ground (right below where it was initially thrown).

You can get creative with graphs by "fusing" together two or more functions to model a real-world situation. Here is an example depicting a moving vehicle.

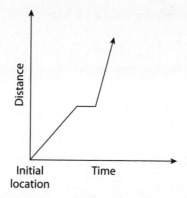

Description: Initially, the vehicle drives at a steady speed for a while, stops for a short while, and then continues on at a faster speed than before.

☞ Try These

1. Verbally describe the following graph depicting a trip on a bicycle.

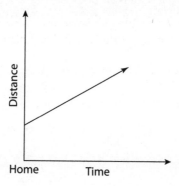

2. Verbally describe the following graph depicting water draining from a pool.

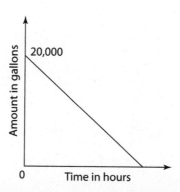

3. Verbally describe the following graph depicting a car trip.

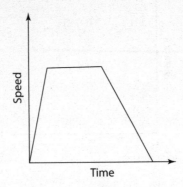

Solutions

1. Initially, the rider is a distance from home. As time increases, the rider's distance from home increases at a steady pace.

2. Initially, the pool contains 20,000 gallons of water. As time increases, the amount of water in the pool decreases at a constant rate until the pool is empty.

3. The driver of the car drives off and steadily increases speed, drives at a constant speed for a period of time, and then steadily decreases speed at a slower rate than before until the speed is zero.

4. Geometry

In this chapter, you will study coordinate rules for geometric transformations and explore congruence and similarity in the context of geometric transformations. You will solve mathematical and real-world problems using the Pythagorean theorem. You also will solve mathematical and real-world problems involving volume of cylinders, cones, and spheres.

Understanding Coordinate Rules for Transformations

(CCSS.Math.Content.8.G.A.1, CCSS.Math.Content.8.G.A.2, CCSS.Math.Content.8.G.A.3)

A **transformation** is a one-to-one matching between the points of a plane and themselves. Each point is associated with itself or with some other point in the plane. A transformation **maps** a **preimage** point, P, onto its corresponding **image** point, P'. In symbols, this mapping is represented as $P \rightarrow P'$ and is read as "the image of P is P prime."

In this chapter you will learn about four common transformations in the plane: reflections, translations, rotations, and dilations.

Understanding Coordinate Rules for Reflections

This section presents coordinate rules for three types of reflection transformations: a reflection over the x-axis, a reflection over the y-axis, and a reflection in the origin.

In the coordinate plane, a **reflection over the x-axis** is a transformation in which $P(x, y) \rightarrow P'(x, -y)$.

Tip: Under a reflection over the x-axis, every x-coordinate stays the same and every y-coordinate is changed to its opposite.

Under a reflection over the x-axis, corresponding points are equidistant from the x-axis, as shown below.

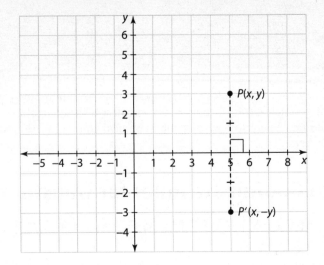

Think of the x-axis as a mirror. Point P' is the reflection of point P in the mirror.

Here is an example.

Find the coordinates of the image of $P(8, 5)$ under a reflection over the x-axis.

$P(8, 5) \rightarrow P'(8, -5)$

In the coordinate plane, a **reflection over the y-axis** is a transformation in which $P(x, y) \rightarrow P'(-x, y)$.

Tip: Under a reflection over the y-axis, every y-coordinate stays the same and every x-coordinate is changed to its opposite.

Under a reflection over the y-axis, corresponding points are equidistant from the y-axis, as shown below.

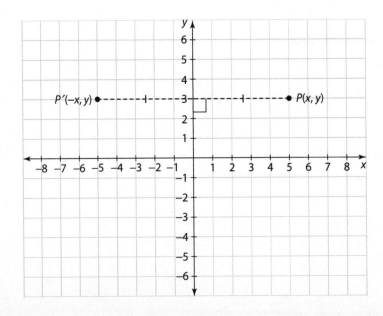

Here is an example.

> In the coordinate plane, construct the image of segment $\overline{AB}$ with endpoints $A(2, 4)$ and $B(5, 1)$ under a reflection over the y-axis.

In the diagram below, segment $\overline{A'B'}$ is the image of segment $\overline{AB}$ under a reflection over the y-axis. Observe that $A(2, 4) \rightarrow A'(-2, 4)$ and $B(5, 1) \rightarrow B'(-5, 1)$.

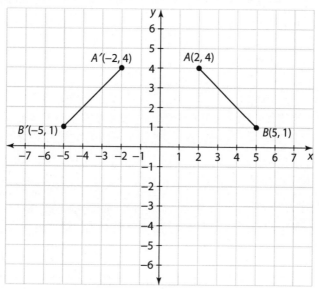

In the coordinate plane, a **reflection in the origin** is a transformation in which $P(x, y) \rightarrow P'(-x, -y)$. *Tip:* Under a reflection in the origin, every x-coordinate and every y-coordinate is changed to its opposite.

Under a reflection in the origin, the origin is the midpoint of segment $\overline{PP'}$ joining corresponding points, as shown below.

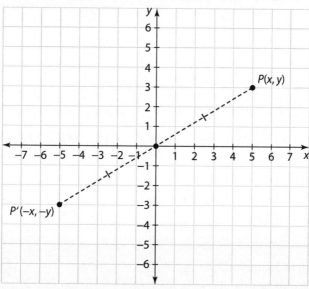

Here is an example.

In the coordinate plane, construct the image of rectangle $ABCD$ with vertices $A(2, -3)$, $B(2, -5)$, $C(5, -5)$, and $D(5, -3)$ under a reflection in the origin.

In the diagram below, rectangle $A'B'C'D'$ is the image of rectangle $ABCD$ under a reflection in the origin. Observe that $A(2, -3) \rightarrow A'(-2, 3)$, $B(2, -5) \rightarrow B'(-2, 5)$, $C(5, -5) \rightarrow C'(-5, 5)$, and $D(5, -3) \rightarrow D'(-5, 3)$.

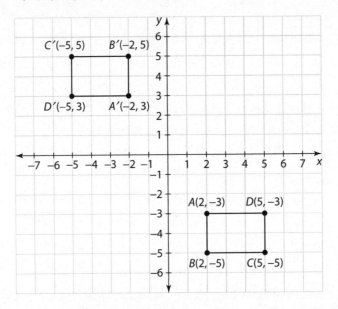

Tip: As the examples in this section illustrate, you can think of reflections as "flips." The image is the result of flipping the preimage over the x- or y-axis or the origin.

☞ Try These

1. Fill in the blank.

   (a) Under a reflection over the x-axis, the image of (x, y) is _____.
   (b) Under a reflection over the y-axis, the image of (x, y) is _____.
   (c) Under a reflection in the origin, the image of (x, y) is _____.

2. Find the coordinates of the image of the point under a reflection over the x-axis.

   (a) $A(5, 3)$
   (b) $B(6, -4)$
   (c) $C(-2, 8)$
   (d) $D(-10, -5)$

3. In the coordinate plane, construct the image of the given figure under a reflection over the x-axis.

   (a) segment $\overline{AB}$ with endpoints $A(2, 4)$ and $B(5, 1)$
   (b) rectangle $ABCD$ with vertices $A(-4, 3)$, $B(-4, 1)$, $C(2, 1)$, and $D(2, 3)$

4. Find the coordinates of the image of the point under a reflection over the *y*-axis.

   (a) $A(5, 3)$
   (b) $B(6, -4)$
   (c) $C(-2, 8)$
   (d) $D(-10, -5)$

5. In the coordinate plane, construct the image of rectangle *ABCD* with vertices $A(-4, 3)$, $B(-4, -1)$, $C(-2, -1)$, and $D(-2, 3)$ under a reflection over the *y*-axis.

6. Find the coordinates of the image of the point under a reflection in the origin.

   (a) $A(5, 3)$
   (b) $B(6, -4)$
   (c) $C(-2, 8)$
   (d) $D(-10, -5)$

7. In the coordinate plane, construct the image of segment $\overline{AB}$ with endpoints $A(2, 4)$ and $B(5, 1)$ under a reflection in the origin.

Solutions

1. **(a)** $(x, -y)$
   (b) $(-x, y)$
   (c) $(-x, -y)$

2. **(a)** $A(5, 3) \rightarrow A'(5, -3)$
   (b) $B(6, -4) \rightarrow B'(6, 4)$
   (c) $C(-2, 8) \rightarrow C'(-2, -8)$
   (d) $D(-10, -5) \rightarrow D'(-10, 5)$

3. **(a)** In the diagram below, segment $\overline{A'B'}$ is the image of segment $\overline{AB}$ under a reflection over the *x*-axis. Observe that $A(2, 4) \rightarrow A'(2, -4)$ and $B(5, 1) \rightarrow B'(5, -1)$.

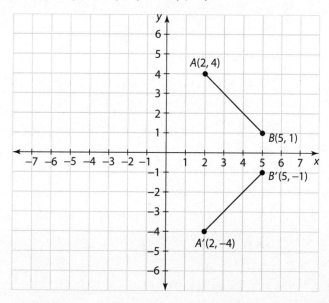

(b) In the diagram below, rectangle $A'B'C'D'$ is the image of rectangle $ABCD$ under a reflection over the x-axis. Observe that $A(-4, 3) \rightarrow A'(-4, -3)$, $B(-4, 1) \rightarrow B'(-4, -1)$, $C(2, 1) \rightarrow C'(2, -1)$, and $D(2, 3) \rightarrow D'(2, -3)$.

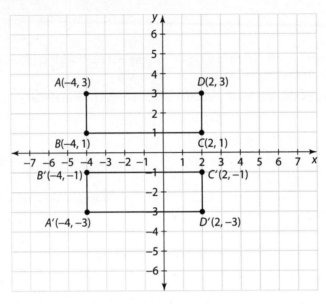

4. **(a)** $A(5, 3) \rightarrow A'(-5, 3)$
   (b) $B(6, -4) \rightarrow B'(-6, -4)$
   (c) $C(-2, 8) \rightarrow C'(2, 8)$
   (d) $D(-10, -5) \rightarrow D'(10, -5)$

5. In the diagram below, rectangle $A'B'C'D'$ is the image of rectangle $ABCD$ under a reflection over the y-axis. Observe that $A(-4, 3) \rightarrow A'(4, 3)$, $B(-4, -1) \rightarrow B'(4, -1)$, $C(-2, -1) \rightarrow C'(2, -1)$, and $D(-2, 3) \rightarrow D'(2, 3)$.

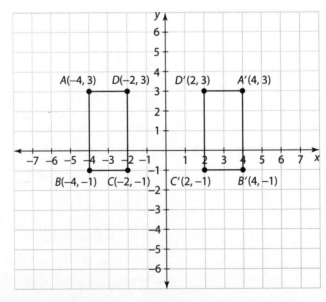

6. **(a)** $A(5, 3) \rightarrow A'(-5, -3)$
   (b) $B(6, -4) \rightarrow B'(-6, 4)$
   (c) $C(-2, 8) \rightarrow C'(2, -8)$
   (d) $D(-10, -5) \rightarrow D'(10, 5)$

7. In the diagram below, segment $\overline{A'B'}$ is the image of segment $\overline{AB}$ under a reflection in the origin. Observe that $A(2, 4) \rightarrow A'(-2, -4)$ and $B(5, 1) \rightarrow B'(-5, -1)$.

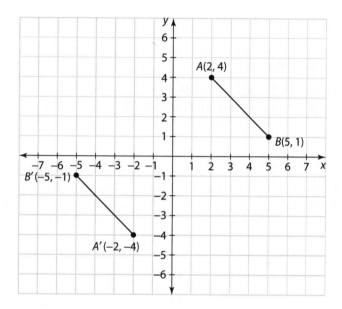

Understanding Coordinate Rules for Translations

This section presents coordinate rules for translations.

In the coordinate plane, a **translation of h units in the horizontal direction and k units in the vertical direction** is a transformation in which $P(x, y) \rightarrow P'(x + h, y + k)$. A translation moves every point h units horizontally and k units vertically.

Tip: In a translation, you merely add h to each x-coordinate and k to each y-coordinate.

Here is an example.

> Find the coordinates of the image of $P(8, 5)$ under a translation of 3 units horizontally and -2 units vertically.

$P(8, 5) \rightarrow P'(8 + 3, 5 - 2) = P'(11, 3)$

☞ Try These

1. Find the coordinates of the image of the point under a translation of 3 units horizontally and –2 units vertically.

    (a) $A(5, 3)$
    (b) $B(6, -4)$
    (c) $C(-2, 8)$
    (d) $D(-10, -5)$

2. In the coordinate plane, construct the image of the given figure under a translation of 3 units horizontally and –2 units vertically.

    (a) segment $\overline{AB}$ with endpoints $A(2, 4)$ and $B(3, 1)$
    (b) rectangle $ABCD$ with vertices $A(-2, 4)$, $B(-2, -1)$, $C(1, -1)$, and $D(1, 4)$

Solutions

1. (a) $A(5, 3) \rightarrow A'(8, 1)$
    (b) $B(6, -4) \rightarrow B'(9, -6)$
    (c) $C(-2, 8) \rightarrow C'(1, 6)$
    (d) $D(-10, -5) \rightarrow D'(-7, -7)$

2. (a) In the diagram below, segment $\overline{A'B'}$ is the image of segment $\overline{AB}$ under a translation of 3 units horizontally and –2 units vertically. Observe that $A(2, 4) \rightarrow A'(5, 2)$ and $B(3, 1) \rightarrow B'(6, -1)$.

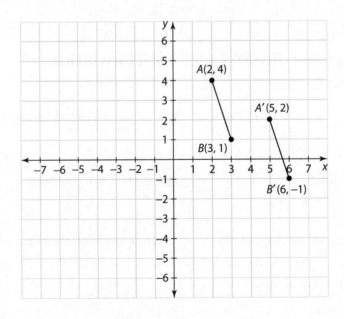

(b) In the diagram below, rectangle $A'B'C'D'$ is the image of rectangle $ABCD$ under a translation of 3 units horizontally and −2 units vertically. Observe that $A(-2, 4) \rightarrow A'(1, 2)$, $B(-2, -1) \rightarrow B'(1, -3)$, $C(1, -1) \rightarrow C'(4, -3)$, and $D(1, 4) \rightarrow D'(4, 2)$.

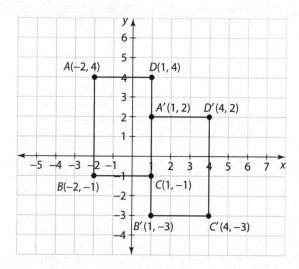

Tip: As the examples in this section illustrate, you can think of translations as "slides." You slide the preimage right or left or up or down, or a combination of these moves. The result is the image.

Understanding Coordinate Rules for Rotations

This section presents coordinate rules for three types of rotations about the origin O: a counterclockwise rotation of 90° about O, a counterclockwise rotation of 180° about O, and a counterclockwise rotation of 270° about O.

Tip: Think of rotations as "turns" around a point.

In the coordinate plane, a **counterclockwise rotation of 90° about the origin O** is a transformation in which $P(x, y) \rightarrow P'(-y, x)$.

117

Under a **rotation of 90° about O,** the angle *POP'* is a right angle, as shown below.

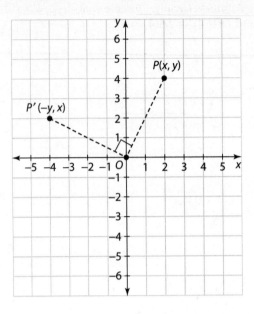

Here is an example.

In the coordinate plane, construct the image of segment $\overline{AB}$ with endpoints $A(2, 4)$ and $B(5, 1)$ under a rotation of 90° about the origin.

In the diagram below, segment $\overline{A'B'}$ is the image of segment $\overline{AB}$ under a rotation of 90° about the origin. Observe that $A(2, 4) \rightarrow A'(-4, 2)$ and $B(5, 1) \rightarrow B'(-1, 5)$.

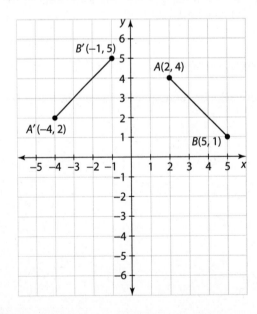

In the coordinate plane, a **counterclockwise rotation of 180° about the origin O** is a transformation in which $P(x, y) \rightarrow P'(-x, -y)$. ***Tip:*** A counterclockwise rotation of 180° about the origin O is equivalent to a reflection in the origin.

Under a **rotation of 180° about O,** the measure of angle POP' is 180° as shown below.

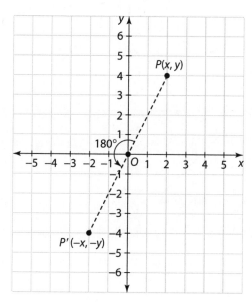

Here is an example.

In the coordinate plane, construct the image of the given figure under a rotation of 180° about the origin.

(a) segment $\overline{AB}$ with endpoints $A(2, 4)$ and $B(5, 1)$

(b) rectangle $ABCD$ with vertices $A(2, -3)$, $B(2, -5)$, $C(5, -5)$, and $D(5, -3)$

(a) In the diagram below, segment $\overline{A'B'}$ is the image of segment $\overline{AB}$ under a rotation of 180° about the origin. Observe that $A(2, 4) \rightarrow A'(-2, -4)$ and $B(5, 1) \rightarrow B'(-5, -1)$.

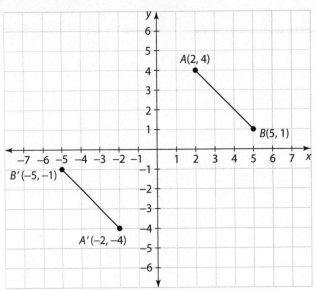

(b) In the diagram below, rectangle $A'B'C'D'$ is the image of rectangle $ABCD$ under a rotation of 180° about the origin. Observe that $A(2, -3) \rightarrow A'(-2, 3)$, $B(2, -5) \rightarrow B'(-2, 5)$, $C(5, -5) \rightarrow C'(-5, 5)$, and $D(5, -3) \rightarrow D'(-5, 3)$.

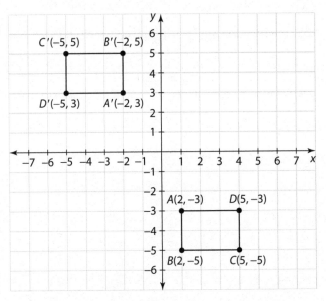

In the coordinate plane, a **counterclockwise rotation of 270° about the origin** O is a transformation in which $P(x, y) \rightarrow P'(y, -x)$.

Under a **rotation of 270° about** O, the measure of angle POP' is 270°, as shown below. *Tip:* The angle is measured *counterclockwise* from $\overline{OP}$ to $\overline{OP'}$.

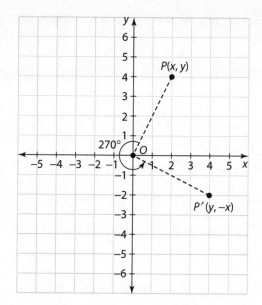

Here is an example.

Find the coordinates of the image of $P(8, 5)$ under a rotation of 270° about the origin.

$P(8, 5) \rightarrow P'(5, -8)$

☞ Try These

1. Fill in the blank.

   (a) Under a counterclockwise rotation of 90° about the origin, the image of (x, y) is _____.
   (b) Under a counterclockwise rotation of 180° about the origin, the image of (x, y) is _____.
   (c) Under a counterclockwise rotation of 270° about the origin, the image of (x, y) is _____.

2. Find the coordinates of the image of the point under a rotation of 90° about the origin.

   (a) $A(5, 3)$
   (b) $B(6, -4)$
   (c) $C(-2, 8)$
   (d) $D(-10, -5)$

3. In the coordinate plane, construct the image of rectangle $ABCD$ with vertices $A(2, -3)$, $B(2, -5)$, $C(5, -5)$, and $D(5, -3)$ under a rotation of 90° about the origin.

4. Find the coordinates of the image of the point under a rotation of 180° about the origin.

   (a) $A(5, 3)$
   (b) $B(6, -4)$
   (c) $C(-2, 8)$
   (d) $D(-10, -5)$

5. In the coordinate plane, construct the image of segment $\overline{AB}$ with endpoints $A(2, 4)$ and $B(5, 1)$ under a rotation of 180° about the origin.

6. Find the coordinates of the image of the point under a rotation of 270° about the origin.

   (a) $A(5, 3)$
   (b) $B(6, -4)$
   (c) $C(-2, 8)$
   (d) $D(-10, -5)$

7. In the coordinate plane, construct the image of the given figure under a rotation of 270° about the origin.

   (a) segment $\overline{AB}$ with endpoints $A(2, 4)$ and $B(5, 1)$
   (b) rectangle $ABCD$ with vertices $A(2, -3)$, $B(2, -5)$, $C(5, -5)$, and $D(5, -3)$

Solutions

1. (a) $(-y, x)$
   (b) $(-x, -y)$
   (c) $(y, -x)$

2. (a) $A(5, 3) \rightarrow A'(-3, 5)$
   (b) $B(6, -4) \rightarrow B'(4, 6)$
   (c) $C(-2, 8) \rightarrow C'(-8, -2)$
   (d) $D(-10, -5) \rightarrow D'(5, -10)$

3. In the diagram below, rectangle $A'B'C'D'$ is the image of rectangle $ABCD$ under a rotation of 90° about the origin. Observe that $A(2, -3) \rightarrow A'(3, 2)$, $B(2, -5) \rightarrow B'(5, 2)$, $C(5, -5) \rightarrow C'(5, 5)$, and $D(5, -3) \rightarrow D'(3, 5)$.

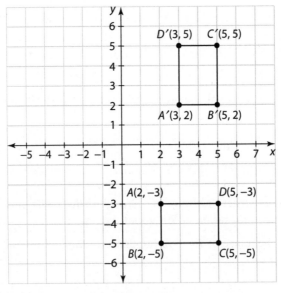

4. (a) $A(5, 3) \rightarrow A'(-5, -3)$
   (b) $B(6, -4) \rightarrow B'(-6, 4)$
   (c) $C(-2, 8) \rightarrow C'(2, -8)$
   (d) $D(-10, -5) \rightarrow D'(10, 5)$

5. In the diagram below, segment $\overline{A'B'}$ is the image of segment $\overline{AB}$ under a rotation of 180° about the origin. Observe that $A(2, 4) \rightarrow A'(-2, -4)$ and $B(5, 1) \rightarrow B'(-5, -1)$.

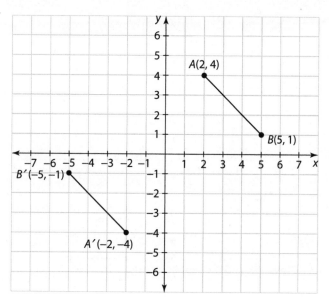

6. **(a)** $A(5, 3) \rightarrow A'(3, -5)$
   (b) $B(6, -4) \rightarrow B'(-4, -6)$
   (c) $C(-2, 8) \rightarrow C'(8, 2)$
   (d) $D(-10, -5) \rightarrow D'(-5, 10)$

7. **(a)** In the diagram below, segment $\overline{A'B'}$ is the image of segment $\overline{AB}$ under a rotation of 270° about the origin. Observe that $A(2, 4) \rightarrow A'(4, -2)$ and $B(5, 1) \rightarrow B'(1, -5)$.

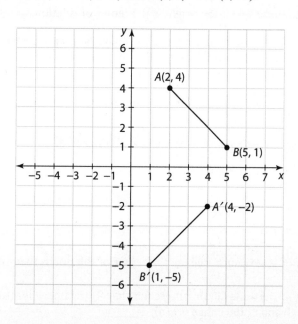

123

(b) In the diagram below, rectangle $A'B'C'D'$ is the image of rectangle $ABCD$ under a rotation of 270° about the origin. Observe that $A(2, -3) \rightarrow A'(-3, -2)$, $B(2, -5) \rightarrow B'(-5, -2)$, $C(5, -5) \rightarrow C'(-5, -5)$, and $D(5, -3) \rightarrow D'(-3, -5)$.

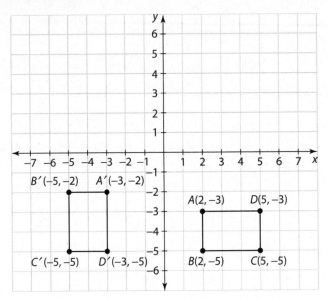

Understanding Coordinate Rules for Dilations

In the coordinate plane, a **dilation of scale factor r where the center of dilation is the origin O** is a transformation in which $P(x, y) \rightarrow P'(rx, ry)$, where $r > 0$. Under a dilation, the ratio of OP' to OP equals the dilation's scale factor r. That is, $\dfrac{OP'}{OP} = r$. ***Note:*** Any point can be chosen as the center of dilation. In this book, dilations are limited to those where the origin is the center of dilation.

Under a dilation, if the scale factor r is greater than 1, the image is an **enlargement** of the preimage and has the same shape. If the scale factor is between 0 and 1, the image is a **reduction** of the preimage and has the same shape. If the scale factor equals 1, the preimage and image are the same size and shape. ***Tip:*** It's uncommon for the scale factor to equal 1.

Here is an example.

Find the coordinates of the image of $P(8, 5)$ under a dilation of 2.

$P(8, 5) \rightarrow P'(16, 10)$

☞ Try These

1. Fill in the blank(s).

   (a) Under a dilation of scale factor r where the center of dilation is the origin, the image of (x, y) is

   _____.

   (b) Under a dilation, if the scale factor r is greater than 1, the image is a(n)_____. If the scale factor is between 0 and 1, the image is a(n)_____.

2. Find the coordinates of the image of the point under a dilation of 2.

   (a) $A(5, 3)$
   (b) $B(6, -4)$

3. Find the coordinates of the image of the point under a dilation of $\frac{1}{2}$.

   (a) $C(-2, 8)$
   (b) $D(-10, -5)$

4. In the coordinate plane, construct the image of segment $\overline{AB}$ with endpoints $A(2, 1)$ and $B(3, -2)$ under a dilation of 2.

5. In the coordinate plane, construct the image of rectangle $ABCD$ with vertices $A(-4, 5)$, $B(-4, -5)$, $C(4, -5)$, and $D(4, 5)$ under a dilation of $\frac{1}{2}$.

Solutions

1. **(a)** (rx, ry)
   (b) enlargement; reduction

2. **(a)** $A(5, 3) \rightarrow A'(10, 6)$
   (b) $B(6, -4) \rightarrow B'(12, -8)$

3. **(a)** $C(-2, 8) \rightarrow C'(-1, 4)$
   (b) $D(-10, -5) \rightarrow D'(-5, -2.5)$

4. In the diagram below, segment $\overline{A'B'}$ is the image of segment $\overline{AB}$ under a dilation of 2. Observe that $A(2, 1) \rightarrow A'(4, 2)$ and $B(3, -2) \rightarrow B'(6, -4)$.

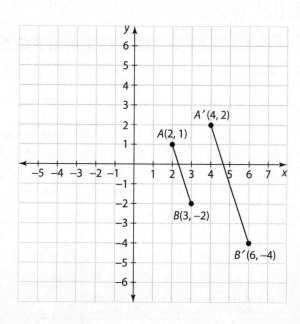

5. In the diagram below, rectangle $A'B'C'D'$ is the image of rectangle $ABCD$ under a dilation of $\frac{1}{2}$.

Observe that $A(-4, 5) \rightarrow A'(-2, 2.5)$, $B(-4, -5) \rightarrow B'(-2, -2.5)$, $C(4, -5) \rightarrow C'(2, -2.5)$, and $D(4, 5) \rightarrow D'(2, 2.5)$.

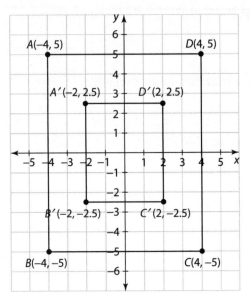

Understanding Properties of Reflections, Translations, Rotations, and Dilations

(CCSS.Math.Content.8.G.A.1.A, CCSS.Math.Content.8.G.A.1.B, CCSS.Math.Content.8.G.A.1.C)

Here is a summary of the coordinate rules for the common transformation types presented in this chapter.

Transformation	Coordinate Rule
Reflection over the x-axis	$P(x, y) \rightarrow P'(x, -y)$
Reflection over the y-axis	$P(x, y) \rightarrow P'(-x, y)$
Reflection in the origin	$P(x, y) \rightarrow P'(-x, -y)$
Counterclockwise rotation of 90° about the origin	$P(x, y) \rightarrow P'(-y, x)$
Counterclockwise rotation of 180° about the origin	$P(x, y) \rightarrow P'(-x, -y)$
Counterclockwise rotation of 270° about the origin	$P(x, y) \rightarrow P'(y, -x)$
Translation of h units in the horizontal direction and k units in the vertical direction	$P(x, y) \rightarrow P'(x + h, y + k)$
Dilation of scale factor r where center of dilation is the origin	$P(x, y) \rightarrow P'(rx, ry), r > 0$

Under transformations, the preimage retains some properties of the image. The five properties **preserved** (meaning "kept") under reflections, translations, and rotations are the following:

1. **Distance**—Lengths in the image equal their corresponding lengths in the preimage.

2. **Angle measure**—Angles in the image have the same measure as their corresponding angles in the preimage.

3. **Parallelism**—The images of two parallel lines are also parallel lines.

4. **Collinearity**—The images of three or more points that lie on a straight line (that is, the points are collinear) will also lie on a straight line in the same order.

5. **Midpoint**—The image of the midpoint of a line segment is the midpoint of the line segment's image.

Understanding Properties of Reflections, Translations, and Rotations

Reflections, translations, and rotations are **rigid motions.** These transformations are rigid motions because they move a figure to a different location in the plane without altering its shape or size. They take lines to lines. They take line segments to line segments of the same length. They take angles to angles of the same measure. They take parallel lines to parallel lines. And they take points to their same relative locations.

For instance, in the diagram below, parallelogram $A'B'C'D'$ is the image of parallelogram $ABCD$ under a reflection over the y-axis. In $ABCD$ and $A'B'C'D'$, corresponding line segments and angles have the same measure. Parallel lines correspond to parallel lines. Points B, M, and D lie on the same line, $\overline{BD}$, and their images lie on $\overline{B'D'}$. Point M is the midpoint of $\overline{BD}$ and point M' is the midpoint of $\overline{B'D'}$. *Tip:* Hash marks identify the corresponding parts. Corresponding parts have the same number of strokes.

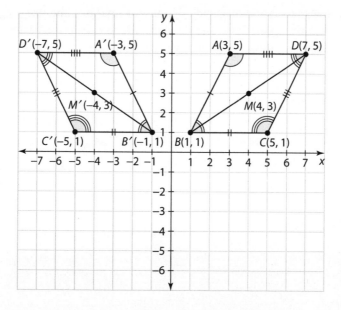

Under reflections, translations, and rotations, figures (preimages) and their corresponding images are congruent. **Congruent figures** have the same shape and size. One can be placed on top of the other without any overlap. Thus, corresponding parts of congruent figures are congruent. Congruent parts have the same measure. That is, corresponding lengths are equal and corresponding angles have the same measure.

Understanding Properties of Dilations

Dilations are *not* rigid motions. Dilations do not preserve distance (except when the scale factor is 1). Lengths in the image figure are equal to their corresponding lengths in the preimage figure multiplied by the scale factor r.

The properties preserved under dilations include only four of the five properties preserved under reflections, translations, and rotations. These properties are angle measure, parallelism, collinearity, and midpoint. Furthermore, a dilation maps a line not containing the center of dilation to a parallel line.

Under dilations, figures (preimages) and their images are similar. **Similar figures** have the same shape, but are not necessarily the same size. Corresponding angles of similar shapes are congruent. Corresponding lengths of similar shapes are proportional. That is, the ratios of the lengths are equal.

☞Try These

1. Fill in the blank(s).

    (a) Reflections, translations, and rotations are _____ motions. These transformations move a figure to a different location in the plane without altering its _____ or _____.

    (b) Reflections, translations, and rotations take line segments to line segments of the _____ length.

    (c) Reflections, translations, rotations, and dilations take angles to angles of the _____ measure.

    (d) Reflections, translations, rotations, and dilations take parallel lines to _____ lines.

    (e) Reflections, translations, rotations, and dilations take points to their same _____ locations.

    (f) Under reflections, translations, and rotations, preimages and their corresponding images are best described as _____ (congruent, similar).

    (g) Under dilations, preimages and their corresponding images are best described as _____ (congruent, similar).

2. In the diagram, triangle $A'B'C'$ is the image of triangle ABC under a reflection over the origin.

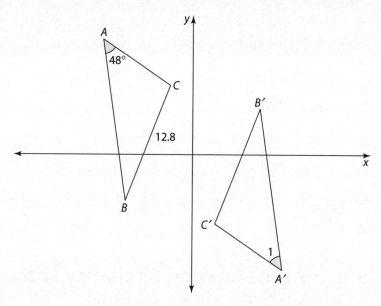

   (a)   What is the length of $\overline{B'C'}$?
   (b)   What is the measure of $\angle 1$?
   (c)   Are the two triangles best described as congruent or similar?

3. In the diagram, triangle $D'E'F'$ is the image of triangle DEF under a dilation of 2.5.

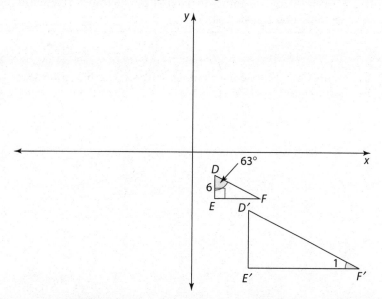

   (a)   What is the length of $\overline{D'E'}$?
   (b)   What is the measure of $\angle 1$?
   (c)   Are the two triangles best described as congruent or similar?

Solutions

1. **(a)** rigid; shape; size
   (b) same
   (c) same
   (d) parallel
   (e) relative
   (f) congruent
   (g) similar

2. **(a)** 12.8 units
   (b) 48°
   (c) congruent

3. **(a)** (6 units)(2.5) = 15 units
   (b) $m\angle 1 = 90° - 63° = 27°$
   (c) similar

Understanding Congruence and Similarity Through the Concepts of Geometric Transformations

(CCSS.Math.Content.8.G.A.2, CCSS.Math.Content.8.G.A.4)

> A two-dimensional figure is congruent to another if the first can be transformed into the second by a sequence of rotations, reflections, and translations.

Here is an example.

> In the diagram, trapezoids I and II are congruent. Describe a possible sequence of transformations that transforms trapezoid I into trapezoid II.

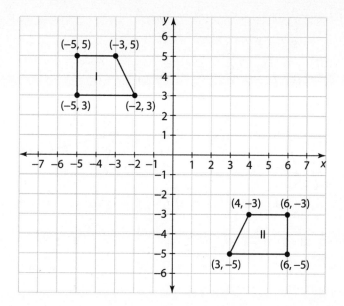

Answers may vary. Trapezoid I can be transformed into trapezoid II by a reflection across the y-axis, followed by a translation of 1 unit right and 8 units down. Specifically, $(-5, 5) \rightarrow (5, 5) \rightarrow (6, -3)$; $(-5, 3) \rightarrow (5, 3) \rightarrow (6, -5)$; $(-2, 3) \rightarrow (2, 3) \rightarrow (3, -5)$; $(-3, 5) \rightarrow (3, 5) \rightarrow (4, -3)$.

A two-dimensional figure is similar to another if the first can be transformed into the second by a sequence of rotations, reflections, translations, and dilations.

Here is an example.

In the diagram, triangles I and II are similar. Describe a possible sequence of transformations that transforms triangle I into triangle II.

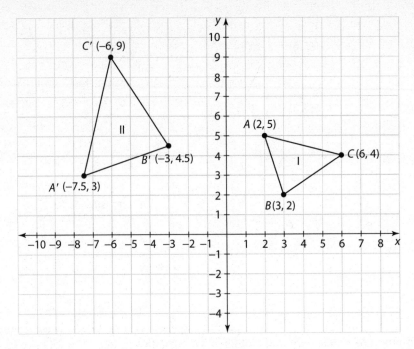

Answers may vary. Triangle I can be transformed into triangle II by a counterclockwise rotation of 90°, followed by a dilation of 1.5. Specifically, $(2, 5) \rightarrow (-5, 2) \rightarrow (-7.5, 3)$; $(3, 2) \rightarrow (-2, 3) \rightarrow (-3, 4.5)$; $(6, 4) \rightarrow (-4, 6) \rightarrow (-6, 9)$.

☞ Try These

1. Fill in the blank.

   (a) A two-dimensional figure is _____ to another if the first can be transformed into the second by a sequence of rotations, reflections, and translations.

   (b) A two-dimensional figure is _____ to another if the first can be transformed into the second by a sequence of rotations, reflections, translations, and dilations.

2. Name a transformation that transforms the point as indicated.

   (a) $(3, -4) \rightarrow (-4, -3)$
   (b) $(10, 2) \rightarrow (10, -2)$
   (c) $(5, -1) \rightarrow (-5, 1)$
   (d) $(-8, 7) \rightarrow (8, 7)$
   (e) $(4, 3) \rightarrow (8, -2)$
   (f) $(-6, -3) \rightarrow (3, -6)$
   (g) $(-15, 25) \rightarrow (-3, 5)$

3. Describe a sequence of transformations that transforms the point as indicated.

   (a) $(2, -5) \rightarrow (4, -10) \rightarrow (-10, -4)$
   (b) $(7, 1) \rightarrow (7, -1) \rightarrow (10, 4)$
   (c) $(6, -2) \rightarrow (-6, 2) \rightarrow (6, 2)$

4. In the diagram, triangles I and II are congruent. Describe a possible sequence of transformations that transforms triangle I into triangle II.

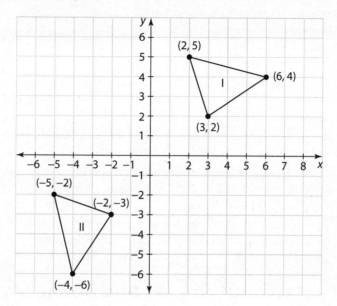

5. In the diagram, squares I and II are similar. Describe a possible sequence of transformations that transforms square I into square II.

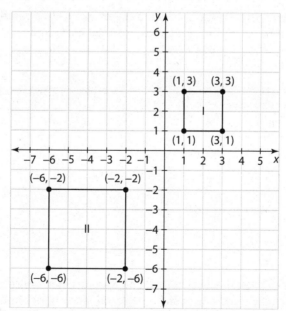

Solutions

1. **(a)** congruent
   (b) similar

2. **(a)** counterclockwise rotation of 270°
   (b) reflection over the *x*-axis
   (c) reflection in the origin or counterclockwise rotation of 180°
   (d) reflection over the *y*-axis
   (e) translation of 4 units right and 5 units down
   (f) counterclockwise rotation of 90°
   (g) dilation of $\frac{1}{5}$

3. **(a)** dilation of 2, followed by counterclockwise rotation of 270°
   (b) reflection over the *x*-axis, followed by translation of 3 units right and 5 units up
   (c) reflection in the origin, followed by reflection over the *y*-axis

4. Answers may vary. Triangle I can be transformed into triangle II by a reflection across the *x*-axis, followed by a counterclockwise rotation of 270°. Specifically, $(2, 5) \rightarrow (2, -5) \rightarrow (-5, -2); (3, 2) \rightarrow (3, -2) \rightarrow (-2, -3); (6, 4) \rightarrow (6, -4) \rightarrow (-4, -6)$.

5. Answers may vary. Square I can be transformed into square II by a dilation of 2 followed by a reflection in the origin (or a counterclockwise rotation of 180°). Specifically, $(1, 3) \rightarrow (2, 6) \rightarrow (-2, -6); (1, 1) \rightarrow (2, 2) \rightarrow (-2, -2); (3, 1) \rightarrow (6, 2) \rightarrow (-6, -2); (3, 3) \rightarrow (6, 6) \rightarrow (-6, -6)$.

Establishing Facts About Angles and Similarity

(CCSS.Math.Content.8.G.A.5)

A line that intersects two lines is a **transversal.** When a transversal cuts two parallel lines, eight angles are formed. In the diagram shown below, the line *t* intersects parallel lines *l* and *m*.

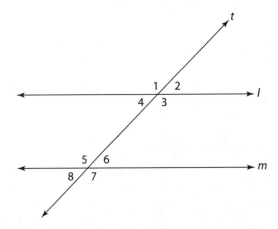

Angles 3, 4, 5, and 6 are **interior angles.** Angles 1, 2, 7, and 8 are **exterior angles. Corresponding angles** are pairs of nonadjacent angles on the same side of the transversal, one exterior and one interior. There are four pairs of corresponding angles: angles 1 and 5, angles 2 and 6, angles 4 and 8, and angles 3 and 7. **Alternate interior angles** are pairs of interior nonadjacent angles on opposite sides of the transversal. There are two pairs of alternate interior angles: angles 3 and 5 and angles 4 and 6. *Tip:* **Adjacent angles** share a common vertex with no overlap.

> If two parallel lines are cut by a transversal, then any pair of corresponding angles are congruent, and any pair of alternate interior angles are congruent.

Here are examples.

In the diagram shown, parallel lines l and m are cut by a transversal t. What is the measure of angle x?

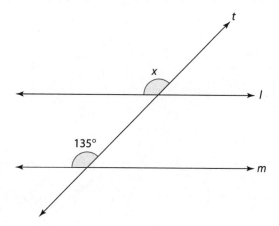

The $m\angle x$ is 135° because a pair of corresponding angles of two parallel lines cut by a transversal are congruent, and therefore the angles have equal measures.

In the diagram shown, parallel lines l and m are cut by a transversal t. What is the measure of angle y?

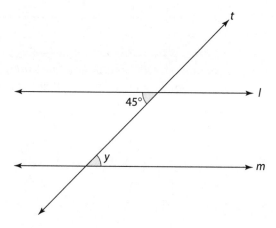

The $m\angle y$ is 45° because a pair of alternate interior angles of two parallel lines cut by a transversal are congruent, and therefore the angles have equal measures.

On the other hand, you might have two lines cut by a transversal, and want to determine whether the two lines are parallel.

If two lines are cut by a transversal so that a pair of corresponding angles are congruent, then the two lines are parallel.

If two lines are cut by a transversal so that a pair of alternate interior angles are congruent, then the two lines are parallel.

For instance, in the diagram below, lines *a* and *b* are parallel because a pair of corresponding angles are congruent.

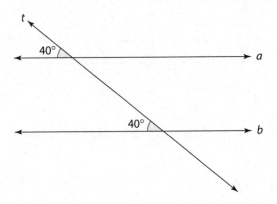

You can use parallel lines and transversals to prove the following:

The sum of the measures of the interior angles of a triangle is 180°.

Here's how to do it.

In triangle ABC, draw a line that contains side $\overline{BC}$ and draw a line through C that is parallel to the line that contains side $\overline{AB}$, as shown below. The aim is to show that $m\angle 1 + m\angle 2 + m\angle 3 = 180°$.

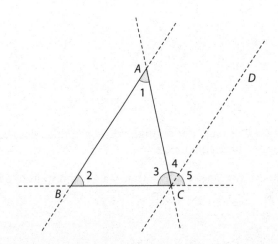

By construction, lines $\overleftrightarrow{AB}$ and $\overleftrightarrow{DC}$ are parallel. The line $\overleftrightarrow{AC}$ is a transversal that cuts these two parallel lines. So $\angle 1$ and $\angle 4$ are congruent because they are alternate interior angles of parallel lines. The line $\overleftrightarrow{BC}$ is a transversal that cuts the same two parallel lines. So $\angle 2$ and $\angle 5$ are congruent because they are corresponding angles of parallel lines. Angles 3, 4, and 5 lie on a straight line, so the sum of their measure is 180°. That is, $m\angle 3 + m\angle 4 + m\angle 5 = 180°$. Congruent angles have equal measures, so you can substitute $m\angle 1$ for $m\angle 4$ and $m\angle 2$ for $m\angle 5$ to obtain $m\angle 3 + m\angle 1 + m\angle 2 = m\angle 1 + m\angle 2 + m\angle 3 = 180°$, which completes the proof.

An **exterior angle** of a triangle is the angle between one side of the triangle and the extension of the side adjacent to it. For example, in the diagram below, $\angle ACE$ and $\angle BCF$ are exterior angles at vertex C of triangle ABC. These two angles are congruent because they are vertical angles of the intersecting lines $\overleftrightarrow{AC}$ and $\overleftrightarrow{BC}$. Therefore, you can select either one to represent the exterior angle at vertex C.

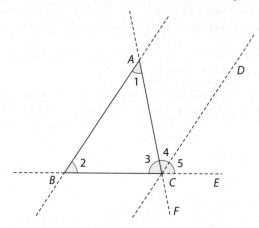

Using the diagram above, you can easily prove the following:

> The measure of an exterior angle of a triangle equals the sum of the measures of the two nonadjacent interior angles.

Without loss of generality, select the exterior angle at C for the proof. Then you must show that $m\angle ACE = m\angle 1 + m\angle 2$. Try it.

At vertex C, the exterior angle ACE at C is composed of angles 4 and 5. Thus, $m\angle ACE = m\angle 4 + m\angle 5$. Angles 1 and 4 are congruent because they are alternate interior angles of parallel lines. Angles 2 and 5 are also congruent because they are corresponding angles of parallel lines. Therefore, by substitution, $m\angle ACE = m\angle 1 + m\angle 2$, which completes the proof. (**Note:** Proofs for angles A and B are similar to this one.)

> The sum of the measures of the exterior angles of a triangle equals 360°.

The proof for this fact is straightforward.

From the section "Understanding Properties of Reflections, Translations, Rotations, and Dilations" earlier in this chapter, you know that corresponding angles of similar figures are congruent and the ratios of the lengths of corresponding sides are equal. Therefore, you have the following.

If triangles ABC and $A'B'C'$ are similar, then

(1) $\angle A \cong \angle A'$, $\angle B \cong \angle B'$, and $\angle C \cong \angle C'$

and

(2) $\dfrac{BC}{B'C'} = \dfrac{AC}{A'C'} = \dfrac{AB}{A'B'}$

Tip: Note the correspondence between the vertices. This correspondence will assist you in identifying corresponding parts.

Conversely, two triangles are similar if either (1) or (2) is true. The reason is that once either one is true, the other is automatically true as well. *Tip:* This fact is true for triangles, but not generally true for all polygons.

Therefore, two triangles are similar if their corresponding angles are congruent. This fact enables you to establish the following **angle-angle (AA) criterion for similarity:**

Two triangles are similar if two angles of one triangle are congruent to two corresponding angles of the other triangle.

☞ Try These

1. Fill in the blank(s).

   (a) If two parallel lines are cut by a transversal, then any pair of corresponding angles or alternate interior angles are _____.

   (b) If two lines are cut by a transversal so that a pair of corresponding angles are congruent, then the two lines are _____.

   (c) If two lines are cut by a transversal so that a pair of alternate interior angles are congruent, then the two lines are _____.

   (d) The measure of an exterior angle of a triangle equals the _____ of the measures of the two nonadjacent interior angles.

   (e) The sum of the measures of the interior angles of a triangle equals _____.

   (f) The sum of the measures of the exterior angles of a triangle equals _____.

   (g) The AA criterion for similarity asserts that two triangles are similar if _____ angles of one triangle are congruent to _____ corresponding angles of the other triangle.

2. In the diagram shown below, lines *l* and *m* are parallel.

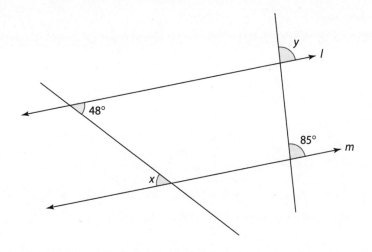

   (a) What is the measure of ∠*x*? Justify your answer.
   (b) What is the measure of ∠*y*? Justify your answer.

3. In the diagram shown below, triangles *ABC* and *A′B′C′* are similar, with corresponding vertices *A* and *A′*, *B* and *B′*, and *C* and *C′*.

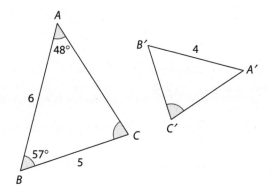

   (a) What is the measure of ∠*C′*? Justify your answer.
   (b) To the nearest unit, what is the measure of $\overline{B'C'}$? Justify your answer.

4. In the diagram shown below, what is the measure of $\angle x$?

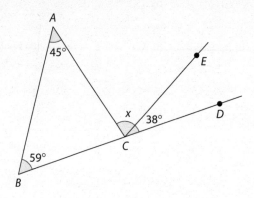

5. Prove the sum of the measures of the exterior angles of a triangle equals 360°.

Solutions

1. **(a)** congruent
   (b) parallel
   (c) parallel
   (d) sum
   (e) 180°
   (f) 360°
   (g) two; two

2. **(a)** 48°, because alternate interior angles of parallel lines cut by a transversal are congruent.
   (b) 85°, because corresponding angles of parallel lines cut by a transversal are congruent.

3. **(a)** 75°
   $\angle C'$ and $\angle C$ are congruent because they are corresponding angles of similar triangles. The measure of $\angle C = 180° - 57° - 48° = 75°$. Thus, the measure of $\angle C'$ is 75°.

   (b) 3 units. The ratios of corresponding sides of similar triangles are equal. Set up a proportion and solve for $B'C'$.

$$\frac{AB}{A'B'} = \frac{BC}{B'C'}$$

$$\frac{6}{4} = \frac{5}{B'C'}$$

$$B'C' = \frac{(4)(5)}{6}$$

$$B'C' = \frac{20}{6}$$

$$B'C' \approx 3$$

The measure of $\overline{B'C'}$ is approximately 3 units.

4. 66°. $\angle ACD$ is an exterior angle at vertex C. So, the $m\angle ACD = 59° + 45° = 104°$. $\angle x + \angle ECD = \angle ACD$. The $m\angle ECD$ is 38°. Thus, $m\angle x = 104° - 38° = 66°$.

5. In triangle ABC, let $x =$ the measure of the exterior angle at A, $y =$ the measure of the exterior angle at B, and $z =$ the measure of the exterior angle at C. The aim is to show $x + y + z = 360°$.

The measure of an exterior angle of a triangle equals the sum of the measures of the two nonadjacent interior angles. Thus, $x = m\angle B + m\angle C$, $y = m\angle A + m\angle C$, and $z = m\angle A + m\angle B$. Adding the three equations yields

$$x + y + z = m\angle B + m\angle C + m\angle A + m\angle C + m\angle A + m\angle B$$
$$x + y + z = (m\angle B + m\angle C + m\angle A) + (m\angle C + m\angle A + m\angle B)$$
$$x + y + z = 180° + 180° \text{ (because a triangle's interior angles sum to } 180°)$$
$$x + y + z = 360°, \text{ which completes the proof.}$$

Understanding and Applying the Pythagorean Theorem

(CCSS.Math.Content.8.G.B.6, CCSS.Math.Content.8.G.B.7, CCSS.Math.Content.8.G.B.8)

In this section, you will learn about the Pythagorean theorem and its applications. A special relationship, named after the famous Greek mathematician Pythagoras, exists between the sides of a right triangle. This special relationship is the Pythagorean theorem.

Understanding the Pythagorean Theorem

In a right triangle, the **hypotenuse** is the side opposite the right angle. The other two sides are the **legs**. *Tip:* The hypotenuse is *always* the longest side in a right triangle.

The **Pythagorean theorem:** In a right triangle, $a^2 + b^2 = c^2$, where c is the length of the hypotenuse and a and b are the lengths of the legs of the right triangle (illustrated below).

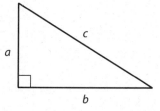

Here is a proof of the Pythagorean theorem using similar triangles.

In the diagram below, triangle ACB is a right triangle, where $\angle ACB$ is a right angle, c is the length of the hypotenuse, and a and b are the lengths of the legs. $\overline{CD}$ is the altitude to the hypotenuse $\overline{AB}$. The aim is to prove that $a^2 + b^2 = c^2$.

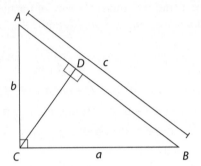

The altitude $\overline{CD}$ divides the right triangle ACB into two right triangles: ADC and CDB.

By the AA criterion for similarity, right triangles ACB and ADC are similar because they both contain right angles and both contain $\angle A$. To set up correct equal ratios based on these two similar triangles, identify corresponding vertices. The vertices A, C, and B of the larger right triangle ACB correspond, respectively, to A (because $\angle A$ is a common angle), D (because D is the vertex of the right angle), and C (because there is no choice left) of the smaller right triangle ADC.

Likewise, by the AA criterion for similarity, right triangles ACB and CDB are similar because they both contain right angles and both contain $\angle B$. The vertices B, C, and A of the larger right triangle ACB correspond, respectively, to B (because $\angle B$ is a common angle), D (because D is the vertex of the right angle), and C (because there is no choice left) of the smaller right triangle CDB.

Here is a diagram showing the three triangles separated. The three triangles are numbered for the convenience of the discussion.

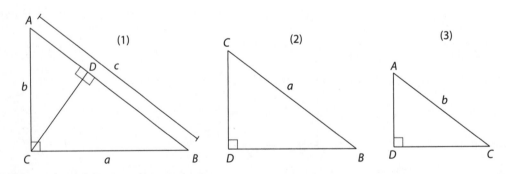

From (1) and (2), $\dfrac{AB}{BC} = \dfrac{BC}{BD}$, which implies $(BC)^2 = (AB)(BD)$; then, by substitution, you have $a^2 = (c)(BD)$.

From (1) and (3), $\dfrac{AB}{AC} = \dfrac{AC}{AD}$, which implies $(AC)^2 = (AB)(AD)$; then, by substitution, $b^2 = (c)(AD)$.

Adding the two equations, $a^2 = (c)(BD)$ and $b^2 = (c)(AD)$, gives

$$a^2 + b^2 = (c)(BD) + (c)(AD) = (c)(BD + AD) = (c)(AD + DB) = (c)(AB) = (c)(c) = c^2,$$

which completes the proof.

The converse of the Pythagorean theorem also is true.

> If the square of the length of the longest side of a triangle equals the sum of the squares of the lengths of the other two sides, the triangle is a right triangle.

For instance, a triangle with sides of lengths 3, 4, and 5 is a right triangle because $3^2 + 4^2 = 9 + 16 = 25 = 5^2$. The numbers (3, 4, 5) are a **Pythagorean triple,** so called because they satisfy the relation $a^2 + b^2 = c^2$. Other well-known Pythagorean triples are (5, 12, 13) and (8, 15, 17).

If each number of a Pythagorean triple is multiplied by a positive number k, the resulting triple also satisfies $a^2 + b^2 = c^2$. Thus, $(3k, 4k, 5k)$, $(5k, 12k, 13k)$, and $(8k, 15k, 17k)$ are Pythagorean triples. For example, let $k = 2$, then $(3k, 4k, 5k)$ equals (6, 8, 10). A triangle with sides of lengths 6, 8, and 10 is a right triangle because $6^2 + 8^2 = 36 + 64 = 100 = 10^2$.

☞ Try These

1. Fill in the blank(s).

    (a) In a right triangle, the _____ is the side opposite the right angle. The other two sides are the _____.

    (b) The longest side of a right triangle is the _____.

    (c) In a right triangle, $a^2 + b^2 = c^2$, where c is the length of the _____ and a and b are the lengths of the _____ of the right triangle.

    (d) If the square of the length of the longest side of a triangle equals the sum of the squares of the lengths of the other two sides, the triangle is a _____ triangle.

2. State "yes" or "no" to whether each set of numbers could be the lengths of the sides of a right triangle. Justify your answer.

    (a) 30, 40, 50
    (b) 13, 5, 12
    (c) 6, 6, 6
    (d) 34, 30, 16
    (e) 1, 1, $\sqrt{2}$
    (f) 2, 1, $\sqrt{3}$
    (g) 5, 6, 7

3. A bike rider leaves camp and travels 14 miles due north, then 6 miles due east, and then 6 miles due south. At this point, the rider stops to rest. What is the rider's true distance from camp in miles?

Solutions

1. **(a)** hypotenuse; legs
    (b) hypotenuse
    (c) hypotenuse; legs
    (d) right

2. **(a)** Yes, because $30^2 + 40^2 = 900 + 1,600 = 2,500 = 50^2$
    (b) Yes, because $5^2 + 12^2 = 25 + 144 = 169 = 13^2$
    (c) No, because $6^2 + 6^2 = 36 + 36 = 72 \neq 6^2 = 36$
    (d) Yes, because $30^2 + 16^2 = 900 + 256 = 1,156 = 34^2$
    (e) Yes, because $1^2 + 1^2 = 1 + 1 = 2 = \left(\sqrt{2}\right)^2$
    (f) Yes, because $1^2 + \left(\sqrt{3}\right)^2 = 1 + 3 = 4 = 2^2$
    (g) No, because $5^2 + 6^2 = 25 + 36 = 61 \neq 7^2 = 49$

3. Let d = the true distance in miles from camp. Make a sketch, filling in the information given in the question.

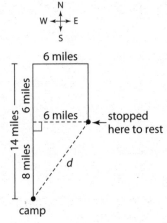

From the sketch, d is the length of the hypotenuse of a right triangle with legs of lengths 6 miles and 8 miles. Therefore, d is 10 miles (because 6, 8, 10 is a Pythagorean triple). The bike rider is 10 miles from camp.

Applying the Pythagorean Theorem to Determine Unknown Side Lengths in a Right Triangle

If you know the length of any two sides of a right triangle, you can use the Pythagorean theorem to find the length of the other side. *Tip:* If the hypotenuse's length is unknown, write the Pythagorean theorem as $c^2 = a^2 + b^2$.

Here are examples of applying the Pythagorean theorem.

A 13-foot wire is anchored 5 feet from the base of a building. How high up the side of the building does the wire reach?

Let x = the height in feet. Make a sketch. *Tip:* Making a sketch is very helpful in application problems involving the Pythagorean theorem.

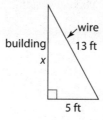

Write an equation that represents the facts.

$$a^2 + b^2 = c^2$$
$$x^2 + (5 \text{ ft})^2 = (13 \text{ ft})^2$$

At this point, you might recognize 5 and 13 as two numbers in the Pythagorean triple, (5, 12, 13). If so, you could write the solution $x = 12$ feet right away. If not, proceed as shown below.

Solve the equation, omitting units for convenience.

$$a^2 + b^2 = c^2$$
$$x^2 + 5^2 = 13^2$$
$$x^2 + 25 = 169$$
$$x^2 + 25 - 25 = 169 - 25$$
$$x^2 = 144$$
$$x = \sqrt{144}$$
$$x = 12$$

The wire goes 12 feet up the wall.

Tip: The number 144 has two square roots, 12 and –12. The negative value is not considered because the length of any side of a triangle cannot be negative.

☞ Try These

Note: In these problems, approximate square roots of irrational answers to the nearest tenth using the method demonstrated in the section "Approximating Irrational Numbers and Expressions" in Chapter 1.

1. A 10-foot ladder is leaning against a wall of a school hallway. The bottom of the ladder is 4 feet from the base of the wall. How high up the wall does the ladder reach?

2. The sizes of the screens of television sets are described by the length of the diagonal across the rectangular screen. The rectangular dimensions of the screen of a portable television set measure 12 inches by 16 inches. What is the size of the television screen?

3. A length of cable is attached to the top of a 30-foot pole. The cable is anchored 10 feet from the base of the pole. What is the length of the cable?

Solutions

1. Let x = the distance up the wall, in feet. Make a sketch.

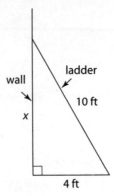

Write an equation that represents the facts.

$$a^2 + b^2 = c^2$$
$$x^2 + (4 \text{ ft})^2 = (10 \text{ ft})^2$$

Solve the equation, omitting units for convenience.

$$a^2 + b^2 = c^2$$
$$x^2 + (4)^2 = (10)^2$$
$$x^2 + 16 = 100$$
$$x^2 + 16 - 16 = 100 - 16$$
$$x^2 = 84$$
$$x = \sqrt{84} \approx 9.2$$

The ladder will reach approximately 9.2 feet up the wall.

2. Let d = the length of the television's diagonal, in inches. Make a sketch.

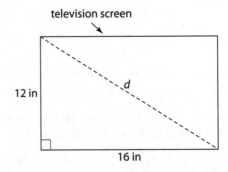

Write an equation that represents the facts.

$$c^2 = a^2 + b^2$$
$$d^2 = (12 \text{ in})^2 + (16 \text{ in})^2$$

At this point, you might recognize 12 and 16 as two numbers in the Pythagorean triple, (12, 16, 20), which is the result of multiplying each number in (3, 4, 5) by 4. If so, you could write the solution $x = 20$ inches right away. If not, proceed as shown below.

Solve the equation, omitting units for convenience.

$$c^2 = a^2 + b^2$$
$$d^2 = (12)^2 + (16)^2$$
$$d^2 = 144 + 256$$
$$d^2 = 400$$
$$d = \sqrt{400}$$
$$d = 20$$

The size of the television screen is 20 inches.

3. Let c = the length of the cable, in feet. Make a sketch.

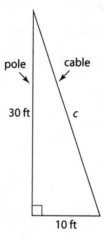

Write an equation that represents the facts.

$$c^2 = a^2 + b^2$$
$$c^2 = (30 \text{ ft})^2 + (10 \text{ ft})^2$$

Solve the equation, omitting units for convenience.

$$c^2 = a^2 + b^2$$
$$c^2 = (30)^2 + (10)^2$$
$$c^2 = 900 + 100$$
$$c^2 = 1,000$$
$$c = \sqrt{1,000} \approx 31.6$$

The length of the cable is approximately 31.6 feet.

Applying the Pythagorean Theorem to Determine the Distance Between Two Points in a Coordinate Plane

Two points that have the same x-coordinate lie on the same vertical line. For instance, $P(-2, 4)$ and $Q(-2, -1)$ lie on the same vertical line. The distance between P and Q is the absolute value of the difference between their y-coordinates. Thus, the distance between P and Q is $|4 - (-1)| = |4 + 1| = |5| = 5$.

Likewise, two points that have the same y-coordinate lie on the same horizontal line. For instance, $Q(-2, -1)$ and $R(5, -1)$ lie on the same horizontal line. The distance between Q and R is the absolute value of the difference between their x-coordinates. Thus, the distance between Q and R is $|-2 - 5| = |-7| = 7$.

> **Tip:** It doesn't matter in which order you subtract the coordinates because $|a - b| = |b - a|$. For instance, $|4 - (-1)| = |4 + 1| = |5| = 5$ and $|-1 - 4| = |-5| = 5$. Similarly, $|-2 - 5| = |-7| = 7$ and $|5 - (-2)| = |5 + 2| = |7| = 7$.

Now consider the distance, d, between P and R. As shown in the coordinate plane below, $\overline{PR}$ is the hypotenuse of a right triangle with legs $\overline{PQ}$ and $\overline{QR}$.

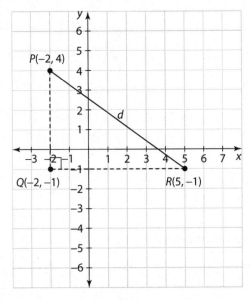

Thus, by the Pythagorean theorem, $d^2 = 5^2 + 7^2$. You solve for d as follows.

$$d^2 = 5^2 + 7^2$$
$$d^2 = 25 + 49$$
$$d^2 = 74$$
$$d = \sqrt{74}$$

In general, you have the following fact.

> If d is the distance between two points (x_1, y_1) and (x_2, y_2) in the coordinate plane, $d = \sqrt{|x_2 - x_1|^2 + |y_2 - y_1|^2}$.

☞ Try These

Note: In these problems, leave irrational square roots in radical form.

1. Fill in the blank.

   (a) Two points with the same _____ (*x*-coordinate, *y*-coordinate) lie on the same vertical line.
   (b) Two points with the same _____ (*x*-coordinate, *y*-coordinate) lie on the same horizontal line.
   (c) The points (–30, 25) and (–30, –18) lie on the same _____ (horizontal, vertical) line.
   (d) The points (14, 20) and (100, 20) lie on the same _____ (horizontal, vertical) line.

2. Find the distance between the two points.

   (a) (8, –15) and (8, –3)
   (b) (75, –12) and (–50, –12)
   (c) (6, –2) and (–8, 3)
   (d) (–3, 4) and (5, –2)
   (e) (–9, –3) and (–5, –1)

3. Find the perimeter of triangle *DEF*.

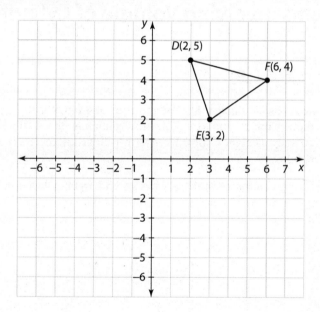

Solutions

1. **(a)** *x*-coordinate
   (b) *y*-coordinate
   (c) vertical
   (d) horizontal

2. **(a)** $|-15 - (-3)| = |-15 + 3| = |-12| = 12$

   (b) $|75 - (-50)| = |75 + 50| = |125| = 125$

   (c) $\sqrt{|-8-6|^2 + |3-(-2)|^2} = \sqrt{|-14|^2 + |3+2|^2} = \sqrt{|-14|^2 + |5|^2} = \sqrt{14^2 + 5^2} = \sqrt{196 + 25} = \sqrt{221}$

   (d) $\sqrt{|5-(-3)|^2 + |-2-4|^2} = \sqrt{|5+3|^2 + |-6|^2} = \sqrt{|8|^2 + |-6|^2} = \sqrt{8^2 + 6^2} = \sqrt{64 + 36} = \sqrt{100} = 10$

   (e) $\sqrt{|-5-(-9)|^2 + |-1-(-3)|^2} = \sqrt{|-5+9|^2 + |-1+3|^2} = \sqrt{|4|^2 + |2|^2} = \sqrt{4^2 + 2^2} = \sqrt{16 + 4} = \sqrt{20}$

3. The perimeter $= DE + EF + FD$.

   $$DE = \sqrt{|3-2|^2 + |2-5|^2} = \sqrt{|1|^2 + |-3|^2} = \sqrt{1^2 + 3^2} = \sqrt{1+9} = \sqrt{10}$$

   $$EF = \sqrt{|6-3|^2 + |4-2|^2} = \sqrt{|3|^2 + |2|^2} = \sqrt{3^2 + 2^2} = \sqrt{9+4} = \sqrt{13}$$

   $$FD = \sqrt{|2-6|^2 + |5-4|^2} = \sqrt{|-4|^2 + |1|^2} = \sqrt{4^2 + 1^2} = \sqrt{16+1} = \sqrt{17}$$

   The triangle's perimeter is $\left(\sqrt{10} + \sqrt{13} + \sqrt{17}\right)$ units.

Solving Problems Involving Volume of Cylinders, Cones, and Spheres

(CCSS.Math.Content.8.G.C.9)

Cylinders, cones, and spheres are **solid figures.** The **volume** of a solid figure is the amount of space inside it. When you use the figure's dimensions to find its volume, the volume units are cubic units, such as cubic inches (in³), cubic feet (ft³), cubic miles (mi³), cubic meters (m³), cubic kilometers (km³), cubic centimeters (cm³), and cubic millimeters (mm³).

A **cylinder** has two parallel congruent bases, which are circles. In a **right cylinder,** the two bases are directly above each other. A rectangular side wraps around and connects the two bases. A cylinder's radius, r, is the radius of one of its circular bases. Its height, h, is the perpendicular distance between the two bases. Here is an example.

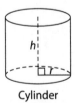

Cylinder

The volume of a cylinder is $V = Bh = (\pi r^2)h$, where $B = \pi r^2$ is the area of one of the cylinder's congruent circular bases and h is the perpendicular distance between the two bases. For example, the approximate volume of a cylinder with a radius of 6 inches and a height of 10 inches is

$$V = Bh = (\pi r^2)h = [\pi(6 \text{ in})^2](10 \text{ in}) = [\pi(36 \text{ in}^2)](10 \text{ in}) \approx [3.14(36 \text{ in}^2)](10 \text{ in}) = 1{,}130.4 \text{ in}^3$$

A **cone** is a three-dimensional solid that has one circular base, from which it tapers smoothly to a single point, its **apex**. In a **right cone,** the apex is directly above the center of the base. A curved side wraps around to form the cone. A cone's radius, r, is the radius of its circular base. Its height, h, is the perpendicular distance from the apex to the base. Here is an example.

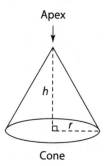

Apex

Cone

The volume of a cone is $V = \frac{1}{3}Bh = \frac{1}{3}(\pi r^2)h$, where $B = \pi r^2$ is the area of the cone's base and h is the perpendicular distance from the apex to the base. For example, the approximate volume of a cone with a radius of 9 meters and a height of 12 meters is

$$V = \frac{1}{3}Bh = \frac{1}{3}(\pi r^2)h = \frac{1}{3}\left[\pi(9 \text{ m})^2\right](12 \text{ m}) = \frac{1}{3}\left[\pi(81 \text{ m}^2)\right](12 \text{ m}) \approx \frac{1}{3}\left[3.14(81 \text{ m}^2)\right](12 \text{ m}) = 1{,}017.36 \text{ m}^3$$

A **sphere** is a three-dimensional solid that is shaped like a ball. Every point on its surface is the same distance from the **center** within the sphere. The sphere's **radius** is a line segment from the center of the sphere to any point on the sphere. The sphere's **diameter** is a line segment joining two points of the sphere and passing through its center. The radius of the sphere is half the diameter. Equivalently, the diameter is twice the radius.

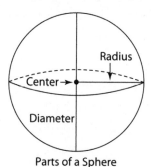

Radius

Center →

Diameter

Parts of a Sphere

The volume of a sphere is $V = \frac{4}{3}\pi r^3$, where r is the radius of the sphere. For example, the approximate volume of a sphere with a radius of 6 feet is

$$V = \frac{4}{3}\pi(6 \text{ ft})^3 = \frac{4}{3}\pi(216 \text{ ft}^3) \approx \frac{4}{3}(3.14)(216 \text{ ft}^3) = 904.32 \text{ ft}^3$$

☞ Try These

1. Find the approximate volume, in cubic centimeters, of a cylindrical jar that is 15 centimeters tall and has a radius of 5 centimeters. (Use $\pi \approx 3.14$.)

2. Find the approximate volume, in cubic feet, of a conical-shaped storage tank that has a radius of 6 feet and a height of 10 feet. (Use $\pi \approx 3.14$.)

3. Rounded to the nearest cubic inch, find the approximate volume of air that will fill to capacity a ball that has a radius of 9.5 inches. (Use $\pi \approx 3.14$.)

Solutions

1. $V = Bh = (\pi r^2)h = [\pi(5\text{ cm})^2](15\text{ cm}) = [\pi(25\text{ cm}^2)](15\text{ cm}) \approx [3.14(25\text{ cm}^2)](15\text{ cm}) = 1{,}177.5\text{ cm}^3$

   The volume of the jar is approximately $1{,}177.5\text{ cm}^3$.

2. $V = \dfrac{1}{3}Bh = \dfrac{1}{3}(\pi r^2)h = \dfrac{1}{3}\left[\pi(6\text{ ft})^2\right](10\text{ ft}) = \dfrac{1}{3}\left[\pi(36\text{ ft}^2)\right](10\text{ ft}) \approx \dfrac{1}{3}\left[3.14(36\text{ ft}^2)\right](10\text{ ft}) = 376.8\text{ ft}^3$

   The volume of the storage tank is approximately 376.8 ft^3.

3. $V = \dfrac{4}{3}\pi(9.5\text{ in})^3 = \dfrac{4}{3}\pi(857.375\text{ in}^3) \approx \dfrac{4}{3}(3.14)(857.375\text{ in}^3) \approx 3{,}590\text{ in}^3$

   The volume of air to fill the ball is approximately $3{,}590\text{ in}^3$.

5. Statistics and Probability

In this chapter, you will investigate patterns of association in bivariate data. You will construct and interpret scatter plots; describe patterns such as clustering, outliers, positive or negative association, linear association, and nonlinear association; and fit linear models to scatter plots. You also will construct and interpret two-way tables of categorical data.

Distinguishing Types of Data

(CCSS.Math.Content.8.SP.A.1, CCSS.Math.Content.8.SP.A.4)

A **statistical question** is one that anticipates the data collected to answer the question will vary. It does not have a specific predetermined answer. For instance, "What are the scores of eighth graders in my classroom on the statewide mathematics test?" is a statistical question. You expect the scores of eighth graders to vary from student to student.

The score of a randomly selected eighth grader in your school on the statewide mathematics test is a **variable.** In statistics, a **variable** is a characteristic (or attribute) that describes a person or thing. The variable's value varies from entity to entity. When you collect information related to a variable, that information is **data.** Data can be **numerical** (such as scores, heights, weights, ages, and other measurements) or it can be **non-numerical** (such as names, labels, colors, and other qualities). Numerical data are **measurement data.** Non-numerical data are **categorical data.**

Bivariate data are paired values of data from two variables. The data are paired in a way that matches each value from one variable with a corresponding value from the other variable. Here is an example.

The following table shows 10 eighth graders' data for the variables MTH (math test score) and ELA (English language arts test score) on the statewide tests.

Student	A	B	C	D	E	F	G	H	I	J
MTH	60	54	84	35	54	26	75	62	44	92
ELA	70	68	85	34	65	28	72	65	46	90

The MTH and ELA score data from the 10 students (A through J) are paired according to the student. Student A had a math test score of 60 and an English language arts test score of 70; student B had a math test score of 54 and an English language arts test score of 68; student C had a math test score of 84 and an English language arts test score of 85; and so on.

☞ Try These

1. Fill in the blank(s).

   (a) A statistical question is one that anticipates the data collected to answer the question will _____.

   (b) A _____ is a characteristic (or attribute) that describes a person or thing.

   (c) Bivariate data are _____ values of data from _____ variables.

2. Classify the data as measurement data or categorical data.

   (a) heights
   (b) ages
   (c) eye colors
   (d) students' first names
   (e) test scores

3. In the bivariate data shown below, describe student G's data. MTH (math test score) and ELA (English language arts test score) are the variables.

Student	A	B	C	D	E	F	G	H	I	J
MTH	60	54	84	35	54	26	75	62	44	92
ELA	70	68	85	34	65	28	72	65	46	90

Solutions

1. (a) vary
   (b) variable
   (c) paired; two

2. (a) measurement
   (b) measurement
   (c) categorical
   (d) categorical
   (e) measurement

3. Student G had a math test score of 75 and an English language arts test score of 72.

Describing Patterns in Scatter Plots

(CCSS.Math.Content.8.SP.A.1)

A **scatter plot** is a graph of bivariate measurement data plotted on a coordinate grid. The data from one variable is plotted along the horizontal axis and the data from the other variable is plotted along the vertical axis. The plotted points are **data points** in the scatter plot. *Tip:* Do not connect the data points in a scatter plot.

The pattern of the data points in a scatter plot can be useful in determining whether there is a **relationship** (or **association**) between the two variables; and, if there is, the nature of that relationship. The data points are often described as forming a "cloud." When the data points in a scatter plot appear to cluster around an imagined line passing through the points, the relationship between the two variables is **linear.**

You should be able to examine scatter plots and distinguish between those indicating linear relationships and those indicating **nonlinear** relationships between two variables. Here is an example.

Which scatter plot clearly shows a nonlinear relationship between variables X and Y?

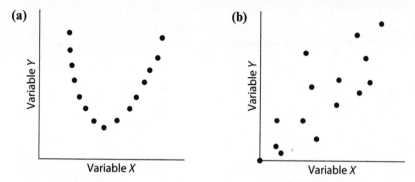

The scatter plot in (a) shows a recognizable curved pattern. This pattern indicates a curved relationship between the variables X and Y. It is clearly nonlinear. The scatter plot in (b) shows a recognizable linear pattern. This pattern indicates a linear relationship between the variables X and Y.

A scatter plot that has no recognizable pattern suggests the two variables have no relationship. Here is an example.

Which scatter plot suggests that there is no relationship between the two variables?

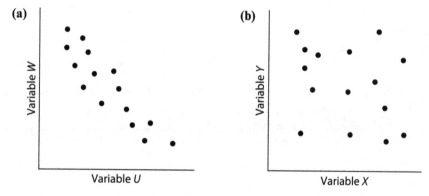

The scatter plot in (a) shows a recognizable linear pattern that suggests a linear relationship between variables U and W. The scatter plot in (b) does not show a recognizable pattern to suggest a relationship between variables X and Y.

If the relationship between two variables is linear, it can be positive or negative. For linear relationships, scatter plots that slant upward from left to right indicate positive linear relationships. In **positive linear relationships,** whenever one of the variables increases, the other variable increases, and when one of the variables decreases, the other variable decreases as well. Scatter plots that slant downward from left to right indicate negative linear relationships. In **negative linear relationships,** whenever one of the two variables increases, the other variable decreases, and conversely. Here is an example.

Describe the scatter plots as having positive or negative linear relationships.

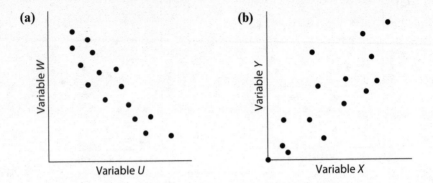

The scatter plot in (a) suggests a negative linear relationship between U and W. The scatter plot in (b) suggests a positive linear relationship between X and Y.

The closer the data points in a scatter plot cluster around an imagined line passing through the points, the stronger the linear relationship is between the two variables. Here is an example.

Which scatter plot suggests the stronger linear relationship between the two variables?

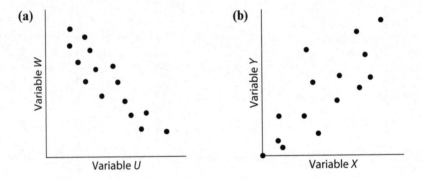

Both scatter plots indicate a linear relationship. The scatter plot in (a) suggests a negative relationship between U and W. The scatter plot in (b) suggests a positive relationship between X and Y. The relationship between U and W is stronger than the relationship between X and Y because the data points in the scatter plot in (a) are clustered closer around an imagined line passing through the points than are the data points in the scatter plot in (b).

In a scatter plot, an **outlier** is a data point that is relatively far away from the rest of the points in the scatter plot. For example, in the scatter plot shown below, the data point marked with an asterisk is a noticeable outlier.

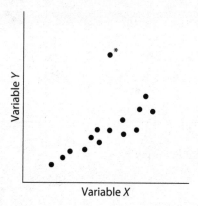

If you have believable information that an outlier doesn't belong with the other data points (perhaps it's the result of an error in collecting the data), you can exclude it when assessing linearity of the scatter plot.

☞ Try These

1. Fill in the blank.

   (a) A scatter plot is a graph of _____ measurement data plotted on a coordinate grid.

   (b) A scatter plot that has no recognizable pattern suggests the two variables have _____ (a negative relationship, a positive relationship, no relationship).

   (c) Scatter plots that slant upward from left to right indicate _____ linear relationships.

   (d) In _____ linear relationships, whenever one of the two variables increases, the other variable decreases, and conversely.

   (e) In a scatter plot, a(n) _____ is a data point that is relatively far away from the rest of the points in the scatter plot.

2. Describe the scatter plot as indicating a linear, nonlinear, or no relationship between the two variables.

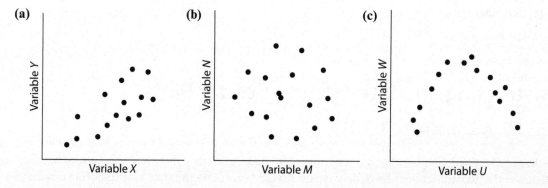

3. Which scatter plot suggests the stronger linear relationship between the two variables?

(a)

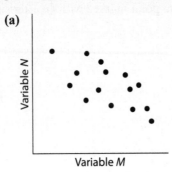

(b)

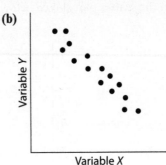

4. Which scatter plot has a noticeable outlier?

(a)

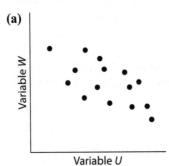

(b)

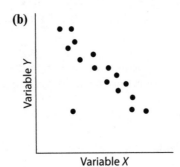

Solutions

1. **(a)** bivariate
   (b) no relationship
   (c) positive
   (d) negative
   (e) outlier

2. **(a)** linear
   (b) no relationship
   (c) nonlinear

3. scatter plot (b)

4. scatter plot (b)

Constructing and Interpreting Scatter Plots

(CCSS.Math.Content.8.SP.A.1)

A teacher is investigating in her classroom of 25 eighth graders whether there is a relationship between their mathematics test scores and their English language arts test scores on the statewide tests. She randomly selects 10 students from her class. To protect their information, she codes each student's name with a letter. The following table shows the 10 students' data for the variables MTH (math test score) and ELA (English language arts test score) on the statewide tests.

Student	A	B	C	D	E	F	G	H	I	J
MTH	60	54	84	35	54	26	75	62	44	92
ELA	70	68	85	34	65	28	72	65	46	90

(a) Construct a scatter plot for the data. Designate the horizontal axis as MTH and the vertical axis as ELA.

(b) Describe patterns in the scatter plot.

(c) Based on the scatter plot, what do the data indicate?

(a) Plot the ordered pairs on a coordinate grid.

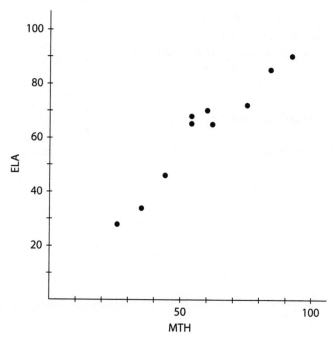

(b) The data points are clustered around an imagined line, which slants upward from left to right. There are no noticeable outliers.

(c) For eighth graders in the teacher's classroom, the scatter plot suggests there is a positive linear relationship between their mathematics scores and their English language arts scores on the statewide tests.

☞ Try These

1. The following table shows the number of hours each of 10 students spent studying for a science test and the student's corresponding score on the test.

Student	A	B	C	D	E	F	G	H	I	J
Hours	1.50	1.00	2.75	3.00	0.50	2.50	2.00	1.75	0.75	2.00
Score	75	65	95	90	45	85	80	70	100	85

(a) Construct a scatter plot for the data.

(b) Describe patterns in the scatter plot.

(c) Based on the scatter plot, what do the data indicate?

2. The following table shows the number of pets in each of 10 students' households and the student's mother's height in inches.

Student	A	B	C	D	E	F	G	H	I	J
Number of Pets	0	3	1	2	0	4	2	3	2	5
Height	70	62	74	55	66	74	70	58	64	57

(a) Construct a scatter plot for the data.

(b) Describe patterns in the scatter plot.

(c) Based on the scatter plot, what do the data indicate?

Solutions

1. (a) Plot the ordered pairs on a coordinate grid.

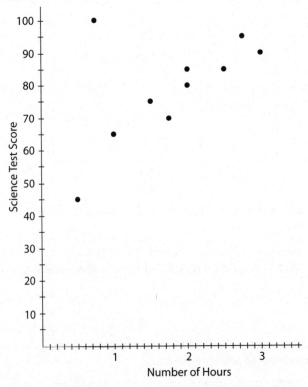

(b) There appears to be one outlier at (0.75, 100). Excluding this outlier as an error in data collection, the data points are clustered around an imagined line, which slants upward from left to right.

(c) The scatter plot suggests a positive linear relationship between number of hours studied and the performance on the science test.

2. **(a)** Plot the ordered pairs on a coordinate grid.

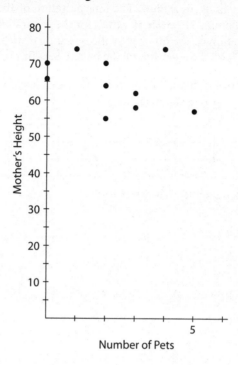

(b) The data points show no recognizable pattern.

(c) The scatter plot suggests there is no relationship between the number of pets in students' households and students' mothers' heights.

Fitting a Linear Model to Scatter Plot Data and Using It to Solve Problems

(CCSS.Math.Content.8.SP.A.2, CCSS.Math.Content.8.SP.A.3)

For scatter plots that suggest a linear relationship, an equation of a line can be used to model the trend shown by the cloud of data points. **The line of best fit** (or **trend line**) is a straight line that best represents the data. It might pass through some of the points, none of the points, or even all of the points.

> **Tip: The line that best fits the data will always pass through the point whose coordinates are the means of the two variables, and you should expect to have "scatter" around the line.**

If X and Y are the two variables under consideration, the equation of the line of best fit has the form $Y = aX + b$, where a is the slope of the line of best fit and b is its vertical intercept. The purpose of determining the equation of the line of best fit is to be able to predict values of variable Y based upon values of variable X (called the **predictor variable**). For statistical reasons, to be safe you should predict only within the range of the predictor variable. When you predict within the range of the plotted data, you are **interpolating**.

The interpretation of the slope of the equation $Y = aX + b$ is that if the X variable increases by one unit, it is predicted that the Y variable will change by a units. The interpretation of the intercept is that when the X variable is zero, the Y variable is b units. However, if values for the X variable near zero would not make sense, then typically the interpretation of the intercept will seem unrealistic in the real world. Nevertheless, the coefficient b is a necessary part of the equation of the line of best fit.

The following table shows 10 eighth graders' data for the variables MTH (math test score) and ELA (English language arts test score) on statewide tests.

Student	A	B	C	D	E	F	G	H	I	J
MTH	60	54	84	35	54	26	75	62	44	92
ELA	70	68	85	34	65	28	72	65	46	90

A scatter plot of the data in the table is shown below.

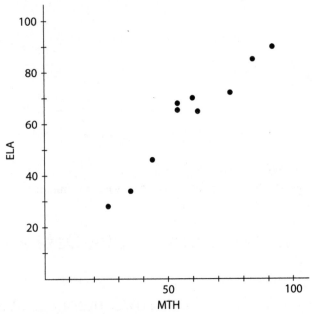

(a) Fit a linear model to the scatter plot data.
(b) Interpret the slope of your fitted line.
(c) Use your linear model to predict the English language arts test score for a student who scored 90 on the math test. *Tip:* Remember, to predict only within the range of the predictor variable, which is MTH in this case.

Note: Answers may vary.

(a) *Step 1.* Compute the means of each variable.

The mean for MTH is mean $_{MTH} = \dfrac{60 + 54 + 84 + 35 + 54 + 26 + 75 + 62 + 44 + 92}{10} = \dfrac{586}{10} = 58.6$

The mean for ELA is mean $_{ELA} = \dfrac{70 + 68 + 85 + 34 + 65 + 28 + 72 + 65 + 46 + 90}{10} = \dfrac{623}{10} = 62.3$

Step 2. Sketch a line through what looks like the center of the cloud of data points. Make sure the line goes through the point $(\text{mean}_{\text{MTH}}, \text{mean}_{\text{ELA}}) = (58.6, 62.3)$. Adjust the line as needed based on balancing the closeness of the data points to the line. Approximate the intercept of the line and label the point (0, intercept).

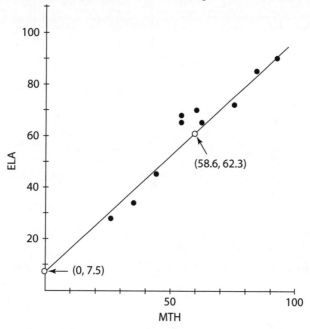

Step 3. Using $(\text{mean}_{\text{MTH}}, \text{mean}_{\text{ELA}}) = (58.6, 62.3)$ and (0, intercept) = (0, 7.5), calculate an approximate value for the slope. *Tip:* The points (58.6, 62.3) and (0, 7.5) are not data points, so do not mark these two points the same way you have marked the actual data points.

The slope is approximately $\dfrac{y_2 - y_1}{x_2 - x_1} = \dfrac{62.3 - 7.5}{58.6 - 0} = \dfrac{54.8}{58.6} \approx 0.94$.

Step 4. Write an equation for the line.

The equation is $Y = 0.94X + 7.5$, where Y is the ELA variable and X is the MTH variable.

(b) The interpretation of the slope of 0.94 is that if the math test score increases by 1 point, it is predicted that the English language arts test score will increase by 0.94 point.

(c) Using the equation $Y = 0.94X + 7.5$, the predicted English language arts test score for a student who scored 90 on the math test is $0.94(90) + 7.5 \approx 92$.

☞ Try These

1. Fill in the blank.

(a) For scatter plots that suggest a linear relationship, an equation of a _____ can be used to model the trend shown by the cloud of data points.

(b) The line that best fits the data in a scatter plot will always pass through the point whose coordinates are the _____ of the two variables.

(c) For statistical reasons, predict only within the _____ of the predictor variable.

2. The following table shows the number of hours each of 10 students spent studying for a science test and the student's corresponding score on the test.

Student	A	B	C	D	E	F	G	H	I	J
Hours	1.50	1.00	2.75	3.00	0.50	2.50	2.00	1.75	0.75	2.00
Score	75	65	95	90	45	85	80	70	100	85

A scatter plot of the data in the table is shown below.

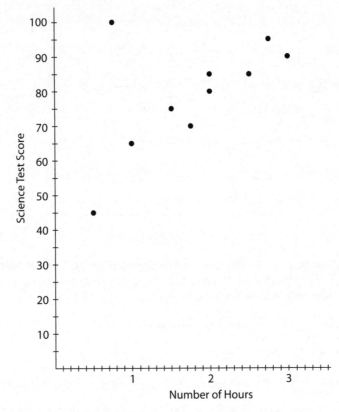

(a) Excluding the outlier (0.75, 100) as an error in data collection, fit a linear model to the scatter plot data.

(b) Interpret the slope of your fitted line.

(c) Use your linear model to predict the science test score for a student who studied for 2.25 hours.

Solutions

1. **(a)** line
   (b) means
   (c) range

2. *Note:* Answers may vary.

   (a) *Step 1.* Excluding the outlier (0.75, 100), compute the means of each variable.
   The mean for the number of hours is

   $$\text{mean}_{\text{HOURS}} = \frac{1.50 + 1.00 + 2.75 + 3.00 + 0.50 + 2.50 + 2.00 + 1.75 + 2.00}{9} = \frac{17}{9} \approx 1.9.$$

   The mean for the science scores is

   $$\text{mean}_{\text{SCIENCE}} = \frac{75 + 65 + 95 + 90 + 45 + 85 + 80 + 70 + 85}{9} = \frac{690}{9} \approx 76.7.$$

   Step 2. Sketch a line through what looks like the center of the cloud of data points. Make sure the line goes through the point $(\text{mean}_{\text{HOURS}}, \text{mean}_{\text{SCIENCE}}) = (1.9, 76.7)$. Adjust the line as needed based on the closeness of the data points to the line. Approximate the intercept of the line and label the point (0, intercept).

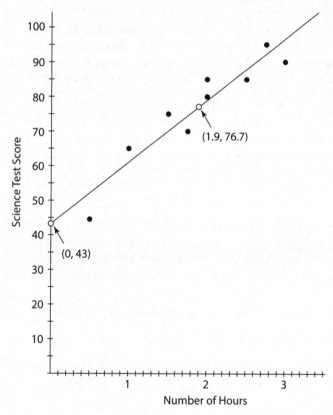

   Step 3. Using $(\text{mean}_{\text{HOURS}}, \text{mean}_{\text{SCIENCE}}) = (1.9, 76.7)$ and (0, y-intercept) = (0, 43), calculate an approximate value for the slope.

   The slope is approximately $\dfrac{y_2 - y_1}{x_2 - x_1} = \dfrac{76.7 - 43}{1.9 - 0} = \dfrac{33.7}{1.9} \approx 17.7.$

Step 4. Write an equation for the line.

The equation is $Y = 17.7X + 43$, where Y is the number of hours studied and X is the science test score.

(b) The interpretation of the slope of 17.7 is that if the study time increases by an additional hour, it is predicted that the science test score will increase by 17.7 points.

(c) Using the equation $Y = 17.7X + 43$, the predicted science test score for a student who studied 2.25 hours is $17.7(2.25) + 43 \approx 83$.

Constructing and Interpreting Two-Way Tables of Categorical Data

(CCSS.Math.Content.8.SP.A.3)

You also can determine patterns of association in **bivariate categorical data.** You collect data on the two variables from the same subjects. These subjects have been randomly selected from the population of interest to you. You display frequencies for the data in a two-way table and calculate row and column totals. Then you use relative frequencies (or proportions) calculated for rows or columns to describe possible associations between the two variables.

Of course, you can't be positive your conclusions are correct because your data are not from the entire population. Your conclusions about a population based on data from a sample are never completely certain. Fortunately, though, random sampling tends to produce representative samples. Representative samples provide meaningful statistical results that will support valid inferences made about the population.

Here is an example.

A random selection of 200 students (100 girls and 100 boys) from a large middle school of 1,500 students was surveyed and asked whether they have an online social media account. Seventy-five of the girls and 56 of the boys responded "yes" to the survey question.

(a) Construct a two-way table that summarizes the survey's results.

Tip: It is customary to use the label "Gender" for a variable that classifies subjects as men/women, boys/girls, or male/female.

(b) Based on the survey data, is there evidence to suggest that, for students in that middle school, gender is associated with having an online social media account?

(a)

Gender	Do you have an online social media account?		
	Yes	**No**	**Row Total**
Female/Girl	75	25	100
Male/Boy	56	44	100
Column Total	131	69	200

(b) The proportion of girls who have an online social media account is $\frac{75}{100} = 0.75$ or 75%. The proportion of boys who have a social media online account is $\frac{56}{100} = 0.56$ or 56%. Note that the two proportions are based on an equal number of students and observe that 0.75 and 0.56 differ by 0.19 or 19%. This difference seems noteworthy. These findings suggest that, for students in that middle school, gender is associated with having an online social media account. It appears that girls are more likely to have a social media account.

☞ Try These

1. Fill in the blank.

   (a) You display frequencies for bivariate categorical data in a _____ table.

   (b) You use _____ frequencies calculated for rows or columns to describe possible associations between bivariate categorical data.

   (c) Conclusions about a population based on data from a sample are _____ (always, never, sometimes) completely certain.

   (d) _____ samples provide meaningful statistical results that will support valid inferences made about the population.

2. In a national random sample of 400 middle school students (200 boys and 200 girls), 40 of the boys and 38 of the girls indicated they want to work a summer job before entering high school.

   (a) Construct a two-way table that summarizes the survey's results.

   (b) Based on the survey data, is there evidence to suggest that, for middle school students, there is an association between gender and preference for working a summer job before entering high school?

3. One hundred fifty sixth graders and 150 eighth graders in a large middle school of 1,000 students were asked whether they have an 8:30 p.m. bedtime on school nights. One hundred twenty of the sixth graders and 75 of the eighth graders responded "yes" to the question.

   (a) Construct a two-way table that summarizes the survey's results.

   (b) Based on the survey data, is there evidence to suggest that, for students in that middle school, there is an association between grade level and having an 8:30 p.m. bedtime on school nights?

Solutions

1. (a) two-way
   (b) relative
   (c) never
   (d) Representative

2. (a)

Gender	Do you want to work a summer job before high school?		
	Yes	No	Row Total
Male/Boy	40	160	200
Female/Girl	38	162	200
Column Total	78	322	400

(b) The proportion of boys who want to work a summer job is $\frac{40}{200} = 0.20$ or 20%. The proportion of girls who want to work a summer job is $\frac{38}{200} = 0.19$ or 19%. Note that the two proportions are based on an equal number of students and observe that 0.20 and 0.19 differ by only 0.01 or 1%. This difference seems negligible. Thus, for students in middle school, these findings fail to indicate an association between gender and preference for working a summer job before entering high school. The data are insufficient to determine whether boys or girls are more likely to want to work a summer job before entering high school.

3. (a)

Grade	Do you have an 8:30 p.m. bedtime on school nights?		
	Yes	No	Row Total
Sixth	120	30	150
Eighth	75	75	150
Column Total	195	105	300

(b) The proportion of sixth graders who have an 8:30 p.m. bedtime on school nights is $\frac{120}{150} = 0.8$ or 80%. The proportion of eighth graders who have an 8:30 p.m. bedtime on school nights is $\frac{75}{150} = 0.5$ or 50%. Note that the two proportions are based on an equal number of students and observe that 0.8 and 0.5 differ by 0.3 or 30%. This difference seems noteworthy. These findings suggest that, for students in that middle school, there is an association between grade level and having an 8:30 p.m. bedtime on school nights. It appears that sixth graders are more likely to have an 8:30 p.m. bedtime on school nights.

6. Practice Test 1

Directions: For questions 1–30, select the best answer choice.

1. Convert $0.\overline{5}$ to an equivalent fractional form.

   A. $\dfrac{1}{5}$

   B. $\dfrac{1}{2}$

   C. $\dfrac{55}{100}$

   D. $\dfrac{5}{9}$

2. Evaluate $10 - 2(-4)^3 + 3(12 - 17) - (-3)^2$.

   A. -142
   B. 114
   C. 132
   D. 144

3. The value of $\sqrt{18}$ is best described as between

   A. 3 and 3.5.
   B. 3.5 and 4.
   C. 4 and 4.5.
   D. 4.5 and 5.

4. Which expression is equivalent to $\dfrac{7^{-10}}{7^{-5}}$?

   A. $\dfrac{1}{7^{15}}$

   B. $\dfrac{1}{7^5}$

   C. 7^2

   D. 7^{15}

5. Solution A contains 3×10^{-2} grams of salt. Solution B contains 6×10^2 grams of salt. The number of grams of salt in solution B is how many times the number of grams of salt in solution A?

   A. 2×10^{-4}
   B. 2×10^{-1}
   C. 2×10^0
   D. 2×10^4

6. Compute $(9 \times 10^7)(4 \times 10^{-2})$.

    A. 3.6×10^{-14}

    B. 36×10^{-5}

    C. 3.6×10^5

    D. 3.6×10^6

7. Jenna is twice as old as Melora. In 5 years, Melora will be $\frac{3}{5}$ as old as Jenna. How old, in years, will Melora be in 5 years?

    A.   10

    B.   15

    C.   20

    D.   25

8. Which equation has both −2 and 2 in the solution set?

    A. $x^2 = 4$

    B. $x^3 = 8$

    C. $x^2 = 16$

    D. $x^3 = 64$

9. Solve $x^2 = 36$.

    A. $x = -6$

    B. $x = -18$

    C. $x = -6$ or $x = 6$

    D. $x = -18$ or $x = 18$

10. Find the slope of the line shown.

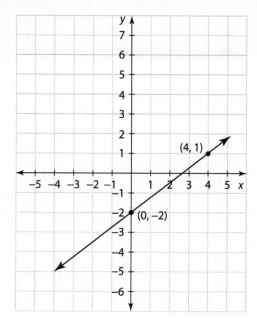

A. $-\dfrac{4}{3}$

B. $-\dfrac{3}{4}$

C. $\dfrac{3}{4}$

D. $\dfrac{4}{3}$

11. Which system of equations has infinitely many solutions?

A. $x - 2y = 5$
   $2x - 4y = 10$

B. $x - 2y = 5$
   $2x - 4y = 8$

C. $x - 2y = 5$
   $2x + 4y = 10$

D. $x - 2y = 5$
   $2x - 4y = -10$

12. The sum of two numbers is 42. Their difference is 6. What is the value of the greater number?

   A.   18
   B.   24
   C.   30
   D.   36

13. Which table could NOT be a partial representation of a function?

A.

x	y
−4	5
−2	6
0	7
2	8
4	9

B.

x	y
5	10
4	10
3	10
2	10
1	10

C.

x	y
5	5
5^2	5
5^3	5
5^4	5
5^5	5

D.

x	y
2	3
3	4
3	5
4	6
5	7

14. The table shows a partial representation of a proportional function showing the relationship between the price, p (in dollars), and the weight, w (in kilograms), of copper.

Weight, w (in kilograms)	Price, p (in dollars)
2	11.02
3	16.53
5	27.55
8	44.08

Write an equation for the function represented in the table.

   A. $w = 5.51p$
   B. $p = 5.51w$
   C. $w = 11.02p$
   D. $p = 11.02w$

15. Which statement about the function $y = \frac{1}{2}x + 5$ is true?

   A.   When the input is 6, the output is 8.
   B.   When the output is −2, the input is 4.
   C.   The graph passes through the origin.
   D.   The rate of change is 5.

16. Which graph is NOT the graph of a function?

A.

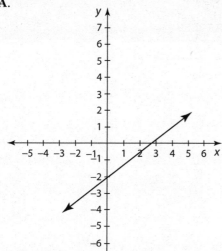

B.

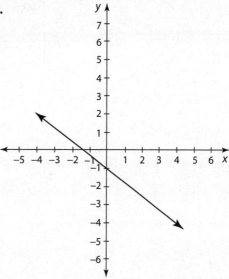

C.

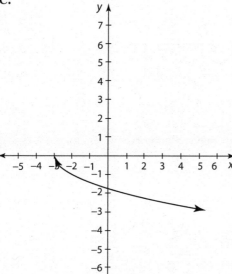

D.

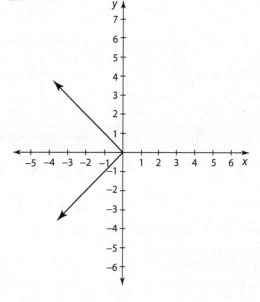

17. The data in the table shown best represents which linear function?

Input x	Output y
−3	−11
0	−5
5	5

    A. $y = x - 8$

    B. $y = x - 5$

    C. $y = x$

    D. $y = 2x - 5$

18. The graph shows y as a function of x.

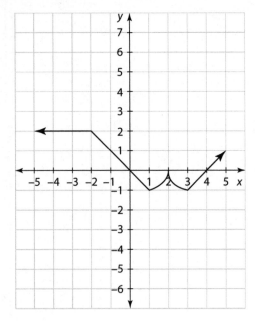

On which intervals is the function decreasing?

    A.   −5 to −2 and 0 to 2

    B.   −2 to 1 and 2 to 3

    C.   0 to 1 and 2 to 3

    D.   1 to 2 and 3 to 5

19. What is the rate of change of the function that has the graph shown?

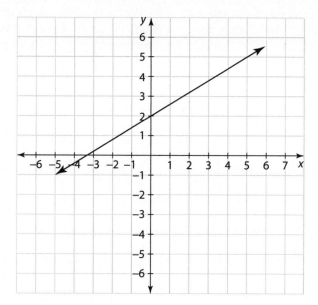

A. $\dfrac{3}{5}$

B. $\dfrac{1}{2}$

C. $\dfrac{5}{3}$

D. 2

20. Function A is a linear function. The table shown is a partial representation of Function A.

x	y
−4	−16
−2	−11
2	−1
4	4

Function B is a linear function. Its graph has slope of $\dfrac{5}{2}$ and intercept of 3. Which statement is true?

A. The rate of change of Function A is greater than the rate of change of Function B.
B. The rate of change of Function B is greater than the rate of change of Function A.
C. The intercept of Function A is greater than the intercept of Function B.
D. The intercept of Function B is greater than the intercept of Function A.

21. In a coordinate plane, triangle *ABC* has vertices *A*(2, 1), *B*(2, 5), and *C*(5, 2).

    Triangle *A′B′C′* is the image of triangle *ABC* after a reflection over the *y*-axis followed by a translation of 4 units to the right and 2 units down. What are the coordinates of *B′*?

    A. (–4, 9)
    B. (0, –1)
    C. (6, –7)
    D. (2, 3)

22. If the point *P*(2, –3) is rotated 90° counterclockwise about the origin, in what quadrant does *P′* lie?

    A. quadrant I
    B. quadrant II
    C. quadrant III
    D. quadrant IV

23. In the diagram shown, right triangle *ABC* is similar to right triangle *DEF*. What is the length of the hypotenuse in triangle *ABC*?

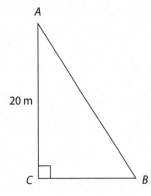
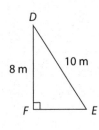

    A. 4 m
    B. 25 m
    C. 28 m
    D. 30 m

24. Use the diagram below to answer the question that follows.

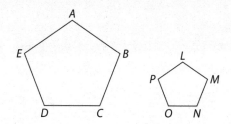

ABCDE and LMNOP are similar regular pentagons. If AB = 9.0 units and LM = 7.5 units, what is the ratio of the perimeter of ABCDE to the perimeter of LMNOP?

A.   0.8
B.   1.1
C.   1.2
D.   1.3

25. Which set of numbers could be the lengths of the sides of a right triangle?

A.   8, 12, 20
B.   16, 9, 24
C.   12, 13, 5
D.   10, 8, 5

26. A 10-foot ladder is leaning against a building. The base of the ladder is 3 feet from the base of the building. Which measurement, in feet, is closest to the distance from the base of the building to the top of the ladder?

A.   6.5 feet
B.   7.0 feet
C.   9.5 feet
D.   10.5 feet

27. Use the diagram below to answer the question that follows.

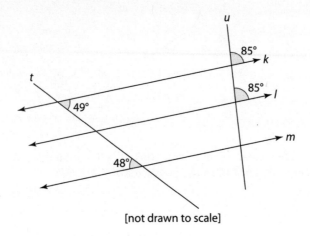

[not drawn to scale]

Based on the diagram, which statement is true?

A. $k \parallel l$
B. $k \parallel m$
C. $l \parallel m$
D. $t \parallel u$

28. A cone-shaped paperweight is made of solid brass. It has a height of 10 inches and a diameter of 8 inches. Which volume is closest to the volume of brass in the paperweight? (Use $\pi \approx 3.14$.)

A. 167 in³
B. 209 in³
C. 502 in³
D. 670 in³

29. Which scatter plot suggests the strongest linear relationship between variables X and Y?

A.

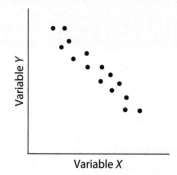

B.

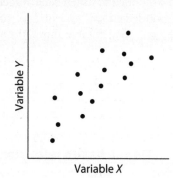

C.

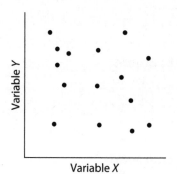

D.

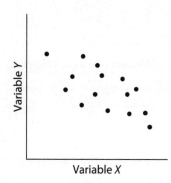

30. A teacher's class of eighth graders conducted a random survey of 50 students (25 boys and 25 girls) in their middle school and asked each student, "Do you have a television in your bedroom?" Every student responded either "yes" or "no" to the survey question. Eighteen of the boys and 15 of the girls responded "yes." Which table shows the approximate relative frequencies of the survey data?

A.

Do you have a television in your bedroom?

Gender	Yes	No	Row Total
Boys	18%	7%	25%
Girls	15%	10%	25%
Column Total	33%	17%	50%

B.

Do you have a television in your bedroom?

Gender	Yes	No	Row Total
Boys	72%	28%	100%
Girls	60%	40%	100%
Column Total	66%	34%	100%

C.

Do you have a television in your bedroom?

Gender	Yes	No	Row Total
Boys	36%	14%	50%
Girls	30%	20%	50%
Column Total	66%	34%	100%

D.

Do you have a television in your bedroom?

Gender	Yes	No	Row Total
Boys	55%	45%	100%
Girls	45%	55%	100%
Column Total	100%	100%	100%

Directions: For questions 31–40, enter your answer in the answer box below the question. Enter the exact answer unless you are told to round your answer.

31. Solve $0.4(x - 5) + 4x = -3(0.2x + 2) - 6$

    [ ]

32. A water tank is in the shape of a right circular cylinder with a height of 10 feet and a volume of 490π cubic feet. What is the radius, in feet, of the water tank?

    [ ] ft

33. As shown in the diagram, to get from home to a local movie theater, Padma and her parents can either walk a graveled path through the rectangular park or walk a rectangular path of sidewalk along the sides of the park.

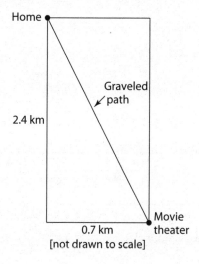

Home •
Graveled
path
2.4 km
Movie
theater
0.7 km
[not drawn to scale]

    How much farther, in kilometers, would they walk by walking along two sides of the park rather than taking the graveled path through the park?

    [ ] km

34. A spherical ball has a radius of approximately 2.1 inches. To the nearest cubic inch, what is the volume of air needed to fill the ball to capacity? (Use $\pi \approx 3.14$.)

$$\boxed{} \ \text{in}^3$$

35. A scatter plot showing the linear relationship between the number of hours of study and the score on a science midterm exam of 10 eighth graders is shown below.

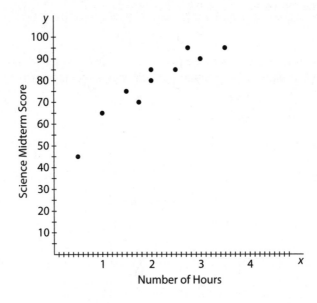

The line of best fit for the data has equation $Y = 16X + 46$. What is the predicted science midterm score for a student who studied $2\frac{1}{4}$ hours?

$$\boxed{}$$

36. In triangle ABC shown, CE is 200 meters and EA is 100 meters. In triangle ADE, DE is 50 meters. What is the area, in square meters, of triangle ABC?

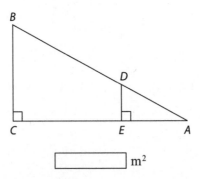

$$\boxed{} \ \text{m}^2$$

37. In the system of equations shown, what is the value of y?

$$6x - 5y = 18$$
$$2x + 3y = -8$$

38. Jason and Phaedra volunteered to build a rectangular sandbox at the neighborhood park. The sandbox's length is 1 foot more than twice its width. The sandbox has a perimeter of 20 feet. What is the width, in feet, of the sandbox?

[   ] ft

39. In the diagram, with the measures of the angles as shown, what is the measure of angle E?

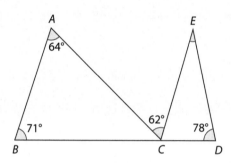

[   ]°

40. If $x = \left(1 + \left(1 + 2^{-1}\right)^{-1}\right)^{-1}$, then $5x =$

[   ]

Answer Key

1. D	11. A	21. D	31. −2
2. B	12. B	22. A	32. 7 ft
3. C	13. D	23. B	33. 0.6 km
4. B	14. B	24. C	34. 39 in³
5. D	15. A	25. C	35. 82
6. D	16. D	26. C	36. 22 500 m²
7. B	17. D	27. A	37. −3
8. A	18. B	28. A	38. 3 ft
9. C	19. A	29. A	39. 29°
10. C	20. D	30. C	40. 3

Answer Explanations

1. **D.** Choice D is the correct response. Let $x = 0.\overline{5} = 0.555\ldots$

   Step 1. Multiply both sides of the equation, $x = 0.555\ldots$, by $10^1 = 10$ (because 1 digit repeats).

   $$x = 0.555\ldots$$
   $$10 \cdot x = 10(0.555\ldots)$$
   $$10x = 5.555\ldots$$

   Step 2. Subtract the original equation from the new equation.

   $$10x = 5.555\ldots$$
   $$-x = -0.555\ldots$$
   $$\overline{}$$
   $$9x = 5$$

   Step 3. Solve for x by dividing both sides of the resulting equation by the coefficient of x.

   $$9x = 5$$
   $$\frac{9x}{9} = \frac{5}{9}$$
   $$x = \frac{5}{9}$$

2. **B.** Choice B is the correct response. Follow the order of operations.

   $$10 - 2(-4)^3 + 3(12-17) - (-3)^2 = 10 - 2(-4)^3 + 3(-5) - (-3)^2$$
   $$= 10 - 2(-64) + 3(-5) - 9$$
   $$= 10 + 128 - 15 - 9$$
   $$= 114$$

3. **C.** Choice C is the correct response. First, find two perfect squares that 18 lies between: $16 < 18 < 25$. Then $\sqrt{16} < \sqrt{18} < \sqrt{25}$, which implies that $4 < \sqrt{18} < 5$. Therefore, you can eliminate choices A and B as too small because $\sqrt{18}$ lies between 4 and 5. Looking at $\sqrt{16} < \sqrt{18} < \sqrt{25}$, consider that 25 and 16 are 9 units apart and 18 and 16 are 2 units apart. So roughly, $\sqrt{18}$ is $\frac{2}{9}$ of the distance between 4 and 5, which is 1 unit. Given that $\frac{2}{9} < \frac{1}{2} = 0.5$, you can safely conclude that $\sqrt{18}$ lies between 4 and 4.5.

4. **B.** Choice B is the correct response. Follow the rules for exponents.

   $$\frac{7^{-10}}{7^{-5}} = 7^{-10-(-5)} = 7^{-10+5} = 7^{-5} = \frac{1}{7^5}$$

5. **D.** Choice D is the correct response. Divide 6×10^2 grams by 3×10^{-2} grams.

   $$\frac{6 \times 10^2 \text{ g}}{3 \times 10^{-2} \text{ g}} = \frac{\overset{2}{\cancel{6}} \times 10^2 \ \cancel{g}}{\underset{1}{\cancel{3}} \times 10^{-2} \ \cancel{g}} = 2 \times 10^{2-(-2)} = 2 \times 10^{2+2} = 2 \times 10^4$$

   The number of grams of salt in solution B is 2×10^4 times the number of grams of salt in solution A.

6. **D.** Choice D is the correct response.

$$(9 \times 10^7)(4 \times 10^{-2}) = 36 \times 10^{7+-2} = 36 \times 10^5 = 3.6 \times 10^1 \times 10^5 = 3.6 \times 10^6$$

7. **B.** Choice B is the correct response. Let m = Melora's age now, in years. Then $2m$ = Jenna's age now, in years. Make a chart to organize the information in the question.

When?	Melora's Age	Jenna's Age
Now	m	$2m$
5 years from now	$m + 5$ years	$2m + 5$ years

Write an equation that represents the facts given.

$$(m + 5 \text{ years}) = \frac{3}{5}(2m + 5 \text{ years})$$

Solve the equation, omitting the units for convenience.

$$(m + 5) = \frac{3}{5}(2m + 5)$$

$$m + 5 = \frac{6}{5}m + 3$$

$$m + 5 - \frac{6}{5}m = \frac{6}{5}m + 3 - \frac{6}{5}m$$

$$\frac{5}{5}m - \frac{6}{5}m + 5 = 3$$

$$-\frac{1}{5}m + 5 = 3$$

$$-\frac{1}{5}m + 5 - 5 = 3 - 5$$

$$-\frac{1}{5}m = -2$$

$$\left(-\frac{5}{1}\right)\left(-\frac{1}{5}m\right) = (-5)(-2)$$

$$\left(-\frac{5}{1}\right)\left(-\frac{1}{5}m\right) = (-5)(-2)$$

$$m = 10$$

$$m + 5 = 15$$

Melora will be 15 years old in 5 years.

8. **A.** Choice A is the correct response. Check the answer choices.

Check A: The solution of $x^2 = 4$ is $x = \sqrt{4} = 2$ or $x = -\sqrt{4} = -2$. Thus, choice A is the correct response.

In a test situation, you should move on to the next question. For your information, here are the checks for the other answer choices.

Check B: The solution of $x^3 = 8$ is $x = \sqrt[3]{8} = 2$.

Check C: The solution of $x^2 = 16$ is $x = \sqrt{16} = 4$ or $x = -\sqrt{16} = -4$.

Check D: The solution of $x^3 = 64$ is $x = \sqrt[3]{64} = 4$.

9. **C.** Choice C is the correct response.

$$x^2 = 36$$
$$x = \sqrt{36} \text{ or } -\sqrt{36}$$
$$x = 6 \text{ or } -6$$

10. **C.** Choice C is the correct response. The line slants upward from left to right, meaning its slope is positive. So eliminate choices A and B.

$$\text{slope} = \frac{\text{vertical change}}{\text{horizontal change}} = \frac{y_2 - y_1}{x_2 - x_1} = \frac{-2-1}{0-4} = \frac{-3}{-4} = \frac{3}{4}$$

11. **A.** Choice A is the correct response. Check the answer choices by comparing the ratios of the coefficients of the two equations.

Check A: $\frac{1}{2}$, $\frac{-2}{-4}$, and $\frac{5}{10}$ are equivalent ratios. Therefore, the system $\begin{array}{l} x - 2y = 5 \\ 2x - 4y = 10 \end{array}$ has infinitely many

solutions. In a test situation, you should move on to the next question. For your information, the systems $\begin{array}{l} x - 2y = 5 \\ 2x - 4y = 8 \end{array}$ (choice B) and $\begin{array}{l} x - 2y = 5 \\ 2x - 4y = -10 \end{array}$ (choice D) have no solution. The system $\begin{array}{l} x - 2y = 5 \\ 2x + 4y = 10 \end{array}$

(choice C) has exactly one solution.

12. **B.** Choice B is the correct response. Let x = the greater of the two numbers. Let y = the lesser of the two numbers. Write two equations that represent the facts given.

$$x + y = 42$$
$$x - y = 6$$

Solve the system.

Using the method of elimination, add the two equations to eliminate y. Then solve for x.

$$\begin{array}{r} x + y = 42 \\ x - y = 6 \\ \hline 2x = 48 \end{array}$$

$$\frac{\cancel{2}x}{\cancel{2}} = \frac{\cancel{48}^{24}}{\cancel{2}}$$

$$x = 24$$

The greater number is 24.

13. **D.** Choice D is the correct response. Only the ordered pairs in choice D could not be a partial representation of a function because the ordered pairs (3, 4) and (3, 5) have the same input value, 3, but different output values, 4 and 5.

14. **B.** Choice B is the correct response. The input-output ordered pairs are (2, 11.02), (3, 16.53), (5, 27.55) and (8, 44.08). A proportional function has the form $y = mx$, where m is the function's rate of change. Using (2, 11.02) and (3, 16.53), the rate of change is $\frac{16.53 - 11.02}{3 - 2} = \frac{5.51}{1} = 5.51$. The function has equation $p = 5.51w$.

15. **A.** Choice A is the correct response. Check the answer choices.

    Check A: When the input is 6, the output is $\frac{1}{2}(6)+5=3+5=8$. None of the other answer choices contains a true statement about the function.

16. **D.** Choice D is the correct response. The graph in choice D is not a function because as shown below, the graph does not pass the vertical line test.

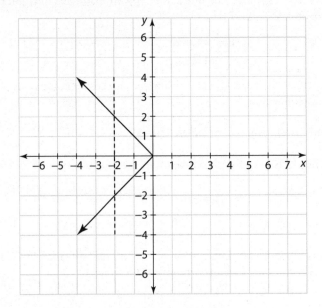

17. **D.** Choice D is the correct response. Check the answer choices.

    Check A: Eliminate A because the ordered pairs (0, –5) and (5, 5) do not satisfy the equation $y = x - 8$.
    Check B: Eliminate B because the ordered pairs (–3, –11) and (5, 5) do not satisfy the equation $y = x - 5$.
    Check C: Eliminate C because the ordered pairs (–3, –11) and (0, –5) do not satisfy the equation $y = x$.
    Check D: The table data best represent $y = 2x - 5$ because all three of the ordered pairs in the table satisfy the equation. ✓

18. **B.** Choice B is the correct response. The graph decreases from left to right as x goes from –2 to 1, and again as x goes from 2 to 3.

19. **A.** Choice A is the correct response. As shown below, for every 5-unit change in x, there is a 3-unit change in y.

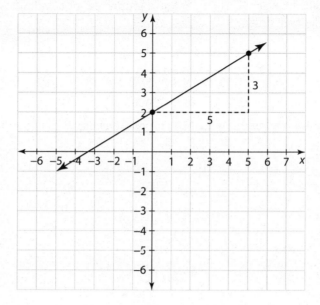

So, the rate of change is $\frac{3}{5}$.

20. **D.** Choice D is the correct response. The rate of change of Function A is $\frac{-11-(-16)}{-2-(-4)} = \frac{-11+16}{-2+4} = \frac{5}{2}$. The rate of change of Function B is $\frac{5}{2}$. The rates of change for the two functions are equal. So eliminate choices A and B. The intercept for Function B is 3. The intercept for Function A occurs when $x = 0$. The value 0 occurs between the input values of -2 and 2. Both of these input values have negative output values. The output value for the input 0 is also negative because a linear function does not change direction. Thus, the intercept, 3, of Function B is greater than the intercept of Function A.

21. **D.** Choice D is the correct response. Under a reflection over the y-axis, $(2, 5) \rightarrow (-2, 5)$. Under a translation of 4 units right and 2 units down, $(-2, 5) \rightarrow (-2 + 4, 5 - 2) = (2, 3)$. The coordinates of B' are $(2, 3)$.

22. **A.** Choice A is the correct response. Under a counterclockwise rotation of 90° about the origin, $P(2, -3) \rightarrow P'(3, 2)$, which lies in quadrant I.

23. **B.** Choice B is the correct response. The corresponding sides of similar triangles are proportional. Side $\overline{AB}$ is the hypotenuse of triangle ABC. Its corresponding side is $\overline{DE}$, the hypotenuse of triangle DEF. The corresponding side for side $\overline{AC}$ is $\overline{DF}$. Set up a proportion of equal ratios. ***Tip:*** Make sure you keep corresponding sides in order.

$$\frac{AB}{DE} = \frac{AC}{DF}$$

$$\frac{AB}{10 \text{ m}} = \frac{20 \text{ m}}{8 \text{ m}}$$

Solve the proportion for AB, omitting the units for convenience.

$$\frac{AB}{10} = \frac{20}{8}$$

$$AB = \frac{(10)(20)}{8}$$

$$AB = \frac{\left(\overset{5}{\cancel{10}}\right)\left(\cancel{20}^{\,5}\right)}{\cancel{8}_{\,4}}$$

$$AB = 25$$

The length of the hypotenuse in triangle ABC is 25 meters.

24. **C.** Choice C is the correct response. The ratio of the perimeters is the same as the ratio of two corresponding sides from the two pentagons because all five sets of corresponding sides have the same ratios. Sides $\overline{AB}$ and $\overline{LM}$ are corresponding sides. So, the ratio of the perimeter of $ABCDE$ to $LMNOP$ is $\frac{AB}{LM} = \frac{9}{7.5} = 1.2$.

25. **C.** Choice C is the correct response. Only choice C satisfies the Pythagorean theorem, $a^2 + b^2 = c^2$, as shown here.

$$5^2 + 12^2 = 25 + 144 = 169 = 13^2$$

26. **C.** Choice C is the correct response. Let x = the distance from the base of the building to the top of the ladder. Make a sketch.

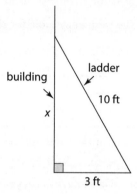

Write an equation that represents the facts.

$$a^2 + b^2 = c^2$$
$$x^2 + (3 \text{ ft})^2 = (10 \text{ ft})^2$$

Solve the equation, omitting units for convenience.

$$a^2 + b^2 = c^2$$
$$x^2 + (3)^2 = (10)^2$$
$$x^2 + 9 = 100$$
$$x^2 + 9 - 9 = 100 - 9$$
$$x^2 = 91$$
$$x = \sqrt{91} \approx 9.5$$

The ladder will reach approximately 9.5 feet up the side of the building.

Tip: You should eliminate choice D from the outset because a leg of a right triangle cannot be longer than the hypotenuse.

27. **A.** Choice A is the correct response. If two lines are cut by a transversal so that a pair of corresponding angles are congruent, then the two lines are parallel. Lines k and l are parallel because they have a pair of congruent corresponding angles. None of the statements in the other answer choices are true.

28. **A.** Choice A is the correct response. The radius is $\frac{1}{2}(8 \text{ in}) = 4 \text{ in}$.

$$V = \frac{1}{3}Bh = \frac{1}{3}(\pi r^2)h = \frac{1}{3}\left[\pi(4 \text{ in})^2\right](10 \text{ in}) = \frac{1}{3}\left[\pi(16 \text{ in}^2)\right](10 \text{ in}) \approx \frac{1}{3}\left[3.14(16 \text{ in}^2)\right](10 \text{ in}) \approx 167 \text{ in}^3$$

The volume of brass in the paperweight is approximately 167 in³.

29. **A.** Choice A is the correct response. The data points in the scatter plot in choice A cluster closer around an imagined line passing through the points than do those in the scatter plots in the other answer choices. This scatter plot suggests the strongest linear relationship between the two variables.

30. **C.** Choice C is the correct response. The frequency table for the data is shown below.

Do you have a television in your bedroom?

Gender	Yes	No	Row Total
Boys	18	7	25
Girls	15	10	25
Column Total	33	17	50

The relative frequencies should be based on the total number of students surveyed, which is 50. Converting each entry in the table to a percentage of 50 yields the relative frequency table in choice C.

Do you have a television in your bedroom?

Gender	Yes	No	Row Total
Boys	36%	14%	50%
Girls	30%	20%	50%
Column Total	66%	34%	100%

Only the table entries in choice C equal the percentage of 50 represented by the survey counts.

31. **–2**

$$0.4(x-5)+4x=-3(0.2x+\ 2)-6$$
$$0.4x-2.0+4x=-0.6x-6-6$$
$$4.4x-2=-0.6x-12$$
$$4.4x-2+0.6x=-0.6x-12+0.6x$$
$$5.0x-2=-12$$
$$5x-2+2=-12+2$$
$$5x=-10$$
$$\frac{\cancel{5}x}{\cancel{5}}=\frac{\cancel{10}^{-2}}{\cancel{5}}$$
$$x=-2$$

32. **7 ft**

The volume of a cylinder is $V = (\pi r^2)h$, where r is the cylinder's radius and h is its height.
Write an equation that represents the facts given.

$$(\pi r^2)h = V$$
$$(\pi r^2)(10 \text{ ft}) = 490\pi \text{ ft}^3$$

Solve the equation for r, omitting the units for convenience.

$$(\pi r^2)(10) = 490\pi$$
$$10\pi r^2 = 490\pi \qquad \text{Simplify.}$$
$$\frac{10\pi r^2}{10\pi} = \frac{\overset{49}{\cancel{490}}\cancel{\pi}}{\cancel{10}\cancel{\pi}} \qquad \text{Divide by the coefficient of } r^2.$$
$$r^2 = 49$$
$$r = 7 \qquad \text{Take the positive square root because length is nonnegative.}$$

The radius of the water tank is 7 feet.

33. **0.6 km**

To answer the question, do three steps. First, determine the distance, s, walking along the two sides.
Next, find the distance, p, taking the graveled path. Then compute $s - p$.

Step 1. The distance walking along the two sides is

$$s = 2.4 \text{ km} + 0.7 \text{ km} = 3.1 \text{ km}$$

Step 2. The distance taking the graveled path is the length of the hypotenuse of a right triangle that
has legs of lengths 2.4 km and 0.7 km. Let c = the length of the hypotenuse. Write an equation that
represents the facts.

$$c^2 = a^2 + b^2$$
$$c^2 = (2.4 \text{ km})^2 + (0.7 \text{ km})^2$$

Solve the equation, omitting the units for convenience.

$$c^2 = (2.4)^2 + (0.7)^2$$
$$c^2 = 5.76 + 0.49$$
$$c^2 = 6.25$$
$$c = 2.5 \qquad \text{Take the positive square root because length is nonnegative.}$$

The distance along the graveled path is 2.5 km.

Step 3. Subtract.

$$3.1 \text{ km} - 2.5 \text{ km} = 0.6 \text{ km}$$

Walking along two sides of the park is 0.6 kilometer farther than taking the graveled path through the
park.

34. **39 in³**

$$V = \frac{4}{3}\pi(2.1 \text{ in})^3 = \frac{4}{3}\pi(9.261 \text{ in}^3) \approx \frac{4}{3}(3.14)(9.261 \text{ in}^3) \approx 39 \text{ in}^3$$

35. **82**

$$2\frac{1}{4} \text{ hours} = 2.25 \text{ hours}$$

The predicted science midterm score for a student who studied 2.25 hours is

$$Y = 16(2.25) + 46 = 36 + 46 = 82$$

36. **22 500 m²**

From the diagram, you can see triangles *ABC* and *ADE* are right triangles. To find the area of right triangle *ABC*, compute $\frac{1}{2}$ the product of the lengths of its two perpendicular legs, $\overline{CA}$ and $\overline{BC}$. The diagram shows that *CA* = *CE* + *EA*. Because right triangles *ABC* and *ADE* have two congruent right angles and an acute angle in common, namely angle *A*, they are similar triangles. Thus, *BC* can be determined by using properties of similar triangles.

To find the area of triangle *ABC*, do three steps. First, find *CA* by adding *CE* and *EA*. Next, find *BC* by using the proportionality of the corresponding sides of similar triangles *ABC* and *ADE*. Then, find the area of triangle *ABC* by computing $\frac{1}{2}(CA)(BC)$.

Step 1. Find *CA*.

$$CA = 200 \text{ m} + 100 \text{ m} = 300 \text{ m}$$

Step 2. Find *BC*, omitting the units for convenience.

$$\frac{BC}{DE} = \frac{CA}{EA}$$
$$\frac{BC}{50} = \frac{300}{100}$$
$$BC = \frac{(50)(300)}{100}$$
$$BC = 150$$
$$BC = 150 \text{ m}$$

Step 3. Find the area of triangle *ABC*.

$$\frac{1}{2}(CA)(BC) = \frac{1}{2}(300 \text{ m})(150 \text{ m}) = 22\ 500 \text{ m}^2$$

The area of triangle *ABC* is 22 500 m².

37. **–3**

$$6x - 5y = 18$$
$$2x + 3y = -8$$

The system has exactly one solution because $\dfrac{6}{2} \neq \dfrac{-5}{3}$.

Step 1. Write both equations in standard form: $Ax + By = C$.

$$6x - 5y = 18$$
$$2x + 3y = -8$$

Step 2. To eliminate x, multiply the second equation by –3.

$$\begin{aligned} 6x - 5y &= 18 \\ 2x + 3y &= -8 \end{aligned} \rightarrow \begin{aligned} 6x - 5y &= 18 \\ -3(2x + 3y) &= -3(-8) \end{aligned} \rightarrow \begin{aligned} 6x - 5y &= 18 \\ -6x - 9y &= 24 \end{aligned}$$

Step 3. Add the transformed equations and solve for y.

$$6x - 5y = 18$$
$$\underline{-6x - 9y = 24}$$
$$0 - 14y = 42$$
$$-14y = 42$$
$$\frac{\cancel{-14}y}{\cancel{-14}} = \frac{\cancel{42}^{-3}}{\cancel{-14}}$$
$$y = -3$$

38. 3 ft

Let w = the width, in feet, of the sandbox. Then $2w + 1$ foot = the length, in feet, of the sandbox. Make a sketch.

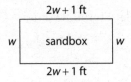

Perimeter = 20 ft

The perimeter is the distance around the sandbox. Write an equation that represents the facts given.

$$2(2w + 1 \text{ ft}) + 2(w) = 20 \text{ ft}$$

Solve the equation, omitting the units for convenience.

$$2(2w+1)+2(w)=20$$
$$4w+2+2w=20$$
$$6w+2=20$$
$$6w+2-2=20-2$$
$$6w=18$$
$$\frac{\cancel{6}w}{\cancel{6}}=\frac{\cancel{18}^{3}}{\cancel{6}}$$
$$w=3$$

The width of the sandbox is 3 feet.

39. 29°

Start with the angles for which you can find the measure by using the given information. As you determine the measure of each angle, you will gain enough information to find the solution.

$$m\angle ACB = 180° - 64° - 71° = 45°$$
$$m\angle BCE = 45° + 62° = 107°$$

The measure of an exterior angle of a triangle equals the sum of the measures of the nonadjacent interior angles. Thus, $m\angle BCE = 107° = 78° + m\angle E$. Hence, $m\angle E = 107° - 78° = 29°$.

40. 3

Substitute the given value of x, and use your knowledge of exponents to solve for $5x$.

$$5x = 5\left(1+\left(1+2^{-1}\right)^{-1}\right)^{-1}$$

$$= 5\left(1+\left(1+\frac{1}{2}\right)^{-1}\right)^{-1} = 5\left(1+\left(\frac{3}{2}\right)^{-1}\right)^{-1} = 5\left(1+\frac{2}{3}\right)^{-1} = 5\left(\frac{5}{3}\right)^{-1} = \cancel{5}\left(\frac{3}{\cancel{5}}\right) = 3$$

7. Practice Test 2

Directions: For questions 1–30, select the best answer choice.

1. Convert $1.\overline{63}$ to an equivalent fractional form.

   A. $\dfrac{11}{9}$

   B. $\dfrac{18}{11}$

   C. $\dfrac{18}{9}$

   D. $\dfrac{163}{99}$

2. Evaluate $20 - 3(-4^2) + \dfrac{8(42-18)}{12} - (-4)^2$.

   A. -28

   B. 36

   C. 68

   D. 100

3. Which expression is NOT equivalent to $\dfrac{5^3}{5^6}$?

   A. 5^{-3}

   B. $\dfrac{1}{125}$

   C. $\dfrac{1}{25}$

   D. $\dfrac{1}{5^3}$

4. Which expression is equivalent to $3^x + 12^x$?

   A. $3^x(1 + 4^x)$

   B. $3(5^x)$

   C. 15^x

   D. 15^{2x}

5. Culture A contains 6×10^4 bacteria. Culture B contains 3×10^6 bacteria. Which statement is correct?

   A. Culture A contains $\dfrac{1}{200}$ as many bacteria as Culture B.

   B. Culture A contains $\dfrac{1}{50}$ as many bacteria as Culture B.

   C. Culture A contains 50 times as many bacteria as Culture B.

   D. Culture A contains 200 times as many bacteria as Culture B.

6. Compute $(6 \times 10^{-3})(8 \times 10^{-5})$.

   A. 4.8×10^{-8}

   B. 4.8×10^{-7}

   C. 4.8×10^{8}

   D. 4.8×10^{15}

7. Which expressions is equivalent to $\sqrt{100}$?

   A. $\sqrt{50} + \sqrt{50}$

   B. $\sqrt{36} + \sqrt{64}$

   C. $\left(\sqrt{10}\right)^2$

   D. $\left(\sqrt{25}\right)^4$

8. Eight less than three times a number is seven more than twice the number. What is the number?

   A. 5

   B. 8

   C. 12

   D. 15

9. Which equation has both –4 and 4 in the solution set?

   A. $x = \sqrt[3]{64}$

   B. $x = \sqrt{16}$

   C. $x^2 = 16$

   D. $x^3 = 64$

10. A collection of dimes and quarters has a value of \$22.50. Ten times as many dimes as quarters are in the collection of coins. How many dimes are in the collection?

   A. 18

   B. 50

   C. 80

   D. 180

11. Find the distance between the two points shown.

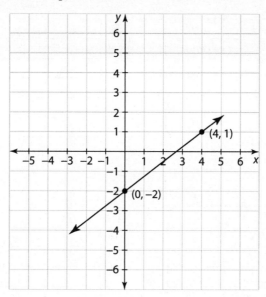

A. $\sqrt{6}$ units
B. 5 units
C. 6 units
D. $\sqrt{37}$ units

12. Which system of equations has no solution?

A. $x - 2y = 5$
$2x - 4y = 10$

B. $x - 2y = 5$
$2x - 4y = 8$

C. $x - 2y = 5$
$2x + 4y = 10$

D. $x + 2y = 5$
$2x - 4y = 3$

13. The one-day admission at a zoo is $8 for adults and $5 for children. On a certain weekend at the zoo, a total of 1,800 adult and children tickets were sold and $11,250 was collected. How many children tickets were sold on that weekend?

A. 750
B. 800
C. 1,000
D. 1,050

14. Which table could NOT be a partial representation of a function?

A.

x	y
-3	$\frac{1}{9}$
-2	$\frac{1}{2}$
-1	1
2	$\frac{1}{2}$
3	$\frac{1}{9}$

B.

x	y
-1	-1
-2	-2
0	0
1	1
2	2

C.

x	y
0	0
20	$-\sqrt{20}$
20	$\sqrt{20}$
30	$-\sqrt{30}$
30	$\sqrt{30}$

D.

x	y
$-\sqrt{30}$	30
$-\sqrt{20}$	20
0	0
$\sqrt{20}$	20
$\sqrt{30}$	30

15. The following table shows a partial representation of a proportional function between volume, v (in cubic centimeters) and the weight, w (in grams), of aluminum.

Volume, v (in cubic centimeters)	Weight, w (in grams)
12	32.4
20	54.0
45	121.5
74	199.8

Write an equation for the function represented in the table.

A. $w = 2.7v$
B. $w = 21.6v$
C. $v = 2.7w$
D. $v = 21.6w$

16. Which statement about the function $y = 3.8x + 1$ is true?

A. For every 1-unit change in the input, there is a 3.8-unit change in the output.
B. For every 1-unit change in the input, there is a 4.8-unit change in the output.
C. For every 1-unit change in the output, there is a 3.8-unit change in the input.
D. For every 1-unit change in the output, there is a 4.8-unit change in the input.

17. Which graph is NOT the graph of a function?

A.

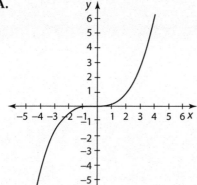

B.

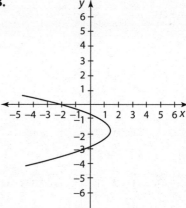

C.

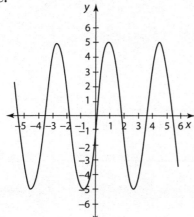

D.

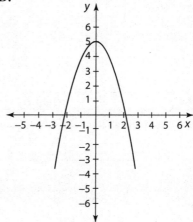

18. The ordered pairs in the following table best represent which linear function?

Input x	Output y
−14	−10
−2	−4
0	−3

A. $y = x + 4$

B. $y = x - 3$

C. $y = \dfrac{1}{2}x - 3$

D. $y = 2x$

19. Compare the following representations of four linear functions. Which function has the greatest rate of change?

A. $y = \dfrac{8}{3}x + 10$

B.

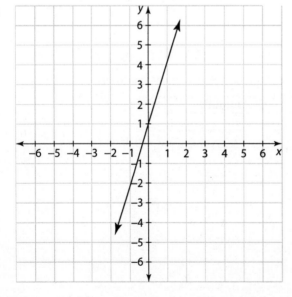

C.

Input x	Output y
−3	−2.7
−1	1.1
2	6.8

D.

20. Using data collected through experimentation, a social scientist develops a function that relates hours of sleep, y (output), to age, x (input). Which statement MUST be true about the scientist's function?

    A. It is a linear function.
    B. Each hours value, y, has one and only one age value, x.
    C. The graph of the function passes through the origin.
    D. Each age value, x, has one and only one hours value, y.

21. The graph of a linear function passes through the points (–3, 3.5) and (3, –11.5). What is the function's rate of change?

    A. $-\dfrac{5}{2}$

    B. $-\dfrac{2}{5}$

    C. $\dfrac{2}{5}$

    D. $\dfrac{5}{2}$

22. In a coordinate plane, segment $\overline{AB}$ has endpoints $A(-5, 1)$ and $B(6, -2)$. Segment $\overline{A'B'}$ is the image of $\overline{AB}$ after a reflection over the x-axis followed by a counterclockwise rotation of 270° about the origin. What are the coordinates of A'?

    A. (–5, –1)
    B. (–1, –5)
    C. (–1, 5)
    D. (5, –1)

23. If the point $P(-2, -4)$ is rotated 90° counterclockwise about the origin, in what quadrant does P' lie?

    A. quadrant I
    B. quadrant II
    C. quadrant III
    D. quadrant IV

24. In the diagram, lines m and n are parallel and $x = 8y$. What is the value of x?

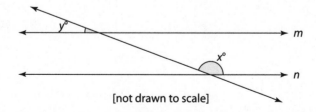

[not drawn to scale]

    A. 10
    B. 20
    C. 160
    D. 170

25. A photograph 8 inches by 10 inches is enlarged so that its longer side measures 15 inches. What is the measure, in inches, of the enlargement's shorter side?

   A. 8 inches
   B. 9 inches
   C. 12 inches
   D. 14 inches

26. Which set of numbers could be the lengths of the sides of a right triangle?

   A. 3, 4, 7
   B. 2, 3, $\sqrt{13}$
   C. 4, 8, 12
   D. 5, 9, $\sqrt{14}$

27. The hypotenuse of a right triangle measures 15 centimeters. One of the legs of the triangle is twice as long as the other. Which length is closest to the measure of the shorter leg of the triangle?

   A. 4.5 centimeters
   B. 6.7 centimeters
   C. 7.5 centimeters
   D. 8.7 centimeters

28. A cylindrical container is filled to capacity with juice. The container has a height of 25 centimeters and a diameter of 12 centimeters. Which volume is closest to the volume of juice in the container? (Use $\pi \approx 3.14$.)

   A. 471 cm^3
   B. 942 cm^3
   C. 1413 cm^3
   D. 2826 cm^3

29. A scatter plot showing the linear relationship between the number of hours of study and the number of questions missed on a mathematics midterm exam by 10 eighth graders is shown below.

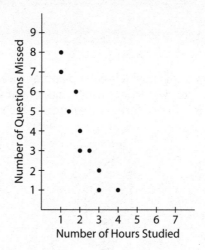

If you were to use the scatter plot to predict the number of questions missed based on the number of hours studied, you should limit the number of hours to between

A. 1 and 4.
B. 1 and 5.
C. 1 and 6.
D. 1 and 7.

30. LeVar and Vince conducted a random survey of 200 students in their middle school and asked each student, "Do you have a weekend curfew?" Every student responded either "yes" or "no" to the survey question. The two-way table shows the relative frequencies of the survey data.

Do you have a weekend curfew?

Gender	Yes	No	Row Total
Boys	46%	4%	50%
Girls	40%	10%	50%
Column Total	86%	14%	100%

How many total students answered "yes" to the survey question?

A. 14
B. 28
C. 86
D. 172

Directions: For questions 31–40, enter your answer in the answer box below the question. Enter the exact answer unless you are told to round your answer.

31. Solve $\frac{1}{2}(3x-4)-20=x-5$.

32. The grain storage bin shown has a right cylindrical top part and a right conical bottom part. The bin's overall height is 20 feet. If the bin's cylindrical top part has a radius of 3 feet and its conical bottom part has a height of 8 feet, what is the approximate volume, to the nearest cubic foot, of the storage bin? (Use $\pi \approx 3.14$.)

$\boxed{}$ ft^3

33. Solve $2x^3 = 432$.

34. In the system of equations shown, what is the value of x?

$$2x+3y=-4$$
$$x+4y=3$$

35. Evaluate $\dfrac{(6\cdot10)^3}{6^2}+\dfrac{(2+3)^{10}}{5^6}$.

36. Find the value of x in the diagram.

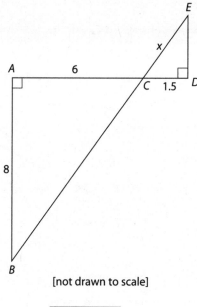

[not drawn to scale]

☐ units

37. The diameter of Earth is approximately 12,700,000 meters. Express this measure in scientific notation.

☐ m

38. Approximate $\sqrt{60}$ to the nearest tenth.

☐

39. For the function $y = \frac{3}{2}x + 15$, find x such that $y = 9$.

☐

40. In the diagram, lines *m* and *n* are parallel and cut by the transversal *t*. What is the measure of angle *y* in degrees?

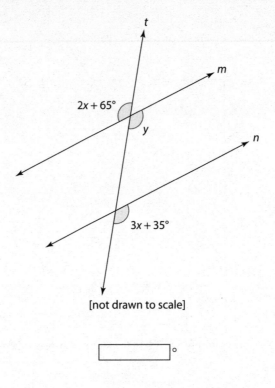

[not drawn to scale]

☐ °

Answer Key

1. B	11. B	21. A	31. 34
2. C	12. B	22. C	32. 414 ft^3
3. C	13. D	23. D	33. 6
4. A	14. C	24. C	34. −5
5. B	15. A	25. C	35. 6,625
6. B	16. A	26. B	36. 2.5 units
7. C	17. B	27. B	37. 1.27×10^7 m
8. D	18. C	28. D	38. 7.7
9. C	19. D	29. A	39. −4
10. D	20. D	30. D	40. 125°

Answer Explanations

1. **B.** Choice B is the correct response. Let $x = 1.\overline{63} = 1.6363\ldots$

   Step 1. Multiply both sides of the equation, $x = 1.6363\ldots$, by $10^2 = 100$ (because 2 digits repeat).

   $$x = 1.6363\ldots$$
   $$100 \cdot x = 100(1.6363\ldots)$$
   $$100x = 163.6363\ldots$$

   Step 2. Subtract the original equation from the new equation.

   $$100x = 163.6363\ldots$$
   $$\underline{-x = -\ 1.6363\ldots}$$
   $$99x = 162$$

   Step 3. Solve for x by dividing both sides of the resulting equation by the coefficient of x.

   $$99x = 162$$
   $$\frac{\cancel{99}x}{\cancel{99}} = \frac{162}{99}$$
   $$x = \frac{162 \div 9}{99 \div 9}$$
   $$x = \frac{18}{11}$$

2. **C.** Choice C is the correct response. Follow the order of operations.

   $$20 - 3(-4^2) + \frac{8(42 - 18)}{12} - (-4)^2 = 20 - 3(-4^2) + \frac{8(24)}{12} - (-4)^2$$
   $$= 20 - 3(-16) + \frac{8(24)}{12} - (16)$$
   $$= 20 + 48 + \frac{8\left(\cancel{24}^{\,2}\right)}{\cancel{12}} - 16$$
   $$= 20 + 48 + 16 - 16$$
   $$= 68$$

   Tip: Notice that $(-4^2) = (-16) = -16$, not 16; and $(-4)^2 = (-4)(-4) = 16$, not -16. An exponent applies only to the number or grouped quantity to which it is attached.

3. **C.** Choice C is the correct response. Follow the rules for exponents.

   $$\frac{5^3}{5^6} = 5^{3-6} = 5^{-3} = \frac{1}{5^3} = \frac{1}{125}$$

   Only $\dfrac{1}{25}$ (choice C) is not equivalent to $\dfrac{5^3}{5^6}$.

4. **A.** Choice A is the correct response. Follow the rules for exponents.

$$3^x + 12^x = 3^x + (3 \cdot 4)^x = 3^x + 3^x 4^x = 3^x(1 + 4^x)$$

5. **B.** Choice B is the correct response. Eliminate choices C and D because 6×10^4 is less than 3×10^6. Divide 6×10^4 by 3×10^6.

$$\frac{6 \times 10^4}{3 \times 10^6} = 2 \times 10^{4-6} = 2 \times 10^{-2} = 2 \times \frac{1}{10^2} = \cancel{2} \times \frac{1}{\cancel{100}_{\,50}} = \frac{1}{50}$$

Culture A contains $\dfrac{1}{50}$ times as many bacteria as Culture B.

6. **B.** Choice B is the correct response.

$$(6 \times 10^{-3})(8 \times 10^{-5}) =$$
$$48 \times 10^{-3\,+\,-5} = 48 \times 10^{-8} = 4.8 \times 10^1 \times 10^{-8} = 4.8 \times 10^{1\,+\,-8} = 4.8 \times 10^{-7}$$

7. **C.** Choice C is the correct response. $\sqrt{100} = 10$. Only choice C is equivalent to 10 because $\left(\sqrt{10}\right)^2 = \left(\sqrt{10}\right)\left(\sqrt{10}\right) = 10$. None of the other answer choices contains an expression that is equivalent to 10.

8. **D.** Choice D is the correct response. Let n = the number.

Write an equation that represents the facts.

$$3n - 8 = 2n + 7$$

Tip: "Eight less than three times a number" is not $8 - 3n$.

Solve the equation.

$$3n - 8 = 2n + 7$$
$$3n - 8 - 2n = 2n + 7 - 2n$$
$$n - 8 = 7$$
$$n - 8 + 8 = 7 + 8$$
$$n = 15$$

The number is 15.

9. **C.** Choice C is the correct response. Check the answer choices.

Check A: The solution of $x = \sqrt[3]{64}$ is 4. Eliminate A.

Check B: The solution of $x = \sqrt{16}$ is 4. Eliminate B. *Tip:* The square root symbol $\left(\sqrt{}\right)$ always returns the principal square root, which is nonnegative.

Check C: The solution of $x^2 = 16$ is $x = \sqrt{16} = 4$ or $x = -\sqrt{16} = -4$. ✓

In a test situation, you should move on to the next question. For your information, the check for choice D is shown below.

Check D: The solution of $x^3 = 64$ is $x = \sqrt[3]{64} = 4$.

10. **D.** Choice D is the correct response. Let q = the number of quarters and $10q$ = the number of dimes.

Make a table to organize the coin information in the question.

Denomination	Dimes	Quarters	Total
Face Value per Coin	$0.10	$0.25	N/A
Number of Coins	$10q$	q	Not given
Value of Coins	$0.10(10q)	$0.25q	$22.50

Using the table information, write an equation that represents the facts.

$$\$0.10(10q) + \$0.25q = \$22.50$$

Solve the equation for q, the number of quarters, omitting the units for convenience. Then compute $10q$, the number of dimes.

$$0.10(10q) + 0.25q = 22.50$$
$$q + 0.25q = 22.50$$
$$1.25q = 22.50$$
$$\frac{\cancel{1.25}q}{\cancel{1.25}} = \frac{\cancel{22.50}^{18}}{\cancel{1.25}}$$
$$q = 18$$
$$10q = 10(18) = 180$$

There are 180 dimes in the collection.

Tip: Be sure to answer the question asked. After you determine the number of quarters, use the result to determine the number of dimes.

11. **B.** Choice B is the correct response.

$$\text{distance} = \sqrt{\left|0-4\right|^2 + \left|-2-1\right|^2} = \sqrt{\left|-4\right|^2 + \left|-3\right|^2} = \sqrt{4^2 + 3^2} = \sqrt{16+9} = \sqrt{25} = 5$$

The distance between the two points is 5 units.

12. **B.** Choice B is the correct response. Check the answer choices by comparing the ratios of the coefficients of the two equations.

Check A: $\frac{1}{2}$, $\frac{-2}{-4}$, and $\frac{5}{10}$ are equivalent ratios; the system $\begin{matrix} x - 2y = 5 \\ 2x - 4y = 10 \end{matrix}$ has infinitely many solutions.

Check B: $\frac{1}{2} = \frac{-2}{-4} \neq \frac{5}{8}$; the system $\begin{matrix} x - 2y = 5 \\ 2x - 4y = 8 \end{matrix}$ has no solution. ✓

In a test situation, you should move on to the next question. For your information, the systems

$\begin{matrix} x - 2y = 5 \\ 2x + 4y = 10 \end{matrix}$ (choice C) and $\begin{matrix} x + 2y = 5 \\ 2x - 4y = 3 \end{matrix}$ (choice D) have exactly one solution.

13. **D.** Choice D is the correct response. Let a = the number of adult tickets and c = the number of children tickets.

Write two equations that represent the facts of the question.

$$a + c = 1,800$$
$$\$8a + \$5c = \$11,250$$

Solve the system, omitting the units for convenience.

Using the method of substitution, solve $a + c = 1,800$ for a in terms of c.

$$a + c = 1,800$$
$$a + c - c = 1,800 - c$$
$$a = 1,800 - c$$

Replace a with $1,800 - c$ in the equation $8a + 5c = 11,250$ and solve for c.

$$8a + 5c = 11,250$$
$$8(1,800 - c) + 5c = 11,250$$
$$14,400 - 8c + 5c = 11,250$$
$$14,400 - 3c = 12,250$$
$$14,400 - 3c - 14,400 = 11,250 - 14,400$$
$$-3c = -3150$$
$$\frac{\cancel{3}c}{\cancel{3}} = \frac{\cancel{-3,150}^{1,050}}{\cancel{3}}$$
$$c = 1,050$$

There were 1,050 children tickets sold.

14. **C.** Choice C is the correct response. The ordered pairs in choice C could not be a partial representation of a function because each of the two input values, 20 and 30, is paired with two different output values.

15. **A.** Choice A is the correct response. The input-output ordered pairs are (12, 32.4), (20, 54.0), (45, 121.5), and (74, 199.8). A proportional function has the form $y = mx$, where m is the function's rate of change. Using (12, 32.4) and (20, 54.0), the constant of proportionality (rate of change) is $\frac{54.0 - 32.4}{20 - 12} = \frac{21.6}{8} = 2.7$. The function has equation $w = 2.7v$.

16. **A.** Choice A is the correct response. The rate of change of $y = 3.8x + 1$ is 3.8. Thus, for every 1-unit change in the input, there is a 3.8-unit change in the output. None of the other answer choices contains a true statement about the function.

17. **B.** Choice B is the correct response. The graph in choice B is not a function because, as shown below, the graph does not pass the vertical line test. The graphs of the functions in the other answer choices do pass the vertical line test.

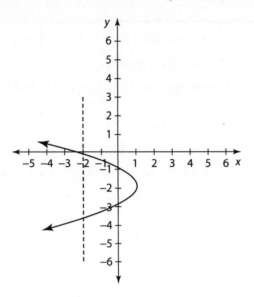

18. **C.** Choice C is the correct response. Check the answer choices.

Check A: Eliminate A because the ordered pairs (–2, –4) and (0, –3) do not satisfy the equation $y = x + 4$.

Check B: Eliminate B because the ordered pairs (–14, –10) and (–2, –4) do not satisfy the equation $y = x – 3$.

Check C: The table data best represent $y = \frac{1}{2}x - 3$ because all three of the ordered pairs in the table satisfy the equation. ✓

In a test situation, you should move on to the next question. For your information, here is the check for choice D.

Check D: Eliminate D because the ordered pairs (–14, –10) and (0, –3) do not satisfy the equation $y = x – 3$.

19. **D.** Choice D is the correct response. Eliminate choice B because by visual inspection, the graph in choice B is not as steep as the graph in choice D, indicating the rate of change for the function represented in choice B is less than the rate of change for the function represented in choice D. Determine the rate of change for the functions in choices A, C, and D.

Choice A: The rate of change is $\dfrac{8}{3}$, the coefficient of x.

Choice C: The rate of change is $\dfrac{\text{change in } y}{\text{change in } x} = \dfrac{1.1 - (-2.7)}{-1 - (-3)} = \dfrac{1.1 + 2.7}{-1 + 3} = \dfrac{3.8}{2} = 1.9$.

Choice D: The rate of change is 3 because the graph shows a 3-unit change in y for every 1-unit change in x. ✓

Therefore, the function represented in choice D has the greatest rate of change.

20. **D.** Choice D is the correct response. Only choice D must be true. Each input value, x, of a function has one and only one output value, y. Eliminate choices A and C because the function does not have to be linear or pass through the origin. Eliminate choice B because, in a function, y values can have different x values.

21. **A.** Choice A is the correct response. The rate of change is

$$\frac{\text{change in } y}{\text{change in } x} = \frac{-11.5 - 3.5}{3 - (-3)} = \frac{-11.5 - 3.5}{3 + 3} = \frac{-15}{6} = -\frac{5}{2}$$

22. **C.** Choice C is the correct response. Under a reflection over the x-axis, $(-5, 1) \to (-5, -1)$. Under a counterclockwise rotation of 270° about the origin, $(-5, -1) \to (-1, 5)$. The coordinates of A' are $(-1, 5)$.

23. **D.** Choice D is the correct response. Under a counterclockwise rotation of 90° about the origin, $P(-2, -4) \to P'(4, -2)$, which lies in quadrant IV.

24. **C.** Choice C is the correct response. Designate angle X as the angle shown whose measure is $x°$ and angle Y as the angle shown whose measure is $y°$. Angles X and Y are formed when parallel lines are cut by a transversal. Angle X and the angle adjacent to it are supplementary angles. Angle Y and the angle adjacent to angle X are congruent because they are corresponding angles. Thus, angles X and Y are supplementary angles. It is given that $x = 8y$. Write two equations that represent the facts.

$$x + y = 180$$
$$x = 8y$$

Solve the system for x. Replace x with $8y$ in the equation $x + y = 180$.

$$x + y = 180$$
$$8y + y = 180$$
$$9y = 180$$
$$\frac{\cancel{9}y}{\cancel{9}} = \frac{\cancel{180}^{20}}{\cancel{9}}$$
$$y = 20$$
$$x = 8y = 8(20) = 160$$

The value of x is 160.

25. **C.** Choice C is the correct response. Let x = the length, in inches, of the shorter side of the enlargement. Make a sketch.

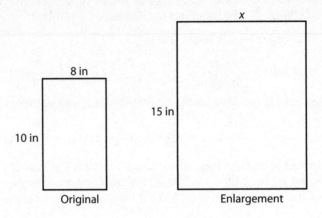

Original	Enlargement

The original photograph and its enlargement are similar. The ratios of corresponding sides are equal. Set up a proportion that represents the facts.

$$\frac{8 \text{ in}}{x} = \frac{10 \text{ in}}{15 \text{ in}}$$

Solve the proportion, omitting the units for convenience.

$$\frac{8}{x} = \frac{10}{15}$$

$$x = \frac{(8)(15)}{10}$$

$$x = \frac{120}{10}$$

$$x = 12$$

The shorter side of the enlargement measures 12 inches.

26. **B.** Choice B is the correct response. Only choice B satisfies the Pythagorean theorem, $a^2 + b^2 = c^2$, as shown here.

$$2^2 + 3^2 = 4 + 9 = 13 = \left(\sqrt{13}\right)^2$$

27. **B.** Choice B is the correct response. Let x = the length, in centimeters, of the shorter leg. Then $2x$ = the length, in centimeters, of the longer leg. Make a sketch.

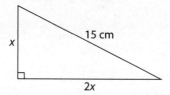

Write an equation that represents the facts.

$$a^2 + b^2 = c^2$$
$$x^2 + (2x)^2 = (15 \text{ cm})^2$$

Solve the equation, omitting the units for convenience.

$$a^2 + b^2 = c^2$$
$$x^2 + (2x)^2 = (15)^2$$
$$x^2 + 4x^2 = 225$$
$$5x^2 = 225$$
$$\frac{\cancel{5}x^2}{\cancel{5}} = \frac{\cancel{225}^{45}}{\cancel{5}}$$
$$x^2 = 45$$
$$x = \sqrt{45}$$

You can determine that $\sqrt{36} < \sqrt{45} < \sqrt{49}$. Thus, $6 < \sqrt{45} < 7$. Only the number in choice B falls between 6 and 7. You do not have to estimate further. You can safely conclude that $\sqrt{45} \approx 6.7$.

The shorter leg measures approximately 6.7 centimeters.

28. **D.** Choice D is the correct response. The radius is $\frac{1}{2}(12 \text{ cm}) = 6$ cm. The volume is

$$V = (\pi r^2)h = [\pi (6 \text{ cm})^2](25 \text{ cm}) = [\pi (36 \text{ cm}^2)](25 \text{ cm}) \approx [3.14(36 \text{ cm}^2)](25 \text{ cm}) = 2826 \text{ cm}^3$$

The volume of juice in the container is approximately 2826 cm³.

29. **A.** Choice A is the correct response. For statistical reasons, you should predict only within the range of the predictor variable, which is the number of hours in this case. The minimum number of hours studied is 1 and the maximum number is 4. You should restrict the number of hours to between 1 and 4.

30. **D.** Choice D is the correct response. The relative frequencies are based on 200, the total number of students surveyed. The total number of students who responded "yes" to the survey question is 86% of $200 = 0.86 \times 200 = 172$.

31. **34**

$$\frac{1}{2}(3x-4)-20=x-5$$

$$\frac{3}{2}x-2-20=x-5$$

$$\frac{3}{2}x-22=x-5$$

$$\frac{3}{2}x-22-x=x-5-x$$

$$\frac{1}{2}x-22=-5$$

$$\frac{1}{2}x-22+22=-5+22$$

$$\frac{1}{2}x=17$$

$$\frac{\cancel{2}}{1}\left(\frac{1}{\cancel{2}}x\right)=2(17)$$

$$x=34$$

32. **414 ft³**

The volume of the storage bin is the volume of the cylindrical top part plus the volume of the conical bottom part. The cylindrical top part has a radius of 3 feet and a height of 20 feet – 8 feet = 12 feet. The conical bottom part has a radius of 3 feet and a height of 8 feet. Therefore, the volume of the storage bin is

$$\left[\pi(3\text{ ft})^2\right](12\text{ ft})+\frac{1}{3}\left[\pi(3\text{ ft})^2\right](8\text{ ft})=$$

$$\left[\pi(9\text{ ft}^2)\right](12\text{ ft})+\frac{1}{3}\left[\pi(9\text{ ft}^2)\right](8\text{ ft})\approx\left[3.14(9\text{ ft}^2)\right](12\text{ ft})+\frac{1}{3}\left[3.14(9\text{ ft}^2)\right](8\text{ ft})\approx 414\text{ ft}^3$$

33. **6**

$$2x^3=432$$

$$\frac{\cancel{2}x^3}{\cancel{2}}=\frac{\cancel{432}^{216}}{\cancel{2}}$$

$$x^3=216$$

$$x=\sqrt[3]{216}$$

$$x=6$$

34. –5

$$2x+3y=-4$$
$$x+4y=3$$

The system has exactly one solution because $\dfrac{2}{1}\neq\dfrac{3}{4}$.

Step 1. Write both equations in standard form: $Ax + By = C$.

$$2x+3y=-4$$
$$x+4y=3$$

Step 2. To eliminate y, multiply the first equation by 4 and the second equation by –3.

$$\begin{array}{c} 2x+3y=-4 \\ x+4y=3 \end{array} \rightarrow \begin{array}{c} 4(2x+3y)=4(-4) \\ -3(x+4y)=-3(3) \end{array} \rightarrow \begin{array}{c} 8x+12y=-16 \\ -3x-12y=-9 \end{array}$$

Step 3. Add the transformed equations and solve for x.

$$8x+12y=-16$$
$$\underline{-3x-12y=-9}$$
$$5x+0=-25$$
$$5x=-25$$
$$\frac{\cancel{5}x}{\cancel{5}}=\frac{\cancel{-25}^{-5}}{\cancel{5}}$$
$$x=-5$$

Tip: In this problem, you could eliminate x first by multiplying the second equation by –2 and then adding the result to the first equation. You will obtain $y = 2$, which you can substitute into one of the two equations to obtain $x = -5$.

35. 6,625

Follow the rules for exponents.

$$\frac{(6\cdot10)^3}{6^2}+\frac{(2+3)^{10}}{5^6}=\frac{6^3\cdot10^3}{6^2}+\frac{(5)^{10}}{5^6}=6^{3-2}\cdot10^3+5^{10-6}=6\cdot1,000+5^4=6,000+625=6,625$$

36. **2.5 units**

From the diagram, triangles BAC and EDC are right triangles. $\overline{BC}$, the hypotenuse of right triangle BAC, has a length of 10 because (6, 8, 10) is a Pythagorean triple. Angles ACB and DCE are vertical angles of intersecting lines, so they are congruent. Thus, triangles BAC and EDC are similar triangles because two angles of the first are congruent to two angles of the second. The ratios of corresponding sides of similar triangles are equal. Set up a proportion that represents the facts.

$$\frac{EC}{BC} = \frac{DC}{AC}$$

$$\frac{x}{10} = \frac{1.5}{6}$$

Solve the proportion.

$$\frac{x}{10} = \frac{1.5}{6}$$

$$x = \frac{(10)(1.5)}{6}$$

$$x = \frac{15}{6}$$

$$x = 2.5$$

The value of x is 2.5 units.

37. **1.27×10^7 m**

Step 1. Create the first factor. Move the decimal point left, to the immediate right of the first *nonzero* digit of the number.

$$1.\ 2700000$$
$$\underbrace{\leftarrow\leftarrow\leftarrow\leftarrow\leftarrow\leftarrow\leftarrow}_{\substack{7 \text{ places} \\ \text{left}}}$$

Step 2. Create the second factor. The exponent for the power of 10 is the number of places you moved the decimal point in Step 1. It will be a positive integer.

$$12{,}700{,}000 = 1.27 \times 10^7$$

The diameter of Earth is approximately 1.27×10^7 meters.

38. **7.7**

Step 1. Approximate $\sqrt{60}$ to the nearest whole number.

Find two consecutive integers such that the square of the first integer is less than 60 and the square of the second integer is greater than 60. You know $7 \times 7 = 49$, which is less than 60, and $8 \times 8 = 64$, which is greater than 60. Thus, $\sqrt{49} < \sqrt{60} < \sqrt{64}$. So, the approximate value of $\sqrt{60}$ is between 7 and 8. It is closer to 8 because 60 is closer to 64 (4 units away) than it is to 49 (11 units away). To the nearest whole number, $\sqrt{60}$ is approximately 8.

Step 2. Approximate $\sqrt{60}$ to the nearest tenth.

Consider that 49 and 64 are 15 units apart and 60 and 49 are 11 units apart. So, 60 is $\frac{11}{15}$ of the distance between 49 and 64. As a rough approximation, $\sqrt{60}$ is about $\frac{11}{15}$ of the distance between 7 and 8, which is 1 unit. So, $\sqrt{60} \approx 7 + \frac{11}{15}(1) \approx 7 + 0.7 \approx 7.7$.

39. **−4**

Given that $y = 9$, substitute 9 into the equation in place of y. Then solve for x.

$$y = \frac{3}{2}x + 15$$
$$9 = \frac{3}{2}x + 15$$
$$9 - 15 = \frac{3}{2}x + 15 - 15$$
$$-6 = \frac{3}{2}x$$
$$\left(\frac{2}{3}\right)(-6^{-2}) = \left(\frac{2}{3}\right)\left(\frac{3}{2}x\right)$$
$$-4 = x$$

40. **125°**

The angle measures y and $2x + 65°$ are equal because vertical angles of intersecting lines are congruent. The angle measures y and $3x + 35°$ are equal because corresponding angles of parallel lines cut by a transversal are congruent. Write two equations that represent the facts. (***Tip:*** Recall, congruent angles have equal measures.)

$$y = 2x + 65°$$
$$y = 3x + 35°$$

Solve the system by substitution. Replace y with $2x + 65°$ in the second equation. Solve for x. Then compute y using either one of the original equations.

$$2x + 65° = 3x + 35°$$
$$2x + 65° - 3x = 3x + 35° - 3x$$
$$-x + 65° = 35°$$
$$-x + 65° - 65° = 35° - 65°$$
$$-x = -30°$$
$$x = 30°$$
$$y = 2x + 65° = 2(30°) + 65° = 60° + 65° = 125°$$

Appendix: Measurement Conversions

U.S. Customary Units	Conversion
Length	
Inch (in)	$1 \text{ in} = \dfrac{1}{12} \text{ ft}$
Foot (ft)	1 ft = 12 in $1 \text{ ft} = \dfrac{1}{3} \text{ yd}$
Yard (yd)	1 yd = 36 in 1 yd = 3 ft
Mile (mi)	1 mi = 5,280 ft 1 mi = 1,760 yd
Weight	
Pound (lb)	1 lb = 16 oz
Ton (T)	1 T = 2,000 lb
Capacity	
Fluid ounce (fl oz)	$1 \text{ fl oz} = \dfrac{1}{8} \text{ c}$
Cup (c)	1 c = 8 fl oz
Pint (pt)	1 pt = 2 c
Quart (qt)	1 qt = 32 fl oz 1 qt = 4 c 1 qt = 2 pt $1 \text{ qt} = \dfrac{1}{4} \text{ gal}$
Gallon (gal)	1 gal = 128 fl oz 1 gal = 16 c 1 gal = 8 pt 1 gal = 4 qt

Metric Units	Conversion
Length	
Millimeter (mm)	$1 \text{ mm} = \dfrac{1}{10} \text{ cm}$ $1 \text{ mm} = \dfrac{1}{1000} \text{ m}$
Centimeter (cm)	$1 \text{ cm} = 10 \text{ mm}$ $1 \text{ cm} = \dfrac{1}{100} \text{ m}$
Meter (m)	$1 \text{ m} = 1000 \text{ mm}$ $1 \text{ m} = 100 \text{ cm}$ $1 \text{ m} = \dfrac{1}{1000} \text{ km}$
Kilometer (km)	$1 \text{ km} = 1000 \text{ m}$
Mass	
Milligram (mg)	$1 \text{ mg} = \dfrac{1}{1000} \text{ g}$
Gram (g)	$1 \text{ g} = 1000 \text{ mg}$ $1 \text{ g} = \dfrac{1}{1000} \text{ kg}$
Kilogram (kg)	$1 \text{ kg} = 1000 \text{ g}$
Capacity	
Milliliter (mL)	$1 \text{ mL} = \dfrac{1}{1000} \text{ L}$
Liter (L)	$1 \text{ L} = 1000 \text{ mL}$

Time	Conversion
Second (s)	$1 \text{ s} = \dfrac{1}{60} \text{ min}$ $1 \text{ s} = \dfrac{1}{3,600} \text{ hr}$
Minute (min)	$1 \text{ min} = 60 \text{ s}$ $1 \text{ min} = \dfrac{1}{60} \text{ hr}$
Hour (hr)	$1 \text{ hr} = 3,600 \text{ s}$ $1 \text{ hr} = 60 \text{ min}$ $1 \text{ hr} = \dfrac{1}{24} \text{ d}$
Day (d)	$1 \text{ d} = 24 \text{ hr}$
Week (wk)	$1 \text{ wk} = 7 \text{ d}$
Year (yr)	$1 \text{ yr} = 365 \text{ d}$ $1 \text{ yr} = 52 \text{ wk}$